Tier **3** of the RTI Model

Dedicated to the memory of my son, Kyle

Tier **3** of the RTI Model

Problem Solving Through a Case Study Approach

Sawyer Hunley
Kathy McNamara

A JOINT PUBLICATION

NASP
NATIONAL
ASSOCIATION OF
SCHOOL
PSYCHOLOGISTS

CORWIN
A SAGE Company

For information:

Corwin
A SAGE Company
2455 Teller Road
Thousand Oaks, California 91320
(800) 233-9936
Fax: (800) 417-2466
www.corwinpress.com

SAGE India Pvt. Ltd.
B 1/I 1 Mohan Cooperative
    Industrial Area
Mathura Road, New Delhi 110 044
India

SAGE Ltd.
1 Oliver's Yard
55 City Road
London EC1Y 1SP
United Kingdom

SAGE Asia-Pacific Pte. Ltd.
33 Pekin Street #02-01
Far East Square
Singapore 048763

Printed in the United States of America.

Library of Congress Cataloging-in-Publication Data

Tier 3 of the RTI model : problem solving through a case study approach / Sawyer Hunley and Kathy McNamara.
      p. cm.
"A Joint Publication With the National Association of School Psychologists."
Includes bibliographical references and index.
ISBN 978-1-4129-5330-6 (cloth)
ISBN 978-1-4129-5331-3 (pbk.)
    1. Problem children—Education—United States—Case studies. 2. Remedial teaching—United States—Case studies. 3. School failure—United States—Prevention—Case studies. 4. Behavior disorders in children—Treatment—United States—Case studies. I. Hunley, Sawyer A. II. McNamara, Kathy. III. National Association of School Psychologists. IV. Title: Tier three of the RTI model.

LC4802.T54 2010
371.9—dc22   2009019910

This book is printed on acid-free paper.

09   10   11   12   13   10 9 8 7 6 5 4 3 2 1

Acquisitions Editor:	Jessica Allan
Editorial Assistant:	Joanna Coelho
Production Editor:	Cassandra Margaret Seibel
Copy Editor:	Adam Dunham
Typesetter:	C&M Digitals (P) Ltd.
Proofreader:	Christina West
Cover Designer:	Scott Van Atta

Contents

Preface

Old wine in new skins. In many ways, this text is an apt reflection of this metaphor: For years, the tenets of applied behavioral analysis and behavioral consultation have informed the services that many of us, as school psychologists, have attempted to provide to children, teachers, and parents. Dissatisfied with the limitations of the special education gatekeeping role, school psychologists have expanded our understanding and applications of assessment beyond the mission of diagnosing and categorizing disorders. With the advent of the response to intervention (RTI) framework for our services, we find—perhaps for the first time—a vehicle that is sufficiently flexible and practical to accommodate these tenets in schools, uniting general and special education in a common effort to address the needs of all learners. The challenge has been to navigate the "research to practice gap"—that is, to translate foundational principles and methods to everyday work in schools.

In the RTI model, assessment serves multiple purposes: First, it reveals the impact of instruction and behavior management practices on all students at what has been termed *Tier 1*. Is the reading curriculum effective in teaching basic and advanced skills? Are students progressing at a rate that will be adequate to attain long-term performance goals? Are students developing social competence, and are they being prepared to successfully meet the demands of adult life? The second purpose of assessment in RTI is to identify students whose level of performance and rate of growth are inadequate: Who is failing, or at risk of failure, in attaining established goals? This is accomplished through the analysis of universal screening and strategic monitoring at Tier 1 and progress-monitoring data gathered for students receiving intervention at Tiers 2 and 3, using assessment methods that directly sample behaviors that are research-based indicators of overall functioning.

The third purpose of assessment is to examine students' skills and the learning environment to pinpoint needs and deficiencies: What is the reason for this student's performance problem, and how can it be addressed? It is this third purpose of assessment that forms the core of a case study that is the subject of this text. As we proceed upward through the three tiers of the RTI model, assessment becomes more sharply focused not only on qualitative aspects of students' academic and behavioral performance but also on modifiable environmental factors that are functionally (or causally) related to performance problems. Thus, assessment might demonstrate that a student's lack of motivation or practice contributes to lack of fluency in reading, leading to interventions using incentives and frequent opportunities for reading practice. Similarly, a finding that the materials used for instruction are poorly matched to the student's current skill level would point to the need for changes in instructional materials.

These purposes of assessment are easily understood as both desirable and appropriate in the contemporary practice of school psychology. However, for a variety of reasons, many practitioners lack the knowledge and skills that would enable them to apply methods well suited to these purposes. This text is intended to provide practical guidance to such practitioners. It is not a foundational text in applied behavior analysis, or even in behavioral consultation (which serves as the basis for our model of the case study), and readers interested in more basic instruction in those models are encouraged to consult sources such as Alberto and Troutman (1982) and Bergan and Kratochwill (1990). However, school psychologists who are familiar with basic principles, but lacking in a practical understanding of their applications in practice, will find support in the material contained in this text.

Readers who prefer to develop their understanding of a concept by moving from part to whole can read this text sequentially, beginning with Chapter 1 and moving through to the end. However, we planned the text by consulting the case study rubric, using it as a guide to generate the content of each chapter. Readers who prefer to start with a holistic understanding of a concept, and then investigate its detailed subset of components, may benefit from first reading the case study rubric and the two case studies presented in Chapter 10. This approach will allow the reader to link the technical material explored in each chapter to the concrete examples already presented in Chapter 10. However the reader chooses to approach the text, it is our hope that it will serve as a comprehensive yet practical guide for students and practitioners alike.

In the first chapter, the context in which RTI has evolved as well as challenges to early implementation efforts are discussed. Explanations of the manner in which the RTI process addresses these challenges are provided. In Chapter 2, the reader is given a brief tour of Tiers 1 and 2 and shown how activities and findings at these tiers serve as a precursor to the Tier 3 case study. Assessment methods that are appropriate for use in the RTI (and case study) process are discussed in detail. The role of the school psychologist as a problem-solving consultant and systems change agent is described in Chapter 3.

Chapters 4 through 8 provide a rationale and detailed procedures for conducting the case study at Tier 3. Although chapters treat stages of the case study process discretely, readers are encouraged to view the stages as a holistic approach to assessing and intervening with students at risk for school failure. The problem identification stage described in Chapter 4 uses data gathered at Tiers 1 and 2 to clarify and confirm the severity of student performance problems. It also gathers and synthesizes data leading to hypotheses about the cause of the problem. In Chapter 5, the procedure for hypothesis testing is explained as the key to determining the reason—and an empirically sound solution—for the problem. Chapter 6 describes various single-case designs that can be used for hypothesis testing and monitoring the progress of students receiving interventions. Chapter 7 highlights the practical aspects of selecting and implementing interventions, with emphasis on intervention integrity as a key aspect of a successful case study. A detailed explanation of methods for evaluating case study outcomes is provided in Chapter 8, along with guidelines for deciding whether outcomes are successful.

The final two chapters of the book address implementation issues. Chapter 9 offers a perspective of special education eligibility determination using the RTI process, with a focus on the nature and outcomes of interventions, as well as the integrity of planning and intervention implementation. Chapter 10 proposes two techniques that can be used for evaluation of case study implementation and outcomes by practitioners or in university training programs. The first technique uses aggregated data across case studies to detect patterns revealing the impact of school psychologists on the students that they serve; the second incorporates a case study evaluation rubric, illustrated with examples of completed case studies.

Acknowledgments

The creation of this book has evolved over the years as a result of support by my colleagues, mentors, and friends Jim Evans, Julie Morrison, and Michael Curtis. I am especially grateful to them for sparking the ideas and conversations that encouraged creative responses to unanswered questions. Thanks to Tracy Spires, Dan Trunk, Marjorie Funk, Heather House, and Julie Rabatsky, who have assisted me in researching, developing, and demonstrating the case study rubric. My appreciation goes to the members of the National Association of School Psychologists, the NCSP Board, and Corwin for their contributions to this effort. My profound gratitude goes to my family; they are my cheerleaders when I succeed and when I struggle. Thanks to my parents, Murray and Mary Frances, for showing me the way, and to my husband, Mike, for allowing me to spend countless hours on this project without complaint. Finally, a very special thanks to my daughter, Kristen, who is my confidant and is following in my professional footsteps.

Sawyer Hunley

My students have been a continuing source of challenge and inspiration, convincing me of the need to carefully assemble what I have referenced over the past decade in hastily-scrawled blackboard and PowerPoint diagrams and tables. I am grateful, too, to colleagues who have helped to sharpen my thinking, especially Colleen McMahon, and to those whose patience and support is being rewarded, finally, by the completion of this text—Dan and Caitlin, and Karen. A word of thanks is due to my coauthor, who invited me to join her in this enterprise while we were attending a National Association of School Psychologists (NASP) meeting in the midst of a tropical storm: There's a metaphor in there somewhere! The staff of the NASP, the editorial staff of Corwin, and anonymous reviewers offered suggestions that focused and improved our writing. Finally, for her certain and abiding faith in me— a limitless store from which I drew comfort and confidence for 54 years—I honor the memory of my mother, Mary Ellen.

Kathy McNamara

PUBLISHER'S ACKNOWLEDGMENTS

Corwin would like to acknowledge the following peer reviewers for their editorial insight and guidance:

Gloria Avolio DePaul, PhD
School Counselor, NBCT
Hillsborough County School District
Tampa, FL

Rachel Brown Chidsey, PhD, NCSP
Associate Professor and Program Coordinator
University of Southern Maine
Portland, ME

Joanne Morgan
Doctoral Candidate
School Psychology Program
University of Massachusetts, Amherst
Amherst, MA

Jane Wagmeister, EdD
Director of Curriculum, Instruction, and Continuous Improvement
RTI Co-Chair Task Force
Ventura County Office of Education
Camarillo, CA

About the Authors

Sawyer Hunley, PhD, NCSP, is an associate professor, the Coordinator of the School Psychology Program, and a Learning Teaching Fellow at the University of Dayton. She is chair of the National Certification Board for the National Association of School Psychologists (NASP) and was instrumental in revising the procedure for obtaining the National Credential of School Psychologists (NCSP). The revised process based on the 2000 NASP Standards includes new case study and portfolio requirements, and was inaugurated in fall, 2005. Dr. Hunley has served as a member of the Program Approval Board for the National Association of School Psychologists, and has participated in the writing of the last three revisions of the NASP Standards. Her professional and research interests include systems change for K–12 and higher education. Her publications and presentations have focused on the nature of the changing field of school psychology, data-based decision making, and the relationship between learning space and teaching/learning. She has over twenty years experience as a school psychologist practitioner, supervisor, and faculty member.

Kathy McNamara, PhD, NCSP, is a professor of psychology at Cleveland State University, where she directs the School Psychology Specialist degree program. She currently serves as chair of the Ethics and Professional Practices Committee of the National Association of School Psychologists, and she has been active in the leadership of the Ohio School Psychologists Association since 1984. She has published chapters on social competence and professional ethics in the NASP Best Practices series. Dr. McNamara's research focuses on intervention-based school psychological services, and her work in this area has been published in *The School Psychology Review,* the *Journal of Educational and Psychological Consultation,* and *Exceptional Children.* She has conducted numerous trainings of school psychologists, teachers, and administrators, and consults with school districts regarding implementation of the RTI model. Dr. McNamara has served for 30 years as a school psychologist practitioner, supervisor, and faculty member.

1

Introduction to RTI and the Case Study Model

Response to intervention (RTI) is a school-based system designed to identify and meet children's needs through increasingly more focused and intensive levels ("tiers") of assessment and intervention. It can be applied to academic, behavioral, and mental health issues. A key principle underlying RTI is the notion that all efforts to evaluate and resolve children's school performance deficits represent "problem solving," and that such efforts should persist until effective solutions are found. Stanley Deno (2002) defines a problem as a difference between *what is* (i.e., the child's low score on a measure of math skill), and *what is expected* (i.e., a score similar to that of the average student, or to a benchmark standard). RTI is a large-scale problem-solving process, which incorporates assessment to identify children who demonstrate deficits, and it provides intervention to reduce or eliminate the deficits.

Assessment in RTI is used in a *preventive* context, to ensure that universal instruction is effective, and to identify students who demonstrate risk for failure. At each successive level, assessment becomes more focused on conditions associated with poor school performance. Decisions (i.e., about the need for intervention, characteristics of appropriate interventions, and effectiveness of interventions) are based not on the judgments or opinions of teachers and other instructional personnel but on data generated in the course of assessment, as well as on the strength of evidence supporting the choice of a particular intervention strategy.

In a *remedial* context, RTI is used to gather information needed to select appropriate interventions and to monitor their effects. Intervention in RTI consists of scientific, research-based strategies to remediate deficient performance, provided on a classroom, group, or individual basis. Increasingly more intensive and specialized forms of intervention are introduced as children demonstrate failure to respond adequately to interventions provided at each successive level. At the most intensive level (Tier 3), the selection of an appropriate and effective intervention requires in-depth study of factors contributing to or maintaining the child's performance deficit. This process—along with procedures to monitor and judge the success of interventions—is implemented in the form of a case study.

CONTEXT AND HISTORY

Although relatively new to the field of school psychology, the conceptual and practical foundations of the RTI model are not new. In the field of special education, attention has long been paid to the need to track children's academic progress and to apply evidence-based interventions to their learning problems (Deno & Mirkin, 1977; Ysseldyke & Algozzine, 1982). In recent years, the shift in attention from procedural accountability (i.e., are schools following the rules?) to accountability for student outcomes (i.e., are students learning?) has created an ideal environment for RTI, with its emphasis on routine and systematic assessment of student performance. The Elementary and Secondary Education Act (ESEA), reauthorized in 2001 as the No Child Left Behind Act (2002), mandated the attainment of satisfactory levels of academic skills by all children, lending a sense of urgency to efforts to improve instruction and intervention for underperforming students.

In the mid-1970s, the behavioral consultation (BC) model was introduced as a method for defining student performance problems, identifying contributing factors, developing interventions targeting those factors, and measuring the success of interventions (Kratochwill & Bergan, 1990) (See Table 1.1 for a summary of the stages of the BC model). Variations of the BC model have evolved over the years and have been adopted by most states in policies requiring intervention in general education, prior to consideration of special education eligibility (Buck, Polloway, Smith-Thomas, & Wilcox Cook, 2003).

Numerous studies support the effectiveness of BC and its procedural offspring for addressing children's school performance problems (Burns & Symington, 2002). The emphasis of these approaches on the collection of data to describe student performance and measure intervention outcomes has been complemented by the growing popularity of assessment techniques such as Curriculum-Based Measurement (CBM), which

Table 1.1   The Four General Stages of Behavioral Consultation

1. Problem identification (definition of the problem in measurable terms, including comparison with some standard or norm that defines "expected" performance)

2. Problem analysis (study of the factors that are contributing to the problem; in functional assessment, this includes developing and testing hypotheses about environmental factors that are functionally related to the problem)

3. Plan implementation (intervention carried out according to a plan that includes frequent measurement of the child's progress during the intervention as well as monitoring of intervention fidelity)

4. Problem evaluation (review and analysis of progress-monitoring results to determine whether the intervention should continue, change, terminate, or be phased out)

Source: Adapted from Bergan and Kratochwill (1990)

directly measure children's academic skills (Hosp, Hosp, & Howell, 2007). These developments provide technical support for RTI, with its dual emphasis on assessment and intervention as key elements of effective educational practice.

A third factor has contributed to the growing influence of the RTI approach: the poor "treatment validity" of so-called "test-and-place" practices, in which diagnostic evaluations often led to special education placement (where appropriate interventions were assumed to occur). Test-and-place practices have been criticized for their use of evaluation procedures that seek to identify deficits in individual aptitudes—often inferred from the results of individual intelligence tests. This, in turn, leads to recommendations for interventions to remediate those deficits (and, by further inference, the academic problems thought to result from aptitude deficiencies).

However, research support for this approach has been limited, and efforts to link test-and-place practices with meaningful and effective intervention have been largely unsuccessful (Reschly & Ysseldyke, 2002). In contrast, RTI employs direct measurement of academic performance and behavior, identifying relationships between problems and environmental factors through a process of hypothesis testing. When appropriate targets for intervention have been identified (e.g., opportunities for students to practice skills, incentives for accurate performance), strategies are devised to modify or create environmental conditions that will optimize the potential for improved student performance.

Finally, while the RTI model can be applied to a range of suspected disabilities, its growing popularity can be traced to concerns about unacceptably high rates of learning disability diagnosis and special education placement. This disability category accounts for just over 50% of children enrolled in special education programs (Vaughn & Fuchs, 2003). Federal government initiatives clearly conveyed concern about problems that were apparent in practices used to identify learning disabilities.

In December, 2003, the National Research Center on Learning Disabilities (NRCLD) (2004) held a symposium to explore alternatives for meeting the needs of children with specific learning disabilities. Created by the U.S. Department of Education (Office of Special Education Programs, OSEP), the NRCLD, a joint endeavor of Vanderbilt University and the University of Kansas, had been given the task of conducting research and helping schools learn about more effective service delivery models. Prior to this symposium, OSEP had sponsored the *Learning Disabilities Summit: Building a Foundation for the Future* in August, 2001, and commissioned a series of white papers and roundtable discussions on the topic (Bradley, Danielson, & Hallahan, 2002).

The *Executive Summary* of the 2003 NRCLD Symposium outlines the problems that led to the OSEP initiative:

> the exponential increases in the number of students who are considered to have learning disabilities, the reliance on IQ tests, the exclusion of environmental factors, the inconsistency in procedures and criteria within school districts and across states, and the reliance on aptitude-achievement discrepancy formulas and the manner in which they are used." (NRCLD, 2004, p. 1)

In addition to these concerns, Kavale and Forness (1999), reported results of a meta-analysis of research on special education suggesting that placement of children with disabilities in special education programs *in itself* often did not result in meaningful improvement, perhaps due in part to lower student performance expectations.

In the 2004 reauthorization of IDEA, legislators addressed these concerns by offering an alternative to traditional test-and-place practices. Specifically, the law allowed schools to "use a process that determines if the child responds to scientific, research-based intervention as part of the evaluation procedures" (Individuals with Disabilities Education Improvement Act, 2004, P.L. No. 108-446, par 614). Commonly interpreted as a reference to RTI, this language suggests that the process of delivering interventions based on ongoing performance assessment can serve as a basis for determining whether a child has a specific learning disability. It shifts emphasis from a determination of disability based on results of diagnostic tests administered at one point in time to an examination of data resulting from the application of interventions over time.

In summary, a variety of factors has created an environment conducive to RTI implementation, including mandates for accountability, the evolution of behavioral consultation and related models for service delivery, the push for evaluation practices with greater "treatment validity," and dissatisfaction with assessment and placement practices for children with specific learning disabilities.

THE RESPONSE TO INTERVENTION PROCESS

Assessment and intervention practices employed in the RTI model are typically described in context of three "tiers," organized hierarchically to reflect increasingly more focused assessment and more intensive intervention (Figure 1.1).

Tier 1. Tier 1 is considered a form of "primary prevention," in that it involves all children in high quality, research-based core instruction, as well as periodic assessment of performance. It is similar to the evidence-based practice of inoculating all children against disease or conducting periodic "well-child" exams to ensure satisfactory development. Tier 1 includes differentiated instruction (e.g., flexible grouping) and classroom accommodations (e.g., study aids) to enhance children's understanding of core instruction. Universal screening at Tier 1 consists of quarterly assessment of

Figure 1.1   Response to Intervention "Pyramid"

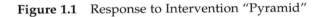

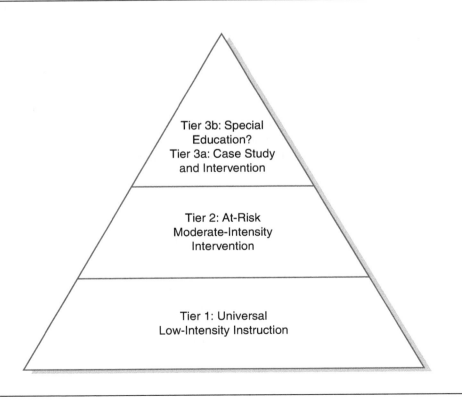

key academic and behavioral targets or skills. Local norms can be generated from these assessment results and, along with benchmark standards, are used to evaluate students' progress toward established goals. Tier 1 assessment also may include strategic monitoring of the performance of students who display moderate performance deficits and of emergent reading skills of students in the primary grades.

Tier 2. When Tier 1 assessment identifies children who are not making adequate progress, the second level of the assessment and intervention process is activated. Tier 2, a form of "secondary prevention," consists of "additional individual instruction, small group instruction, and/or technology-assisted instruction to support and reinforce skills taught by the classroom teacher" (McCook, 2006, p. 30) or interventions to reduce the occurrence of behavior problems among individuals known to be at risk. Tier 2 interventions are generally chosen from a set of research-based strategies selected by the school for remediation of targeted academic and behavior problems. They are considered to be of moderate intensity because they involve more resources than would be available to entire classes, but do not require the highly specialized resources and strategies that are delivered at Tier 3.

What kinds of intervention are used at Tier 2? In some cases, Tier 2 interventions—which are always offered *in addition to* the instruction of Tier 1—consist simply of additional time and opportunity for review and practice of skills, which can be provided by the general education teacher, a classroom aid, or even the student or the student's classmate. Other Tier 2 interventions make use of ancillary personnel, such as federally funded reading and math tutors, who provide additional instruction for students having difficulty acquiring skills, or classroom aids who monitor and provide feedback and incentives for targeted behaviors. However, the mere assignment of a student to an existing remedial program does not guarantee that a valid, research-based intervention will be used at Tier 2. Instead, instructional practices and materials and behavior plans should be reviewed to ensure that they have research support and that the intervention strategies themselves are used in an appropriate and consistent manner.

Still other Tier 2 interventions are drawn from the "standard treatment protocols" developed by literacy experts, particularly for use with children in the primary grades. The "empirical approach" to problem solving also can be used; in it, general education teachers or teams select interventions from an array of strategies that research has shown to be effective for various types of problems, without testing their effectiveness for specific children (e.g., repeated readings or listening previewing for reading fluency problems, active teaching of classroom rules with incentives for compliance in the case of behavior problems).

Tier 3. The topmost area of the pyramid-shaped RTI model is reserved for those (relatively few) students who do not make adequate progress at Tier 2. The assumption underlying Tier 3 is that instruction and interventions delivered at Tiers 1 and 2 have not targeted the actual cause of the problem, so further assessment is needed. The case study model provides a framework for this assessment. It uses a planning process that takes into consideration children's unique needs and circumstances, in contrast to Tiers 1 and 2, where *standardized* interventions are offered to children who demonstrate risk for failure.

Unlike Tiers 1 and 2, Tier 3 has not received much attention in discussions of the RTI model, probably because it is often considered to be equivalent to special education. In fact, The National Research Center on Learning Disabilities (2007) observes that, "in most schools, Tier 3 might be synonymous with special education," although the author goes on to describe it as "sustained, intensive support in the specified area of need . . . tailored to the individual student . . . [which] may continue for much longer periods, depending on student need" (p. 7). The difficulty with equating Tier 3 with special education placement is that it does not allow for the conceptual framework of RTI as a problem-solving model to be incorporated into the third tier of the process. Although special education services and comprehensive evaluation to determine eligibility may occur at Tier 3, the tier is defined in more general terms as individual assessment and intervention to meet children's unique and specific needs, without regard for the setting (special vs. general education) in which it occurs.

The case study procedure in this text presents Tier 3 in two phases (see Figure 1.2); Tier 3a consists of the application of the case study procedure to generate and test explanations (hypotheses) for the child's performance problem. When a "high probability" hypothesis has been identified, interventions targeting factors implicated in that hypothesis can be developed and monitored to evaluate effectiveness. Interventions may vary in intensity, from low (e.g., additional practice opportunities in a peer-assisted learning context, based on a hypothesis of "insufficient practice"), to moderate (e.g., daily small group instruction to teach decoding or comprehension skills, based on a hypothesis of "insufficient help/instruction"), to high intensity (e.g., daily one-to-one instruction using curricular materials from a lower grade level). Children who require high-intensity interventions receive them in context of Tier 3 (often, but not always, on an individual basis), while those requiring less intensive intervention might be assigned to participate in intervention activities already in place for children at Tiers 1 and 2. When a high-intensity intervention is required, it may be of such a specialized nature that a disability is suspected, triggering an evaluation to determine whether entitlement to the intervention—in the form of an individual education plan—is warranted.

Figure 1.2   Tier 3 of the RTI Model

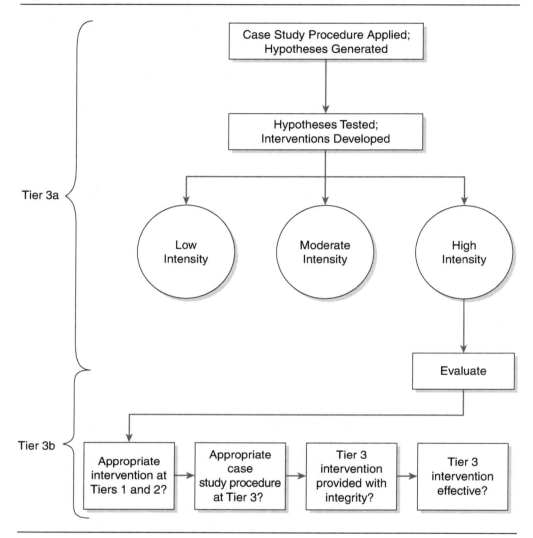

To determine whether a disability is present, interventions of high intensity should be evaluated (Tier 3b) across several criteria: First, whether appropriate, evidence-based interventions were provided as intended at Tiers 1 and 2; second, whether the case study procedure at Tier 3 was applied in an appropriate manner (i.e., with "fidelity"); third, whether the intervention resulting from the case study procedure was provided as intended (i.e., with "integrity"); and, fourth, whether progress-monitoring results indicate that the intervention was effective (successful or promising). These conditions all must be met before the question of eligibility for special education (i.e., legal entitlement to intervention using specialized resources, based on an individual education plan) should be considered. The decision-making process associated with special education eligibility determination is described in more detail in Chapter 9.

Although the focus of most of the literature is on academic performance problems, the RTI framework also can be used to address behavior problems. Tier 1 "instruction" would include the behavior management techniques used on a schoolwide or classwide basis, with all students. Schools employing positive behavior supports (PBS), for example, might post the names of students who have demonstrated exemplary behavior or award points to students or classes that have low rates of disciplinary referrals. As long as these methods are used with all students in the class, grade level, or school, they are considered to be Tier 1 instruction.

Students who fail to demonstrate acceptable levels of appropriate behavior under Tier 1 conditions alone are moved to Tier 2, where interventions known to be effective with behavior problems are introduced. An example of a Tier 2 intervention is differential reinforcement, a research-based strategy that involves reinforcement of desired behavior and planned ignoring of undesired behavior. As a Tier 2 intervention, differential reinforcement would be used by teachers with those few students who continue to display unacceptable levels of problem behavior, in contrast to their peers, for whom Tier 1 instruction has proven adequate.

At the next level—Tier 3—assessment is needed to clearly define the problem behavior (and its target or replacement behavior), certify its severity, and identify factors that are causing or maintaining the problem behavior. This information is used to generate hypotheses that are then linked to interventions. In a manner similar to that employed for academic problems, behavioral interventions are monitored through frequent observations of student performance, with comparison to baseline levels of performance and goals established by intervention planners. Inadequate progress toward specified goals is evidence that an effective intervention has not yet been identified, and there is a need to improve or replace the intervention until a satisfactory level of performance has been attained.

THE CASE STUDY MODEL AND PREREFERRAL INTERVENTION

The five-stage process used in this text to describe the case study conducted at Tier 3 is a modified version of the model described by Bergan and Kratochwill (1990) summarized in Table 1.1. It also addresses several problematic features of *prereferral intervention*, an early version of the case study process outlined in the work of Graden, Casey, and Bonstrom (1985a).

Initially conceived as a dyadic consultation process (e.g., involving a teacher and school psychologist), prereferral intervention came to be associated with a team-based delivery model, in which a group of teachers, administrators, and specialists served as consultants, typically to the general education teacher who referred the student. Many terms have been used to describe this model, including *mainstream assistance teams, intervention assistance teams, instructional assistance teams,* and *intervention-based assessment teams.* What they all have in common is a step-by-step problem-solving sequence, typically some derivative of behavioral consultation (Bergan & Kratochwill, 1990). This problem-solving process is used in prereferral intervention to develop and deliver interventions to children in the general education setting. Prereferral intervention, which occurs in general education settings, reported success in reducing referrals to special education, and enhancing student achievement (Graden, Casey, & Bonstrom, 1985a; Fuchs, Fuchs, Bahr, Fernstrom, & Stecker, 1990; McNamara & Hollinger, 2003).

As more states adopted some form of team-based prereferral intervention, it began to be treated as a recommended or mandatory prerequisite to referral for evaluation for a suspected disability (Truscott, Cohen, Sams, Sanborn, & Frank, 2005). This fact, combined with the problems that accompany the transition from laboratory to field (sometimes termed the "research to practice gap"), led to a number of problems that continue to plague field-based prereferral intervention practices. The five most salient problems are related to student outcomes, collaboration and teaming, interventions, decision making, and special education focus; these are explained below, along with the manner in which they are addressed in the case study model employed at Tier 3 of the RTI process.

Student outcomes. Although team-based prereferral intervention received positive reviews from educators and, especially, parents, studies using *actual student outcomes* are lacking, and those that do exist report equivocal results (Fuchs, Mock, Morgan, & Young, 2003; McNamara, 1998). In contrast, studies have shown that application of the RTI model in general, and the case study procedure employed at Tier 3 in particular, result in improved student outcomes (Burns, Appleton, & Stehouwer, 2005; Gresham, 2002; MacLeod, Jones, Somers, & Havey, 2001).

Within the case study procedure itself, numerous provisions are made for data-based decision making about the nature and severity of student problems, factors contributing to problems, and the effectiveness of intervention outcomes. These provisions include the use of single-subject designs for hypothesis testing and progress monitoring, as well as decision rules for determining whether the intervention has been successful. In every instance, student performance data are drawn from direct measures such as Curriculum-Based Measurement or behavioral observation. In addition, technical adequacy of the case study can be monitored for fidelity of implementation by using the case study rubric that is presented in this text. All of these provisions enable researchers to link application of the case study procedure—embedded within the RTI model—to data demonstrating improved student outcomes.

Collaboration and teaming. Collaboration among stakeholders in the problem-solving process has been cited as a critical component of intervention success (Allen & Graden, 2002). This would seem to be especially important for classroom teachers, who are typically given responsibility for implementing interventions (Slonski-Fowler & Truscott, 2004). However, enthusiasm for team-based "collaborative problem-solving" has been dampened somewhat by observations that many studies demonstrating successful prereferral intervention employed a dyadic consultation model, which does not necessarily translate to the team-based practices currently employed in most schools. Research has shown that the success of teams depends on knowledge and skills, which members may not possess (Flugum & Reschly, 1994; Telzrow, McNamara, & Hollinger, 2000), and that collaboration may not be necessary for successful problem solving (Schulte & Osborne, 2003). Teams report problems in functioning (e.g., inadequate leadership, inequitable task distribution, conflict) that could limit their effectiveness, to the extent that issues related to team dynamics detract from the quality of a team's problem-solving performance (McNamara, Rasheed, & DeLamatre, 2008). Consistent with this observation, Lee and Jamison (2003) found that the fidelity with which a problem-solving sequence was applied was influenced by patterns of interaction among team members. So, although collaborative problem solving was conceived as a coequal partnership between specialists and general educators, in practice, it often did not live up to initial expectations.

In contrast, the RTI model invites collaboration in several ways that are well matched to the strengths of teams, beginning with examination of the results of universal assessments to determine whether instruction is effective and to identify students in need of intervention. Teams also play a key role in creating structures to support the delivery of interventions at Tier 2; Burns and Gibbons (2008), for example, have suggested that grade-level teacher teams should meet regularly to examine the progress of students and troubleshoot interventions. However, the RTI process is not limited to deployment in team meetings focusing on the needs of a small subset of students, but it is a part of the everyday operation of the school.

The RTI model, including the Tier 3 case study procedure, offers two features that restore and enhance the collaborative partnership between consultants (such as school psychologists) and teachers. First, it reconfigures the role of the school psychologist to become a problem solver who works with general education teachers in both preventive and remedial capacities. Instead of serving primarily as a gatekeeper for special education, school psychologists working as consultants within an RTI framework help teachers accomplish their classroom goals. As the relationship between a teacher and the school psychologist develops, a level of trust and mutual understanding facilitates the selection and use of assessment and intervention strategies that are not only appropriate to the needs of students but also feasible for classroom use.

The nature of Tier 2 interventions also holds promise in eliciting a greater degree of cooperation from classroom teachers. General education teachers may have limited knowledge of alternative strategies, and they are sometimes unwilling to attempt interventions, particularly if they view them as complicated and demanding. At Tier 2, interventions that are appropriate for use in general education settings, many of them standard protocols designed for small groups of students, are recommended. If teachers themselves are responsible for delivering Tier 2 interventions, they need only learn those strategies selected for implementation at their grade level or for targeted deficits (e.g., standard protocols or methods such as peer-assisted learning) and techniques for enhancing their effectiveness (e.g., adding rewards, increasing frequency of intervention sessions).

In some cases, the instructional interventions used at Tier 2 can be adapted for use with an entire class. These qualities make it easier and more practical for teachers to deliver interventions to students in general education settings. By reducing the demand on teachers to provide individual accommodations for students who will instead receive small group intervention at Tier 2, the RTI process may lead to greater willingness on the part of teachers to provide individualized intervention for those few students who reach Tier 3.

Interventions. Clearly, the quality and integrity of interventions are key elements of success. There is substantial concern about the *quality and integrity of interventions* in the prereferral model. Despite the call for the use of research-based practices, interventions often are of poor quality, inadequately defined, and poorly communicated to those responsible for providing the interventions (Flugum & Reschly, 1994; Telzrow et al., 2000). Interventions also suffer from a lack of infrastructure to support them, resulting in inadequate integrity; that is, those delivering interventions often do so in ways that differ significantly from the initial plan, if they deliver them at all (Gresham, 1989). Since many prereferral teams fail to collect appropriate progress-monitoring data, they have no means to determine on a timely basis whether interventions are having the desired effect (Telzrow et al., 2000).

As a systematic procedure for creating and supporting feasible interventions in general education at Tier 2, the RTI process is likely to yield greater degrees of intervention integrity; that is, classroom teachers may be more likely to implement them as designed. Since the needs of a greater proportion of students can be adequately addressed at Tier 2, teachers may be better able to manage the demands for individualized intervention at Tier 3. The case study model requires that interventions be monitored for implementation integrity and offers recommendations for doing so (e.g., the use of observers, performance feedback, and implementation checklists). This provision increases the likelihood that interventions will be administered appropriately and consistently. Finally, a growing network of resources supports the selection and delivery of scientific, research-based interventions.

Currently, sources of empirical evidence for intervention efficacy are found in various literatures and sponsored Web sites (Kratochwill, Clements, & Kalymon, 2007). The Clearinghouse of Evidence-based Practices (Kratochwill, 2007), although in its infancy, is planned to evaluate and organize interventions in an easy-to-use, convenient location. In a meta-analysis of available research, Swanson, Hoskyn, and Lee (1999) identified a number of interventions found to be effective for children with academic performance problems; these and other studies are a rich source of information about evidence-based strategies that can be embedded at various tiers of intervention. In addition to the selection of quality interventions, the case study model employs data collection and progress-monitoring procedures (as well as clear decision rules) that identify ineffective interventions several weeks (rather than months) after their initiation, so they can be improved or replaced with more effective strategies on a timelier basis.

Biased decision making. Most prereferral models depend on subjective referrals or biased decision making to identify students who need additional help. For example, studies have shown that teachers are influenced by children's characteristics when deciding whether to refer children for evaluation (Bahr, Fuchs, Stecker, & Fuchs, 1991; Clarizio, 1992). Concern also has been expressed about teachers' ability to reliably identify all students needing assistance, as well as their willingness to do so (Slonski-Fowler & Truscott, 2004). At the other end of the spectrum are concerns about the referral of students whose problems really don't require the intensive problem-solving process used in prereferral intervention. In some instances, the failure of poorly planned or inadequate interventions led teams to conclude that evaluation for a learning disability was the only route to meaningful intervention for many students (McNamara, DeLamatre, & Rasheed, 2002; McNamara & Hollinger, 2003).

Biased decision making regarding referral and program placement leads to over or under representation of diverse student populations and to unreliable application of standards for determining children's need and eligibility for services requiring scarce educational resources (e.g., special education and related services). The remedy for bias lies in the use of a structured, data-based process that provides clear, explicit rules for decision making, not only eliminating bias from decision making but also providing accountability information.

At Tiers 1 and 2 of the RTI model, student learning is assessed periodically using measures directly related to the general education curriculum. Data are displayed on a graph that can be used to decide whether adequate progress toward curricular goals is occurring either for groups of students (Tier 1) or for those receiving more intensive services (Tier 2). When growth is inadequate, intervention can be changed or intensified. At Tier 3, data already collected at Tiers 1 and 2 can be used to define a child's problem in behavioral terms. With bias eliminated and a commitment to effective intervention for all children, schools can modify instructional practices and adjust decision rules so that appropriate proportions of the student population are represented at each tier of the RTI model.

The most common three-tier RTI model (see Figure 1.1) suggests that Tier 1 instruction will elicit an adequate response from 80% of the student population; Tier 2 intervention will be sufficient for 15%; and Tier 3 intervention will be needed by 5% of the school population (Reschly, 2008). These cutoff points are somewhat arbitrary, and it may be prudent to adjust them according to the needs of the school population, since it may not always be feasible to strengthen instruction to the degree required for success at Tiers 1 and 2. For example, a school with a large proportion of students who are functioning well below the expected national benchmark may choose to increase the proportion of students in Tiers 2 and 3. In this way, the RTI system allows for regulation of stable numbers of students who qualify for special education services (a subset of those receiving intensive intervention at Tier 3).

When properly applied, the research-based instruction and supports of Tiers 1 and 2 will have been successful for some children, thereby enabling problem-solving teams to address only the problems of those children who need individualized assessment and intervention. This *gating function* is one of the most valuable features of RTI. Without it, intervention teams receive referrals to conduct evaluations and plan individualized interventions for children who might have been successful with intensified small-group instruction, thereby consuming time and resources needed elsewhere.

Special education focus. Prereferral intervention has been plagued by a narrow view of it as a *prerequisite to special education evaluation.* Many educators persist in believing that special education placement in itself will solve children's academic and behavior problems, and they are not motivated to implement "general education" interventions that they expect to fail (Eidle, Truscott, Meyers, & Boyd, 1998). Financial incentives promote special education placement (i.e., federal funds based on annual counts of children with disabilities), and teachers may be motivated to seek placement that will relieve them of responsibility for children who are difficult to teach. Consequently, the prereferral intervention process is sometimes regarded as a necessary evil on the way to the *real* intervention known as special education, and prereferral intervention is undertaken with an expectation of failure.

Apart from findings consistently demonstrating that special education has not been effective in resolving children's academic problems, labeling children with a disability is a high-stakes decision that should not be undertaken without adequate justification (Burns, Jacob, & Wagner, 2008). In addition, as the law places increasingly greater demands on schools to show evidence of actual gains in student performance, special education placement may be less likely to be regarded as a panacea.

When it is necessary to use information generated in an RTI framework for making special education eligibility and classification decisions about individual students, such information should be interpreted as *an indicator of the student's need for intensive interventions* rather than a diagnostic tool. RTI is a better source of information about effective instruction and intervention than it is for the classification of children's abilities and disabilities. Essentially, it is a "rule-in strategy" to find the most appropriate intervention, not a "rule-out strategy" for identifying what does not work. The second phase of Tier 3 (which we have termed *Tier 3b*) is not a series of actions that is separate from and *follows* the RTI process but an evaluation of the nature of effective interventions that have been developed through the case study process. Although Tier 3 is not equivalent to special education, as some interpretations suggest, it can lead to and inform the eligibility determination process.

The case study model has been structured to include a detailed series of requirements and has been transformed into the case study rubric (presented in Chapter 10) to guide implementation and to ensure that all student concerns are addressed in a consistent manner. Key elements of the model include collaborative problem solving, data-based decision making, logical linkage between the stages, and fidelity of case study procedures.

In the first phase of the case study, facilitators verify that data gathered from Tiers 1 and 2 are sufficient to initiate a more focused and intensive problem-solving process. Also during this phase, the behavior is operationally defined and quantified in terms of both current and desired levels of performance, and the severity and importance of the problem are documented ("problem identification and certification"). In the second phase ("problem analysis"), data from various sources are used to generate hypotheses for academic and behavior problems, based on both skill and performance perspectives. Resulting "high probability" hypotheses are tested to verify the cause of the problem; these hypotheses can be linked to appropriate intervention strategies. In the third phase ("plan implementation"), research-based interventions are implemented, while treatment integrity and intervention effectiveness are monitored. Finally, in the fourth and last phase ("plan evaluation"), progress-monitoring data are evaluated to determine intervention effectiveness; successful interventions may be continued or faded, while those that are less successful may be modified. At this final stage of the process, it also is important to evaluate the fidelity with which the case study procedure was applied since, in some cases, the apparent failure of an intervention may in fact be due to inappropriate or inadequate problem solving.

SUMMARY

The RTI framework holds considerable promise in addressing the concerns described in this chapter—specifically, those having to do with biased referral, unwieldy prereferral team caseloads, the need for more and better research-based interventions that teachers actually will use, and the unfounded notion that every child experiencing problems needs an individualized intervention. The case study model was constructed as a structured, data-based decision-making process to find solutions to problems and to overcome unproven assumptions about special education as the only effective solution to the problems of children who are difficult to teach.

2

Assessment Principles and Practices

All of the structures and processes comprising the RTI model are grounded in assessment. Universal screening at Tier 1—used to ensure that instruction is meeting specified goals and to identify students at risk for failure—employs periodic assessment of student performance, judging it against benchmarks and normative standards. At Tier 2, assessment is used to identify deficiencies that will be the target of supplemental intervention and to monitor progress toward grade-level goals of students receiving intervention. Finally, at Tier 3, assessment identifies environmental factors that explain students' performance problems, tests hypotheses to confirm the role played by those factors, and measures progress toward specific goals while intervention is being provided. For each of these applications, direct measures of academic performance, behavior, and environmental conditions and events are recommended.

ASSESSMENT METHODS

Assessment techniques can be located on a continuum of directness to indirectness. The more direct the measure, the lower the degree of inference associated with that measure. The term *inference* refers to the degree of dissimilarity between what is measured and the behavior of interest. Thus, a "low-inference" measurement of the social skill of "conversing with peers" might include a frequency count, based on direct observation, of the number of times the student initiates a verbal interaction with a peer that lasts longer than 10 seconds—although it is doubtful that most general education teachers would have the resources or patience to evaluate behavior with this degree of specificity! A higher-inference measurement of the same skill might consist of the administration of a rating instrument that includes a "peer interaction" scale, where items describe typical peer interactions and ask the respondent to indicate how frequently the student displays such behavior. Finally, a very high inference measure of the skill would be reflected in administration of a self-report inventory measuring introversion versus extroversion, where high scores on the extroversion scale are assumed to be indicative of a tendency to engage in frequent and skillful peer interaction. Similarly, obtaining a sample of a student's actual reading performance (by listening to the student read text aloud) represents a low-inference measurement of reading skill, while the use of an IQ score to estimate the likelihood of successful reading involves a much higher level of inference.

It is important to use direct measures of academic skills and behavior to the greatest extent possible because they provide an estimate of performance that is both reliable (i.e., measured with accuracy) and valid (i.e., measures the actual phenomenon of interest). They also make it possible to measure and evaluate progress in a precise, unambiguous manner. In the case study process, repeated measures of performance are used—first, to obtain a description of the behavior at baseline, prior to intervention, and then, on multiple occasions, to determine how much progress is being made toward intervention goals. It is important to note that published, nationally-normed achievement tests are not considered useful for purposes of behavioral description, whether for problem identification, baseline measurement, or progress monitoring purposes, as they lack the degree of precision needed in a case study. More specifically, such tests (1) do not include adequate samples of test items reflecting the curriculum in which the child is being instructed; (2) have relatively few items at their lowest (floor) and highest (ceiling) levels, compounding the problem of inadequate item sampling for children at both extremes; (3) are not responsive to small changes in performance and may not discriminate subtle performance differences; and (4) yield scores that are descriptive of the child's performance relative to a national norm group, rather than of the child's performance relative to expected outcomes in his or her own setting (Shapiro, 2004).

When developing an assessment plan for a school, classroom, or individual at any tier of the RTI model, it is important to keep in mind several essential features:

1. The method must measure skills and behaviors that are the same as those students are expected to learn (i.e., curriculum overlap or content validity).

2. The method must be sensitive to small changes in performance, so that even a minimal degree of improvement in skills will be evident upon readministration.

3. The method must be easily administered, and appropriate for frequent, repeated use; it need not be diagnostic, but only an indicator of overall skill in the domain being assessed.

Frequent and repeated administration of measures is important because the purpose of formative assessment is to inform instruction as it occurs rather than after it has been completed (Shapiro, 2004). It allows educators to determine whether instruction is having the desired effect for all students (Tier 1 assessment) and to measure the progress of those students receiving intervention services (Tiers 2 and 3).

When formative assessment is used properly, it is possible to identify students who are *at risk* for failure. It also enables educators to decide whether an intervention is working relatively early in the process. Consequently, students receive assistance before their problems escalate, and interventions can be modified if data collected over a period of several weeks indicate that the interventions are not working as well as expected. These benefits eliminate the "wait to fail" phenomenon that plagues traditional practices requiring documentation of failure prior to the introduction of meaningful intervention.

Several formative assessment methods are appropriate for use in an RTI framework; for academic assessment, the focus of this text is on *Curriculum-Based Measurement,* which can be supplemented with Subskill Mastery Measurement to pinpoint specific deficits. For behavior (rather than academic) problems, behavioral measurement methods and their applications at Tiers 1, 2, and 3 also will be described.

Curriculum-Based Measurement (CBM), developed by Deno and Mirkin (1977) and elaborated by Shinn (1989), was designed specifically to satisfy the three criteria presented above. All three tiers in the RTI process can employ CBM for decision making. CBM procedures involve the administration of brief measures of basic skills using materials known as "probes." The content of probes varies depending on the type of CBM that is being used. The first type, CBM *General-Outcome Measures* (GOM), includes reading and writing assessments, which enable educators to track students' performance over time on a capstone task that subsumes a broad range of skills in an academic domain; GOM does not provide information about progress toward mastery of specific subskills (Hosp, Hosp, & Howell, 2007).

A second type of CBM, *Skill-Based Measures* (SBM), also tracks students' performance over time, but each probe consists of a random selection of items that represent, on a proportionally equal basis, all of the subskills comprising the long-term goals of instruction. SBMs are used for academic domains in which there is no single capstone measure of successful performance. They are appropriate measures of the academic domains of math and spelling, where end-of-year goals are attained through mastery of a set of subskills. For example, success in a second-grade math curriculum might depend on fluent performance of several subskills, including knowledge of addition and subtraction facts as well as the ability to calculate double-digit addition with and without regrouping.

Tasks used for measurement in GOM and SBM forms of Curriculum-Based Measurement include oral reading (a passage read aloud by the student for one minute), writing (a three-minute written story produced by the student in response to a brief "story starter" or prompt), math (a sheet of problems reflecting basic math skills, completed by the student in two- to five-minute administration, and, if desired, problems involving math concepts and applications), and spelling (a list of words written by the student in response to dictation at varying rates, depending on the grade level). A measure of reading comprehension known as "maze" also is available, although oral reading fluency is a good predictor of overall reading skill, making comprehension measures optional, particularly for screening of students in the primary and elementary grades (Joseph, 2007).

All of the formative assessment methods used in an RTI framework measure fluency in the targeted skill, which reports performance as a rate within a given time period. Thus, CBM scores are reported as "number of words read correctly *per minute*," or "number of digits correct *per minute*," and so on. Fluency has been shown to be a reliable predictor of overall skill, although it does not give detailed or diagnostic information about aspects of performance such as the types of errors made by students, or prerequisite skills that may be lacking (Shinn, 1989).

A measure originally designed as a downward extension of CBM, known as DIBELS (Dynamic Indicators of Basic Early Literacy Skills), is used by educators who wish to focus on the development of reading skills (Good, Gruba, & Kaminski, 2002). The original DIBELS measured prereading skills in the area of phonemic awareness (i.e., initial sound fluency, letter sound fluency, phoneme segmentation fluency), based on research demonstrating the predictive validity of these skills for success in acquiring reading skills (Joseph, 2007). DIBELS includes other measures of literacy, including oral reading fluency, word identification fluency, and retell fluency.

Assessment procedures for DIBELS Oral Reading Fluency (DORF) are identical to those used in CBM: Students read three different passages aloud for one minute. Fluency is calculated as the number of words read correctly in one minute, with the median score from the three passages recorded as the fluency score for that administration (Good et al., 2002). Retell fluency is determined by asking the student to retell the details of a passage in one minute after reading the passage aloud for one minute. A retell score is then determined by counting the number of words the student uses to retell the story. A retell percentage score can be calculated by dividing the retell score by the oral reading fluency score (Good et al., 2002).

Extensive information, including measurement probes useful for both universal screening and progress monitoring, as well as directions for administration and scoring, are available for Curriculum-Based Measurement (at no cost) from the Intervention Central (http://www.interventioncentral.org), DIBELS (http://dibels.uoregon.edu), and Easy CBM (http://www.easycbm.com) Web sites. Table 2.1 summarizes features of GOM, SBM, and DIBELS that are consistent with the "essential features" criteria described earlier.

Table 2.1 Features of Curriculum-Based Measurement (CBM): General-Outcome Measures (GOM), Skills-Based Measures (SBM), and Dynamic Indicators of Basic Early Literacy Skills (DIBELS)

Essential Features of Assessment Method	General-Outcome Measure (GOM)	Skills-Based Measure (SBM)	Both GOM and SBM	DIBELS
Measures the same skills as those students are expected to learn (curriculum overlap or alignment, content validity).	Samples capstone skill requiring application of contributing subskills (e.g., oral reading fluency), but does not discretely sample those subskills.	Samples, at each assessment session, an equivalent proportion of subskills (presented in random order) that compose long-term curricular goals (e.g., math computation).	Probes created from the student's own curriculum materials. Or Standard, published probes selected to reflect the same levels of difficulty as materials in the student's own curriculum (GOM), or the same array of subskills composing long-term instructional goals (SBM).	Samples early literacy skills, including phonemic awareness and oral reading fluency and comprehension. Measures correspond to "Big Ideas" underlying successful reading (National Reading Panel, 2000): phonemic awareness, alphabetic principle, fluency with text, vocabulary, and comprehension. Oral reading fluency and comprehension tasks use standard, published reading probes selected for difficulty corresponding to grade levels.
Sensitive to small changes in performance.	Fluency scores generated include number of words read correctly (oral reading fluency) and, for writing, total number of words written, number of words spelled correctly, and number of correct writing sequences.	Scores include number of digits correct (math) and number of correct letter sequences (spelling).	Scores fluctuate with even minimal changes in students' skills.	Fluency scores for phonemic awareness measures (e.g., number of correct letter sounds per minute) and for oral reading, word identification, and comprehension (oral retell). Scores fluctuate with even minimal changes in students' skills.

(Continued)

Table 2.1 (Continued)

Essential Features of Assessment Method	General-Outcome Measure (GOM)	Skills-Based Measure (SBM)	Both GOM and SBM	DIBELS
Easily administered and appropriate for frequent, repeated use; a non-diagnostic indicator of academic skills in a specific domain.	Brief measures consisting of a one-minute oral reading sample, and a three-minute writing task. Research indicates that "words read correctly," "total words written," and "correct writing sequences" predict performance in the domains of reading and writing. No information about discrete subskills (e.g., inferential reading comprehension).	Brief measures consisting of a two- to five-minute paper-and-pencil math task, and a two-minute dictated spelling task. Research indicates that "digits correct" and "correct letter sequences" predict performance in the domains of math and spelling. Results can be evaluated in terms of overall performance in the domain measured, as well as mastery of specific subskills.	Administration and scoring procedures are simple; administration can be done with large groups of students, except oral reading fluency, which is administered individually. Because alternate forms of probes are used, "practice effects" are not observed when measures are administered repeatedly.	Administration and scoring procedures are simple; phonemic awareness, oral reading, and retell fluency probes are administered individually. Because alternate forms of probes are used, "practice effects" are not observed when measures are administered repeatedly. Research indicates that phonemic awareness scores accurately predict performance in the acquisition of literacy skills. No information about discrete subskills is provided except for phonemic awareness and comprehension tasks.

CBM can track both long- and short-term goal attainment, and it is useful in determining the effectiveness of interventions. Scores are graphed, and decision rules can be used to decide whether student progress is sufficient for goal attainment or below expected levels and rates. The original CBM system required educators to create their own measurement materials (probes) from curriculum materials being used for instruction. Although this is still possible, in recent years, standard probes have been created for various skill areas, and they are considered to be valid measures of skills taught at various grade levels (Hosp, Hosp, & Howell, 2007; Howe & Shinn, 2002). Standard probes are available online and from commercial publishers.

A sample graph showing progress monitoring scores over time on a Skills-Based CBM is presented in Figure 2.1. (Note that a graph displaying results of a GOM used for progress monitoring would look identical to this graph.) SBM results can be interpreted as both General-Outcome Measures (GOM) and Mastery Measures (MM). As a GOM, results can be analyzed in terms of the increase in scores over time, showing that the student has learned more and more of the year's curriculum as the weeks go by. For example, on probes containing a mixture of math problems drawn from the entire year's curriculum, scores would be expected to gradually rise because, as the year goes on, instruction in skills that were previously unknown has occurred. Ideally, by the end of the school year, students would demonstrate high levels of accuracy on every mixed-skill probe administered. Performance on this measure also can be analyzed for mastery of specific subskills (MM), which would require inspection of "subscores" on items representing each subskill. For example, a mixed-skill probe containing items requiring both addition and subtraction with regrouping could be examined first for performance on all of the addition items, without regard to the subtraction items.

A final type of formative assessment is *Subskill Mastery Measurement* (SMM), which is useful when a teacher wishes to track student performance on specific subskills and focus instruction on identified areas of weakness. It is well suited to Tier 2 interventions, which should target deficiencies in student performance. There are several SMM methods available, including CBA (Gickling & Havertape, 1981). These measures are similar to CBM in many ways, but as Subskill Mastery model methods, they measure, in sequential order, subskills that make up a broader skill domain (Shapiro, 2004). For example, an evaluation of math skills of first-grade students using CBA might begin with a probe measuring number recognition only, followed by a later probe containing only one-digit addition problems, and so on. The task analysis methods described in Chapter 3 also represent a SMM model of assessment. For reading, SMM measures performance using a series of reading passages (probes) at successively greater levels of difficulty.

Figure 2.1   Progress-Monitoring Data Using CBM Mixed-Skill Math Probes

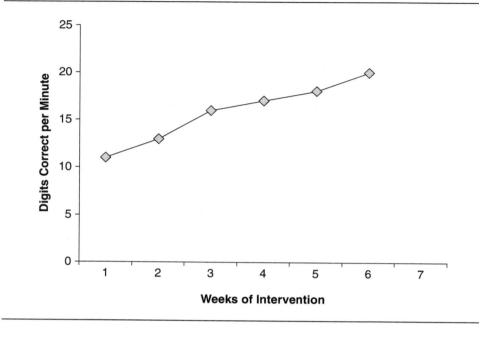

SMM can be especially useful to classroom teachers because it gives more specific information about students' current levels of skill development, and because it is closely matched to the instruction that is actually occurring in the classroom at the time the measure is administered. General education teachers who use this approach for Tier 2 assessment in their own classrooms create or select probes reflecting the subskill that is currently being taught, or, for reading, probes at the level of difficulty currently used for classroom instruction.

Students are tested on the subskill (using alternate forms of subskill probes) until they achieve a predetermined mastery criterion. Then, the next subskill in the hierarchy is assessed in the same manner. This sequence of assessment is depicted in Figure 2.2. Note that, as mastery in each skill is attained (e.g., 40 digits written correctly per minute, the Deno and Mirkin, 1977, mastery criterion for fourth grade math), assessment on that skill is discontinued. In addition to identifying students whose performance falls short of mastery, Subskill Mastery Measurement can be used to track students' rate of progress through a sequence of subskills—defined as the length of time required for the attainment of mastery, which is depicted in the graph of assessment results. Extensive information and guidelines for different versions of Subskill Mastery Measurement are provided by Shapiro (2004), in his text *Academic Skills Problems: Direct Assessment*

Figure 2.2   Progress-Monitoring Data Using Single-Skill Subskill Mastery
Measurement Probes

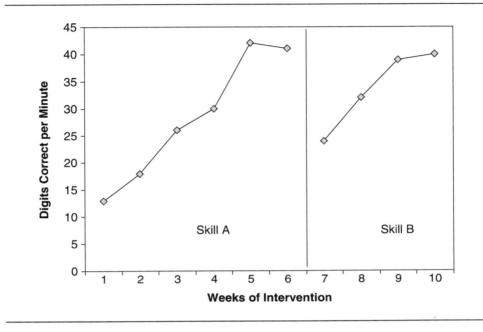

and Intervention. Table 2.2 summarizes features of SMM corresponding
to the "essential features" criteria described earlier.

SMM may be more labor intensive and time consuming than GOM,
SBM, or DIBELS because it requires repeated measurement of subskills
using alternate forms of probes until mastery of each subskill is attained.
Then, the same procedure must be followed for successive subskills, in the
same order as they are addressed in the curriculum. Since subskills are not
sampled again once the mastery criterion has been attained, SMM does not
assess maintenance of subskill mastery over time. In addition, the Subskill
Mastery model requires the establishment of a criterion (a task for which
adequate empirical guidelines are lacking), is time consuming, and
assumes a hierarchical ordering of subskills that may or may not be a valid
representation of the actual sequence of skill development. Because of limitations on the reliability and validity of some SMMs, they should be
supplemented with other measures, such as CBM, especially when high-
stakes decisions are being considered. As noted earlier, however, teachers
often prefer SMM methods because they provide more specific and
instructionally relevant information about skills in which students are not
yet proficient.

Planning for the use of an RTI framework with academic problems
requires the selection of one of the above methods for assessment purposes.

Table 2.2   Features of Subskill Mastery Measurement (SMM)

Essential Features of Assessment Method	Subskill Mastery Measurement (SMM)
Measures the same skills as those being taught to students (curriculum overlap or alignment; content validity).	Samples subskills in an academic domain, presented sequentially as mastery is demonstrated for each subskill.
	Probes constructed from student's curriculum materials representing a single subskill in which students are currently being instructed (except reading, where probes differ on difficulty level of material, rather than discrete subskills).
	Can use standard, published probes selected to reflect subskills appearing in student's curriculum.
	Does not allow repeated measurement of progress toward long-term goals (measures progress only toward short-term subskill mastery objectives).
	Hierarchy of subskills is not empirically derived, and measures (especially those created by teachers) may lack adequate reliability and validity.
Sensitive to small changes in performance.	Subskill probes yield fluency scores identical to those produced by CBM measures (number of words read correctly per minute, number of digits correct per minute, etc.).
	These scores fluctuate with even minimal changes in students' skills.
Easily administered and appropriate for frequent, repeated use; a nondiagnostic indicator of academic skill.	Amount of time and complexity of administration and scoring procedures vary, depending on the measure used.
	Alternate forms of a subskill probe are administered until student achieves mastery criterion. Then, probes of the next subskill in the sequence are administered.
	A subskill probe cannot be repeated once subskill mastery has been attained.
	Because alternate forms of subskill probes are used, "practice effects" are not observed when measures are administered repeatedly until mastery criterion is attained.
	Provides some information of a diagnostic nature (i.e., specific subskills that may be deficient).

Any of the methods described above can be used to track students' progress in the curriculum (Tier 1), identify deficient performance as a target for intervention, or to monitor the progress of students receiving intervention at Tiers 2 or 3. However, CBMs (GOM, SBM, or DIBELS) are the most useful methods for tracking overall performance levels and rates of growth, whether for groups of students or for individual students for whom long-term intervention goals have been established.

ASSESSMENT AT TIER 1

At Tier 1, the purpose of assessment is two fold: first, to measure and track the progress of groups of students (classrooms or grade levels within a school or district) to ensure that curriculum and instructional practices are effective, and, second, to identify students who are at risk for failure because their performance falls below expected levels for either level of scores or rates of growth.

How is *expected performance* defined? Recall Deno's definition of a "problem" as a discrepancy between what is and what is expected (Deno, 2002). In traditional test-and-place models, "expected" performance is specified on the basis of intelligence test scores. A student scoring within the average range on an IQ test is expected to perform within the average range on a measure of age- or grade-appropriate academic achievement (although IQ scores are not intended for use as predictors of academic performance for individual students but as indicators of students' aptitude relative to a comparison group). Similarly, students who earn IQ scores in the below-average range are expected to demonstrate academic achievement at below-average levels. In the RTI model, IQ scores are not employed; instead, expected levels of performance are established in one or more of three ways: one, through the use of peer comparisons or norms, particularly if local norms are available; two, by considering research-based benchmark standards; or three, by consulting research-based instructional standards. With respect to behavior, "expected" performance can be established by considering the quality of behavior that is characteristic of, or normative for, students of similar age, based on developmental benchmarks or comparisons with typically developing peers.

Peer norms and comparisons. The development of local norms for performance on CBMs is recommended to create a framework for peer comparisons, especially when decisions about allocation of resources must be made. However, at least 100 students must be included at each grade level participating in a screening, which is possible only if norming activities are conducted on a schoolwide or districtwide basis. Assuming that such norms are available, a cut score of a certain percentile rank is specified—often, the 16th, 10th, or 8th percentile. In this text, the average range of scores is assumed to fall between the 25th and 75th percentiles, with significantly better-than-average performance attained at the 90th percentile and very poor performance revealed at or below the 10th percentile. Students whose scores fall below the specified percentile rank are considered to be at risk for failure, and they are likely candidates for more intensive intervention. In cases where local norms are not available, or where average scores fall at very high or very low levels, national norms can be used. The National Center on Response to Intervention offers information about performance standards (available at http://www.rti4success.org).

Another method for analyzing assessment results is based on calculation of the discrepancy between the target student's performance score and the median score of the entire class. This method is sometimes used when RTI and universal screening have not been adopted on a schoolwide or districtwide basis, but a classroom teacher wishes to implement aspects of the model. If the ratio of the class average to the target student's score exceeds +2.0, the target student would be considered to be at risk for failure. For example, the ratio of a class average score of 56 words read correctly per minute to a target student's obtained score of 22 words read correctly per minute would equal +2.55, a discrepancy that exceeds +2.0 and is therefore considered an indicator of risk that may warrant intervention. However, it is important to note that this discrepancy method results in different proportions of students who are at risk at different grade levels, such that the degree of discrepancy for a particular student is likely to increase as the student moves to higher grade levels. Another limitation of this approach is the relatively small number of students composing the "sample" against which a target student's score is being compared; this would raise questions about both reliability and validity. Certainly, this method should not be used to make high-stakes decisions, such as determining eligibility for special education.

Benchmark standards. Published and online resources often provide benchmarks for curriculum-referenced measures, along with measurement probes and instructions for administration. Benchmarks specify the expected level of performance for students in various grade levels at different points in time across the school year (typically, fall, winter, and spring). They are based on the notion of predictive validity, in that the benchmark score is a research-based predictor of success in the domain being measured. Thus, a student scoring at or above the benchmark in reading is expected to become a skilled and successful reader. The performance of students who fail to demonstrate scores at or above benchmark levels should be monitored periodically; if students' scores are well below benchmarks (based on decision rules adopted by schools and/or standards available from published sources), those students are at risk for failure and should be regarded as candidates for intervention.

Instructional standards. Instructional standards for reading, math, and writing are available from a variety of sources (Shapiro, 2004). Instructional standards describe the skill levels of students by defining independent (or mastery), instructional, and frustration score ranges for curriculum materials at various grade levels. For example, the instructional range for second-grade-level reading passages is typically set at between 40 and 60 words read correctly per minute (wcpm). If a student earns a score of 72 wcpm (which exceeds the 40–60 wcpm instructional range for that grade level), the second-grade level material would represent that student's independent (mastery) level. For a student earning a score of 53 wcpm, second-grade-level material would be considered "instructional," or the level of difficulty at which instruction should be occurring. Students whose scores in grade-level materials fall below the lower limit of the instructional range (i.e., are in the frustration range) could be candidates for intervention.

Burns and Gibbons (2008) question the utility of instructional standards for purposes of judging the adequacy of student performance, suggesting that national norms may be the best standard for comparison. Thus, instructional standards might best be used to certify the severity of a student's performance problem (e.g., a fourth-grade student whose instructional level in reading falls at the beginning second-grade level) or to assist interventionists in selecting instructional materials at an appropriate level of difficulty, while other criteria—such as benchmarks and norms—should be used to establish expectations for student performance levels and rates of growth.

Defining *satisfactory rate of growth* **in skills.** Just as *levels of performance* can be examined in comparison to average peer performance, *rate of growth* in skills also can be evaluated in comparison to peers, although this procedure requires repeated classwide (or school- or systemwide) assessment of skills using a CBM. In the graph presented in Figure 2.3, the Winter benchmark standard of 98 wcpm has been attained, with a class average or median score of 102 wcpm. This graph also shows satisfactory progress over time, in that the fall average score of 87 wcpm has risen at an acceptable rate to meet or surpass the winter benchmark. If testing yields unsatisfactory results for either levels of performance or rates of growth, then general educators should study the curriculum and instructional methods to identify deficiencies that are hampering student performance.

However, if the average performance of students indicates that, as a group, they possess adequate skills and are making satisfactory progress, then results can be used for a third purpose—to identify students whose performance fails to meet expectations. Analyzing the performance of individual students in Figure 2.3, observe that Jonathan's score falls below the 10th percentile (and well below the benchmark) in the fall assessment, as does his winter score, although he is progressing at a rate exceeding that of his classmates. Suzanne, on the other hand, who also has earned scores that fall well below the class average range (and benchmark) in both the fall and winter tests, is demonstrating progress at a much slower rate than that of her classmates. Note that progress is judged according to the slope of the line connecting fall and winter data points: The flatter the line, the slower the progress.

The performance of students whose problems (discrepancies) are less severe might be monitored on a semimonthly or monthly basis to determine whether adequate growth rates occur under conditions of appropriate Tier 1 instruction. This procedure, known as "strategic monitoring," confirms the risk status of students who demonstrate inadequate growth and therefore require supplemental instruction.

If peer comparison data are unavailable, the target student's rate of progress can be calculated by a simple mathematical formula yielding a *percentage of improvement.* The earlier progress monitoring score (e.g., 40 wcpm) is subtracted from the later progress monitoring score (e.g., 50 wcpm); the result is divided by the earlier score, and multiplied by 100 (50 − 40 = 10; 10/40 × 100 = 25%). A standard for satisfactory growth using this method must be established, taking into consideration the length of time between the earlier and later assessments. Alternatively, as

Figure 2.3   Fall and Winter Assessment Results in Reading Showing Satisfactory Classwide Performance and Comparisons With Individual Student Performance

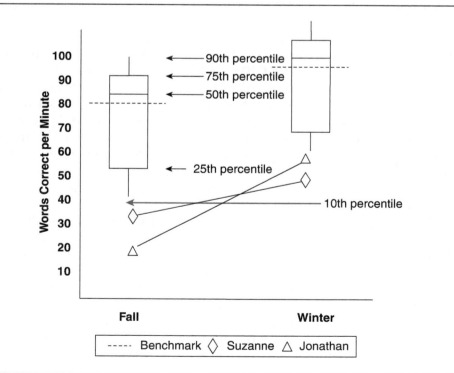

suggested earlier, the *slope of the trend line* connecting progress monitoring data points can be estimated and analyzed as an indicator of improvement in performance. In this formula, the earlier score (e.g., 40 wcpm) is subtracted from the later score (e.g., 50 wcpm); the result is divided by the number of weeks over which intervention has been provided to yield an estimate of the slope of the progress line (50 − 40 = 10; 10 divided by 6 weeks of intervention = +1.67). A value of at least +1.0 represents a minimum standard for satisfactory improvement. Additional standards for judging the adequacy of rates of improvement and trend line slopes are available from various published and online sources, including the National Center on Response to Intervention, mentioned earlier.

ASSESSMENT AT TIER 2

Students who fail to demonstrate either satisfactory levels of performance or rates of growth may be referred (by their test scores, not by instructional personnel) to Tier 2. As indicated by the midsection of the RTI pyramid, approximately 15%–20% of students might be expected to obtain adequate benefit from Tier 2 intervention. At Tier 2, the 20%–25% of students who did not demonstrate adequate performance at Tier 1 receive targeted, research-based interventions in addition to Tier 1 core instruction, typically in a small-group format. Students receiving Tier 2 interventions also participate in more frequent assessment, using the same type of measure as that employed at Tier 1. At Tier 2, this frequent assessment is known as *progress monitoring* and is typically administered—at minimum—on a biweekly basis. Results are plotted on a graph that will show whether Tier 2 interventions are working as well as the rate at which improvement is occurring.

Figure 2.4 shows the performance scores of three students who display various levels of improvement. Visual inspection of Ben's progress-monitoring results show that Tier 2 intervention has resulted in a greatly improved test score, as well as a satisfactory rate of improvement, when considered in comparison to the class average score. On the other hand, while showing a satisfactory rate of improvement, Judi is still unable to demonstrate skill at the expected level. Finally, Andrew's progress-monitoring scores clearly indicate not only that his skills still fall short of expectations but also that the rate of growth in skills during Tier 2 intervention is inadequate. Of these three students, Ben is likely to be phased out of his Tier 2 intervention, Judi will continue the intervention she is receiving, and Andrew needs either an intensified Tier 2 intervention or the individualized interventions planned during a case study at Tier 3.

The reader may wonder how long a Tier 2 intervention should last. Expert opinions vary, with Brown-Chidsey and Steege (2005) recommending a three-week period, and McCook (2006) suggesting that nine to

Figure 2.4   Progress Monitoring Data for Three Students Receiving Tier 2
Intervention and Comparison With Class Average for Fall and
Winter Assessments

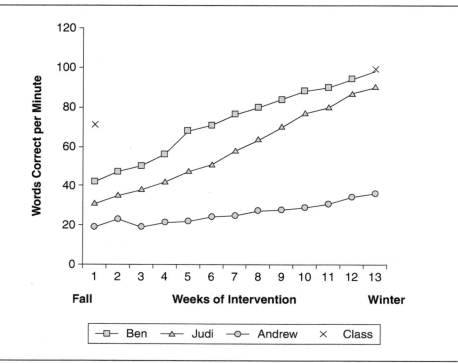

twelve weeks of intervention are needed before it is possible to draw conclusions about the success of interventions. Burns and Gibbons (2008)
address this question directly, recommending three to five 30-minute intervention sessions per week, with a minimum of eight weeks of twice-
weekly progress monitoring. However, Christ and Hintze (2007) caution
against decision making based on fewer than 10 weekly data points
because of the sizable standard error of measurement associated with
shorter timeframes. Thus, it seems reasonable to recommend that, while
trends in students' performance resulting from Tier 2 intervention might
be examined on a tentative basis after eight weeks (with progress monitoring conducted at least weekly), decisions regarding actions to be taken
on the basis of progress-monitoring results should be postponed until the
intervention has been in place for ten weeks.

ASSESSING BEHAVIOR

The rationale for using behavioral assessment methods is similar to
that underlying the use of CBM. Direct measures of behavior, such as

frequency counts or duration recording, are low-inference methods that can be used to identify a problem and certify its severity or significance. They also can be used on a frequent, repeated basis to monitor progress toward the goals of a behavioral intervention. For example, progress toward the behavioral goal of increased rates of appropriate bids for teacher attention might be measured through a frequency or event recording or direct behavior ratings completed by the teacher at the conclusion of a class period.

Behavioral measures, when embedded in functional assessment conducted in a Tier 3 case study, also can reveal relationships between problematic behavior and the function of such behavior. For example, direct observation of disruptive classroom behavior in which instances of the behavior's occurrence are recorded, along with the events immediately preceding and following the behavior, might demonstrate that the function of the disruptive behavior is to escape aversive tasks. As will be discussed in more detail in Chapters 4 and 5, this information is critical to the creation of an effective intervention plan, which must target either or both the aversive nature of the task from which escape is sought and an alternative behavior that will provide relief in a more appropriate manner.

Behavioral assessment methods include behavioral interviews, permanent product or record review, systematic direct observation of behavior, and direct behavior ratings or performance-based recording. Interviews can be conducted with teachers, parents, and students; their purpose is to clearly define specific behaviors of concern, establish the relative frequency or severity of the behaviors in various settings, and to tentatively identify environmental circumstances or events that may be functionally (i.e., causally) related to the occurrence of the behavior. Review or inspection of records and products generated by behavior has a similar purpose, with two additional advantages. First, record review can reveal a point in time at which a pattern emerged or changed (e.g., failing grades beginning in third grade); second, it can be used in tandem with direct observation to clarify the relationship between behavior and student performance outcomes (e.g., a high rate of disengagement during an independent work period associated with a low rate of work completion or a high error rate on the assigned task).

The other two forms of behavioral assessment—systematic direct observation, and direct behavior ratings and performance-based recording (which are based on direct observation)—are the focus of the remainder of this section. These methods involve the observation of behavior in the settings in which it naturally occurs and the recording of behavior in a manner suited to characteristics of the behavior and the resources (time, personnel, attention) available for assessment activities.

Although a great deal is known about behavioral assessment methods that can be used with individual students, it is sometimes difficult to apply these methods to groups of students, as would be necessary at Tier 1 of the RTI process. A promising method that is being used in some schools is the School-Wide Information System (SWIS) (Irvin et al., 2006) in which behavior problems are tracked across the entire student body through the use of office disciplinary referral records. SWIS can be used as a measure of overall student performance at Tier 1; in addition, results reveal particular aspects of problem behavior (i.e., types of behavior, settings, and identities of involved students) that may require modifications of Tier 1 behavior-management practices, or that may be targeted for Tier 2 intervention. SWIS also can be used to monitor the progress of students in Tier 2, as it can be coded and reported for individual students.

Even when used for data collection with individual students, direct observation of student behavior by teachers requires a degree of attention that teachers may find impractical. And, since some methods of behavioral observation are susceptible to reliability error, readers are encouraged to design measurement plans that include multiple sources and methods of data collection for behavior problems. When selecting observational techniques for behavior problems, several decisions are made.

1. What phenomenon should be measured, how will it be measured, and by whom? If concern about the behavior is expressed in quantitative terms, frequency or event recording (i.e., how many times does the behavior occur?), duration recording (i.e., how long does the behavior last?), or latency recording (i.e., how long does it take for the student to perform the behavior after receiving a prompt?) would be appropriate. Discrete behaviors (brief events, easily detected, such as "calling out") that occur on a regular basis are best measured using frequency recording. If concern about the behavior is based on a qualitative dimension, intensity recording (i.e., how loud, intense, or severe is the behavior?), topography recording (i.e., what does the behavior look like; how well does it match a template?), or performance-based recording or direct behavior rating (i.e., to what extent does the behavior match a specified standard?) should be employed.

Some observation methods measure samples of behavior rather than every occurrence of the behavior. Partial interval recording, for example, requires observation of the student during a specified time interval (e.g., three minutes); if the behavior occurs at any time during that interval, the observer records the occurrence and stops observing and recording until the next interval begins. Only one instance of a behavior can be recorded per interval. For example, observations of engagement behavior (defined as eyes oriented toward teacher and task) could be recorded within 15-second intervals, and the frequency count would be converted to a percent of engagement intervals across all observations. Data from the target student can be compared with the normative data gathered by observing peers in the same setting. Several recording observation systems are based on the interval recording method, including the Behavioral Observation of Students in Schools (BOSS) (Shapiro, 1996), and the State-Event Classroom Observation System (SECOS) (Saudargas, 1992).

Some behaviors are not emitted spontaneously; they require a prompt or "opportunity" to occur. For example, giving the correct answer to a question can't occur unless a question has been asked. When planning behavioral observation, it is important to determine whether the behavior is "free" or "controlled;" if it is controlled (and therefore requires an opportunity to occur), it will be necessary to keep track of opportunities to perform the behavior as well as the occurrence of the behavior itself. In the example above, the observation record might include a hash mark for each question asked by the teacher, with circles drawn around the hash marks representing questions to which the student gave an answer. The behavioral "score" would be the proportion of questions answered of the total number of questions asked.

Observation by a third party (i.e., someone other than the classroom teacher) is desirable for many reasons, including maximum flexibility in choice of methods as well as potentially greater reliability and validity of measurement. In schools, however, limited time and personnel may make third-party observation impossible. Two methods for behavioral observation are more feasible for use by teachers and are therefore recommended when observation by a third party is undesirable or impractical. Momentary time sampling is a form of frequency or event recording in which the observer (teacher) looks at the target student at specified time intervals and records the student's behavior at that moment. For example, the plan might call for the teacher to look at the target at the end of every five-minute interval, on average, and place a check mark on a card if the student is actively engaged in an academic task.

A second method is performance-based recording or direct behavior rating in which a scale is created with numeric values assigned to correspond with varying levels of performance. Observers (teachers) are then directed to circle the number that corresponds to the student's performance over a specified time period. For example, performance-based recording of social interaction during the morning and afternoon of a school day might employ the following scale:

4 Student initiated situationally appropriate, reciprocated conversation with a peer on five or more occasions during the time period; resulting interaction lasted for at least 30 seconds.

3 Student initiated conversation with a peer on five or more occasions during the time period, but peer response on two or more of these occasions was absent or minimal.

2 Student initiated conversation with a peer on three or four occasions during the time period.

1 Student initiated conversation with a peer on one to two occasions during the time period.

0 Student did not initiate conversation with peers at all during the time period.

The reader might correctly note that that this kind of recording implies a greater degree of inference, as observer (teacher) judgment is involved in assigning ratings to performance. Thus, it may be a less reliable method, and scores may not be truly representative of the phenomenon in which we are interested. A solution to this problem is to ask the teacher to complete the rating protocol more frequently (e.g., at the end of the morning and at the end of the afternoon, across a week-long period) because an increased number of measurements is associated with higher reliability.

2. Where, and how often, will the observation be conducted? For purposes of baseline measurement of behavior, observation should occur in the settings in which the behavior is most problematic. (Note that this recommendation differs from what might be suggested if the observation were for purposes of problem analysis, which seeks to identify factors that may be prompting or maintaining the problem behavior. For problem analysis, observation of the behavior in settings in which it is both most and least likely to occur is desirable because differences between those settings will provide clues as to the function of the behavior.) As a general rule, it is desirable to conduct behavioral observations across several days; at least 3 data points obtained over a two- to five-day period are recommended for an adequate baseline measurement.

However, adequacy (and, therefore, usefulness) of the baseline depends on several conditions. First, the score must accurately describe the behavior of interest. If the student has a problem in reading fluency, the score must describe the current level of reading fluency. If the student has a problem with disrupting class discussions, the baseline score must describe the frequency of disruptive behavior during class discussions. Although on the surface this seems to be an obvious condition, observers sometimes target a behavior for intervention that is different from the behavior that has been cited as problematic. While this is not necessarily inappropriate, as in the case of secondary dependent variables, discussed in more detail in Chapter 5, the behavior of initial interest should always be measured. For example, a school's intervention assistance team might design an intervention plan that includes strategies to increase the frequency of assignment completion although disengaged, inattentive classroom behavior was the problem of initial interest. While assignment completion may be a desirable objective in itself, and requires engaged, attentive behavior, the behavior that should be operationally defined and measured for baseline and progress-monitoring purposes should be either "disengaged, inattentive classroom behavior" or its replacement, "engaged, attentive classroom behavior," or both, as these are the behaviors of primary concern.

The exception to this rule lies in circumstances in which a behavior has been identified as a factor that contributes to an *academic* performance problem. In such cases, academic performance criteria should be used for goal setting and measurement. For example, if a student's disengaged behavior has been identified as a factor contributing to poor performance in math (e.g., talking with peers, being out of seat), the team should measure performance and set a goal for accuracy in math, although the intervention plan would include strategies to increase engagement.

The second condition that must be satisfied in baseline measurement is reliability of the score. The reader is undoubtedly familiar with the notion of reliability as the accuracy with which the behavior of interest is measured. When behavior is measured, it is important that fluctuations in "scores" be the result of actual changes in the behavior rather than an unintended consequence of poor or erratic measurement procedures. For example, if a student is not feeling well on the day of testing, or if construction workers are making noise outside the window, test scores might have been unduly influenced by these extraneous factors. This introduces the likelihood of measurement error, and it calls into question the reliability of the performance scores.

Enhancing the reliability of measurement occurs in several ways: First, the effects of extraneous factors should be minimized (i.e., postpone testing or observation of an ill student until he or she is feeling better). Second, the phenomenon that is being measured must be clearly defined, and procedures for measuring the phenomenon must be used in a consistent manner. Imprecise definitions of behavior, or modifications in the manner in which measurement occurs, will result in different results, especially if more than one person is involved in the measurement process.

While it is relatively easy to define what is being measured and to standardize the measurement procedure when evaluating academic skills using CBM, it is more challenging in the case of behavioral observation. When measuring behavior, the Stranger Test (Kaplan, 1995) can be used to ensure that the behavior definition is clear: If anyone (i.e., a stranger) were to read the behavioral description of the problem and apply it in the same way as its author, the description would pass the Stranger Test. For example, if the problem behavior was defined as "aggression," another person unfamiliar with the target student might apply a more general interpretation than that intended by the author, such that even mild teasing would be counted as "aggression." In contrast, a description of the problem behavior as "pushing, hitting, or pinching" is sufficiently specific as to be interpreted and applied in the same way by any person observing the target student: This definition passes the Stranger Test.

The measurement technique should also be explained and demonstrated to all those who might be involved in the process. A procedure that can be used to ensure the reliability of behavioral measurement across several observers involves the calculation of *interobserver agreement*, which reports the degree of similarity in the observations of two independent parties. Figure 2.5 demonstrates how to calculate interobserver agreement for several types of behavioral measures; agreement of at least 80% is considered desirable.

Figure 2.5   Calculating Interobserver Agreement

Procedure. Two observers measure behavior at the same time, in the same setting, using the same procedure.

1. When recording the frequency or duration of a behavior, calculate interobserver agreement by dividing the smaller frequency or duration (obtained by one of the observers) by the larger frequency or duration (obtained by the other observer), and multiply by 100 (e.g., 9/10 × 100 = 90% agreement; 48 min/50 min × 100 = 96% agreement).

2. When an interval or time sampling recording method has been used, count the number of intervals (or sampling events) in which the observers agreed on the result (i.e., both observers recorded the occurrence of the behavior, or neither observer recorded the occurrence of the behavior), and divide that number by the total number of intervals or sampling events (e.g., 20 intervals, with 17 agreements and 3 disagreements, would yield 85% agreement, calculated as 17 agreements divided by 20 total intervals, × 100).

The third condition that must be satisfied in baseline measurement is that performance should be measured across several sessions or days so as to minimize the effects of unusual or irrelevant factors on the final (average) score. If behavior is measured only on Monday morning, for example, the fatigue created by a busy weekend schedule might make the behavior less likely to occur, thereby yielding an inaccurate estimate of its typical frequency. (The reader might also recall that reliability is enhanced when the number of measurement events is increased.)

SUMMARY

This chapter provided a detailed discussion of assessment methods that are appropriate for uses at all three tiers of the RTI model. Data-based decisions that govern the progression of students through the tiered sequence of intervention were explained. At Tier 1, assessment is useful for examining overall levels and rates of performance for groups of students and for identifying those whose performance falls below expected levels. Tier 1 assessment results also can be used for purposes of instructional planning or to design appropriate behavior management plans.

At Tier 2, assessment reveals areas of deficiency that should be targeted for intervention among students at risk for failure, and it tracks the progress of students toward expected levels of performance. At Tier 3, the purpose of assessment varies, depending on the case study stage for which it is being used. At the first stage, problem identification, assessment is used to clearly define and certify the severity of a problem; at the second stage, problem analysis, it reveals causal relationships between problematic performance and environmental factors and tests hypotheses describing these relationships. The third stage of the case study, plan implementation, uses assessment to monitor progress toward goals and to ensure that interventions are being delivered with integrity. Finally, at the fourth stage, problem evaluation, data generated through progress monitoring are analyzed to determine whether interventions have been effective.

For academic problems, assessment takes the form of direct measurement of students' academic skills, typically through the use of Curriculum-Based Measurement. For behavior problems (and to measure behaviors contributing to poor academic performance), assessment might include behavioral interviews, permanent product or record review, direct behavioral observation, and direct behavior ratings or performance-based recording. Selection of appropriate assessment methods requires careful consideration of the nature of the phenomenon to be measured, the purposes for which assessment is being conducted, and the resources available for measurement activities.

3

Facilitating Response to Intervention in Schools

R TI has relevance in general, compensatory, and special education, but one of its defining and most revolutionary features is its potential for improving general education practices. This is an exciting prospect but a daunting one as well, especially for school psychologists and special educators accustomed to schools where general and special education are separated by a seemingly insurmountable wall. The RTI framework offers an opportunity for a partnership between general and special education, and between school psychologists and classroom teachers, recognizing that everyone stands to benefit from enhanced communication and shared resources and expertise.

In addition to its potential for creating partnerships, RTI is an invaluable resource for educators anxious to meet the requirements of the No Child Left Behind Act. The assessment procedures employed with RTI can be used to effectively identify children at risk of failure on high-stakes tests (Burns & Gibbons, 2008), and its research-based early-intervention practices can close the achievement gap for these students. Administrators and school personnel are more receptive to RTI as they become aware of its potential for meeting performance goals for all students.

School psychologists play two critical roles in facilitating the RTI process. The first is to act as a systems change agent by working with teachers and administrators to facilitate prevention and intervention activities as well as related assessments at the universal (Tier 1) and small-group

(Tier 2) levels. The second role is to facilitate case studies conducted at Tier 3 when a student does not respond adequately to interventions at Tiers 1 and 2. Through the case study, specific reasons for a student's problem and individualized solutions can be identified. Case study facilitation is the focus of this book and will be discussed in depth in the following chapters. This chapter emphasizes the skills and processes entailed in the change agent role.

SCHOOL PSYCHOLOGIST AS SYSTEMS CHANGE AGENT

In situations where RTI is being implemented on a schoolwide basis, consultation typically occurs with a team of planners who consider a broad range of issues associated with assessment and intervention practices in the school, at various grade levels, and in individual classrooms. The school psychologist's objectives as a change agent at Tiers 1 and 2 are to (1) establish trust, (2) gather information about instructional practices from teacher interviews and observations, (3) assist in defining universal goals for student academic and behavioral performance, (4) facilitate and interpret assessments of all students, and (5) identify empirically sound instructional and intervention strategies for classwide or small-group implementation.

The initial purpose of collaborative consultation is to identify school-wide goals for students and to gather related information. In the initial stage of the process, teachers are clients as well as consultees. As *clients,* teachers expect the school psychologist to help them accomplish their professional goals. Attention to the teacher as the client personalizes the process, increases the likelihood that teachers will feel valued, and results in increased engagement. As *consultees,* teachers work with the school psychologist to accomplish student goals. A collaborative relationship is critical for both system change and individual problem solving.

Teachers should be regarded as the guides at the beginning of this process, and they need to trust that school psychologists are working in their best interest. The school psychologist depends on teachers to gather and report information accurately and to implement prevention and intervention strategies with integrity in the classroom. Positive working relationships tend to increase (1) acceptance of the consultation, assessment, and intervention processes; (2) the probability that interventions will be implemented with integrity; and (3) the effectiveness of interventions for student improvement (Kratochwill, Elliott, & Callan-Stoiber, 2002).

The importance of a trusting relationship cannot be overemphasized, and it must be the school psychologist's first priority as the consultation process begins. Interpersonal skills that serve as a foundation for trust and a good working relationship include empathy, active listening, appropriate questioning, and understanding factors that contribute to resistance (Kampwirth, 1987). Collaborative consultation with members of the school community helps establish a strong relationship that has the essential characteristics of equal power, reciprocity, openness, realistic expectations, trust, involvement of all relevant parties, and a structure for planning and addressing differences of opinion.

EVALUATING THE SYSTEM

Early in the consultation process, it is important to gain an understanding of the learning environment. The purpose of this information-gathering focus is to determine what works for most students and what requires attention in the classroom. Demographic characteristics of the students and the community are available from school records. But qualitative information, which can be richer, is more appropriately obtained through interviews and observations. For example, teacher styles (e.g., innovative versus traditional) and readiness for change (novice versus experienced) are important considerations in guiding the consultation approach.

As a change agent, the school psychologist is alert to signs of readiness for change. If the entire school is not ready for RTI to be initiated, a possible alternative is to begin the innovation on a small scale in one or more classrooms.

Signals of readiness include recognition of concerns, rational problem solving, and coherent planning. Havelock (2005) has identified danger signals that could impede the process: history of unresponsiveness to change, political agendas, pathology or ineffectiveness, and direct antagonism. Estimates of readiness can be gleaned through interviews and observations in the learning environment.

The general education learning environment is the vehicle through which the preventive goals of Tier 1 are accomplished. It includes aspects of the physical space, characteristics of the individuals inhabiting the school, social-system variables, and cultural norms (Lehr & Christenson, 2002). Instructional methods, curricula, rules of operation, inconsistencies in behavioral expectations, ability grouping, rapport, decision-making procedures, communication style, and relationships are all Tier 1 factors that can be potential targets for systematic change in the RTI process (Lehr & Christenson, 2002).

When a mismatch between the learning environment and student needs is suspected, clarifying information is gathered. For example, data from classwide academic assessment can be used to determine whether instructional methods and curricula that are used in the classroom are yielding the expected results, as assessment should measure what is being taught. Similarly, information obtained from interviews, observations, and data from classwide behavioral assessments can be used to guide environmental modifications for optimum impact on both student learning and interpersonal development.

A positive learning environment engages students and teachers in the learning experience. Anderson, Christenson, Sinclair, and Lehr (2004) define student engagement in four areas: behavioral, academic, cognitive, and psychological. School cultural norms related to behavioral engagement include classroom and extracurricular participation, attendance, and other proacademic and prosocial behaviors. Academic engagement norms involve time on task, while cognitive engagement norms incorporate expectations of self-regulated learning, student responsibility, and appropriate use of learning strategies. Psychological engagement occurs when students have a sense of belonging and are involved in a culture of positive interpersonal relationships.

Teacher consultation and observations in the classroom should include information about the often-neglected aspect of physical context (Hunley & Schaller, 2006). For example, classroom seating arrangements can be evaluated for congruence with learning goals and instructional methods. Seating arranged in rows is consistent with didactic instructional methods, while circular seating patterns tend to be more appropriate for group discussion activities. Face-to-face, digital, or virtual learning provide different opportunities for a variety of interactions that can enhance or detract from academic and behavioral goals as well. In addition to the typical issue of class size, factors in the physical environment such as air quality, lighting, acoustics, comfort, and aesthetics can increase engagement (Hunley, 2008; Webb, Schaller, & Hunley, 2008) and improve learning and productivity (Zandvliet & Fraser, 2005). Research has demonstrated that these factors have a profound effect on health, learning, and behavior.

GOAL SETTING

In the first meeting with teachers, the school psychologist should address four basic questions:

1. What are your key academic goals for your students?

2. What are your key behavioral goals for your students?

3. How do you know when your students accomplish the goals?

4. How can I assist you to accomplish these goals?

It is important to frame the questions as open ended, as this will encourage teachers to have maximum input into the conversation, minimize feelings of threat or defensiveness, and convey the school psychologist's intent to be of assistance.

Teachers who have experience with data-based decision making will give responses to the questions that differ from those given by teachers who are novices in this process. For example, schools that are using an RTI framework to measure students' reading progress, and to provide effective instruction at Tier 1 and research-based interventions at Tier 2, will already have specified reading goals as well as data to show which students have benefited from classwide instruction. These teachers also can provide data to demonstrate the progress of students who have received more intensive intervention and more frequent assessment. Together, data from the first and second tiers of RTI are used by the school psychologist and teacher to identify students who have not progressed at expected rates. In this scenario, the school psychologist must be prepared to rapidly move the consultation process into the third tier to individualize assessment and intervention. In other words, a case study may be needed.

Similarly, teachers who participate in schoolwide positive behavior support (PBS) initiatives will have data identifying students who have and have not responded well to PBS initiatives. A well-executed PBS system has a set of goals for student behavior, and it has procedures for gathering data relative to those goals. Students who continue to have documented behavior problems even after they have received targeted interventions (Tier 2) would be referred for a case study for individualized assessment and intervention design.

Teachers who are novices in data-based decision making need more extensive support. Initially, they may neither understand nor welcome the RTI approach. Historically, teachers expect to meet with the school psychologist to discuss individual students who have been referred because of specific problems. Frequently, they anticipate that, at the time of referral, the school psychologist will immediately begin to administer tests to determine eligibility for special education services. Instead, the school psychologist works to assist the teacher to establish academic and behavioral goals and adopt alternate assessment practices.

Goals are based on curricular guidelines, research and theory, data from the previous school year, and specific needs of the teacher, the class, and the school. They are used to guide instruction and curriculum development, to direct learners, and to structure evaluation and accountability (Fuchs, 2002). Academic and behavioral goals are either adopted from existing sources or developed on a local basis. Academic goal development is a process in which goals center on student mastery of clearly defined, specific behaviors (Fuchs, 2002; McKevitt & Braaksma, 2008). In other words, the behaviors specified in goal statements must be observable and measurable.

Long-term goals. The long-term goal approach specifies a set of goals to be attained on an annual basis. This approach constitutes a simple system of academic and behavioral targets that can be consistently measured over time. Annual prioritized goals are the same for all students, and they are measured periodically to indicate both students' rate of growth and relative standing in academic skills, such as reading or math. The key to long-term goal development is to identify keystone skills that are developmentally significant, related to the curriculum and instruction, and can be measured over time. See Figure 3.1 for an example of a long-term classwide goal. Long-term goals for a class also can be stated in terms of the number or percentage of students who will demonstrate proficiency on a high-stakes test or attain a universal screening score at or above a research-based benchmark (e.g., 90% of students at or above the benchmark score by the spring of the current school year). If the school has universal screening scores and high-stakes test data for an adequate sample of students, cut scores predicting success or failure on the high-stakes test can be calculated (Burns & Gibbons, 2008). These cut scores can then be used to establish goal levels of performance on universal screening measures.

Although academic goals for various grade levels may be fairly consistent across schools, the characteristics of the school's student population must be considered for the development of behavioral goals. Well-written goals include five aspects: (1) condition, (2) learner or learners, (3) behavior, (4) criterion, and (5) time. The goal-setting process begins with the identification of classwide goals to be measured at Tiers 1 and 2, while goals for individual students are developed and used at Tier 3.

Figure 3.1   Example of a Long-Term Classwide Performance Goal

Classwide Goal: In 30 weeks, the class, on average, will read fourth-grade text fluently at 100 words correct per minute.	**Condition:** Given a fourth-grade reading passage
	Learner(s): The class
	Behavior: Will fluently read aloud
	Criterion: Read correctly 100 words per minute
	Time: 30 weeks

Short-term goals. Teachers may prefer the gradual implementation of RTI through the use of a short-term goal approach (Fuchs, 2002) based on the Subskill-Mastery model of assessment described in Chapter 2. In this approach, the teacher identifies a sequence, hierarchy, or list of subskills embedded in a broader skill (e.g., decoding words) as well as target dates for achieving student mastery of each of the subskills. One advantage to this approach is that it can be initiated at any time during the school year. Collaborative construction of a task analysis by the teacher and the school psychologist allows the teacher to analyze the detailed components of the task and provide input into the development of the goals.

A task analysis provides detailed subskill targets to assess and monitor for academic (Carter & Kemp, 1996) or behavioral (Browder, 1991, 2001) performance. Information from a task analysis can be used for general planning at Tiers 1 and 2 and for more individualized preparation of assessment and intervention strategies at Tier 3. There are several different types of task analyses: component task analysis, task complexity analysis, and prerequisite task analysis (Carter & Kemp, 1996).

A *component task analysis* requires that a general task be broken into the subskills needed for completion (Carter & Kemp, 1996). This type of task analysis is conducted through direct observation of the complete task being performed competently. The skills needed to complete the task are listed in order. An example of a task that would be appropriate for a component task analysis would be shoe tying. This type of task analysis is especially useful for teachers who are working with students with severe disabilities.

A *task complexity analysis* is used to modify procedures to increase fluency by making a known skill easier to perform (Carter & Kemp, 1996). The analysis is conducted through observation to determine what types of modifications would improve student performance. Modifications could include, but are not limited to, changing performance conditions, level of behavior performed, or criteria for acceptable performance. For example, an observation and task complexity analysis might reveal that students have difficulty with spelling, grammar, and handwriting when completing creative writing assignments. The solution for this problem could result in a modification of the requirements by allowing the students to use the computer to increase fluency and productivity for creative writing assignments.

A *prerequisite task analysis* is desirable for tasks requiring mastery of a set of subskills prior to applying them to the culminating target skill (Carter & Kemp, 1996). This procedure is the basis for the Subskill-Mastery model of assessment described in Chapter 2. Consider the difference between a determination that a student's oral reading fluency problems are due to a lack of prerequisite skills in decoding words with vowel-consonant-vowel combinations versus an inadequate fund of recognized sight words. Although both are examples of reading fluency prerequisites, they require different interventions.

A task analysis should be validated to ensure that it is appropriate and complete. There are several ways to validate the construction of a task analysis. One might be to consult with someone knowledgeable in the task that is being assessed, using theory, research, and curriculum as a basis for construction. Another method would be to observe someone who is competent in completing the task for which the task analysis is being developed (Browder, 1991). A third option is the trial-and-error method (Cooper, Heron, & Heward, 1987) in which the developer figures out the steps firsthand by actually carrying out the task.

The school psychologist assists teachers in the collection, evaluation, and interpretation of the data. Chapters 1 and 2 provide a review of assessment considerations for RTI. However, when a school is not ready for systemwide implementation of RTI, it is possible to address it on a smaller scale with just one teacher. For example, data gathered from assessments administered once or twice a week over a three-week period allow a calculation of weekly rates of improvement. If improvement is not noted across the three-week period, the lack of growth may be due to ineffective instruction, inconsistency between what is being measured and the curriculum, insufficient time to detect small changes in skill levels, or measures that are not sensitive to small changes in performance. There are weaknesses in this approach, but it does serve as a pilot for RTI, and the teacher can learn the potential value of the process implemented on a broader scale.

RTI IMPLEMENTATION

The extent and sophistication of RTI model implementation by the school and district is a major factor that determines the school psychologist's role. There exists an extensive literature regarding systems change in schools generally (e.g., Curtis, Castillo, & Cohen, 2008; Fullen, 1991; Hall & Hord, 1987) and with regard to the RTI model in particular (e.g., Batsche, Curtis, Dorman, Castillo, & Porter, 2007; Graden, Stollar, & Poth, 2007; Marston, Lau, & Muyskens, 2007). Proper implementation of the three-tiered model requires adoption of the RTI framework on a broad scale. Large-scale adoption of the RTI model requires consideration of several conceptual and practical issues. Of critical importance is the point made by Gresham, VanDerHeyden, and Witt (2005), who emphasize a conceptual shift from the "refer-test-place" approach to a "refer-intervene-evaluate" approach.

The manner in which decision-making activities are conducted is determined by the school and district in which they are applied. Procedures adopted by schools delineate a coordinated system of screening, intervention, and entitlement (Fletcher, Lyon, Fuchs, & Barnes, 2007). In addition, data-based decision rules address (1) moving from tier to tier, (2) Tier 3a problem solving; and (3) Tier 3b special education determination. For instance, Kovaleski (2007) recommends that the strategic orchestration in deploying special education personnel and resources must be tempered by flexibility. Assignment and reassignment of staff must be responsive to the changing needs of the students they serve. The system will be most efficient when personnel evolve from the specialist perspective (e.g., teachers of children with learning disabilities) to more generic service providers (e.g., literacy coaches) who can respond to multiple needs as a result of cross-training in a variety of instructional and intervention practices.

Practical implications include consideration of academic and behavioral targets, assessment measures, empirically validated instruction and intervention methods, as well as decision-making rules. Within the general education framework, key academic and behavior targets must be identified and assessed routinely through the brief administration of valid and reliable instruments. Progress-monitoring data are analyzed regularly, and results should be interpreted and used for making instructional decisions. Scientifically sound instruction and intervention methods are used at all three tiers. However, Tier 3 is distinguished from Tiers 1 and 2 by the implementation of high-intensity, individualized strategies. At Tier 3, intervention selection is guided by the individualized problem-solving procedures characteristic of the case study.

Special education eligibility determination in the RTI model requires the collaboration of all school personnel, without regard for general or special education designations or boundaries. When implemented well, the RTI process should provide an equitable system for helping all students achieve school success, be responsive to legal mandates, and lead to fiscally responsible decisions about the allocation of scarce educational resources.

SUMMARY

Implementation of the RTI model in schools requires a new way of thinking about the relationship between school psychologists and teachers. The collaboration must begin *before* an individual student is referred for assistance. The school psychologist should no longer wait until concerns escalate to severe levels before becoming involved in problem-solving efforts. Early collaboration encourages the implementation of preventive strategies and allows for data-based identification of students who may be at risk for failure. Collaborative consultation first attends to prevention issues through proactive strategies and then moves to more targeted, intensive intervention strategies.

This chapter emphasized that expertise is not enough to evoke a successful shift from "refer-test-place" to "refer-intervene-evaluate." Consultation skills are essential to the acceptance of the model by the educators who will implement the process. The consultation skills and strategies described in this chapter are not just a part of the school psychologist's repertoire of tools to do the job; they represent best practices for systems change and consultation, and they become a "way of being a professional." The intention of this chapter is not to reiterate issues associated with systems change but to offer general strategies for school psychologists to work as general change agents at Tiers 1 and 2 of the RTI model, which facilitate the successful completion of Tier 3 case studies.

4

Problem Identification

R ecall that a problem is defined as a discrepancy between a student's actual and expected performance, and that problem solving is intended to reduce or eliminate this discrepancy. Research has shown that a clearly defined problem statement (i.e., description of the performance discrepancy) is a critical element in successful problem solving (Telzrow, McNamara, & Hollinger, 2000). In Behavioral Consultation, problem identification is accomplished through an interview conducted with a consultee (i.e., classroom teacher); questions are designed to elicit information about the specific nature and severity of the problem as well as factors that may be contributing to its occurrence (Kratochwill & Bergan, 1990). The case study method described in this text generates similar information, but as a component of Tier 3 of the RTI model, its problem identification phase also incorporates data collected at Tiers 1 and 2.

TIER 1

The results of universal screenings conducted at different points in the school year (fall, winter, and spring) can be analyzed in terms of performance levels and growth trends for an entire grade level of students as well as discrepancies in performance between typical learners and those who are experiencing problems. Thus, problem identification at Tier 1 is applied in three ways: to identify classwide performance levels and rates of growth that may indicate a problem with the curriculum or instructional practices, to identify individual students whose performance levels are so low as to warrant immediate Tier 2 intervention, and for academic problems, to interpret strategic monitoring results to identify students whose unsatisfactory rates of growth reveal a need for Tier 2 intervention.

As discussed in Chapters 2 and 3, the level of performance (i.e., average score) and rate of progress of the entire class should first be evaluated to determine whether the curriculum and instructional practices are effective. If not, changes in classwide instruction should be undertaken. Assuming that the level of performance and rate of growth of the entire class are adequate, the performance of students whose scores are discrepant from expected levels should be examined to determine whether strategic monitoring is desirable or whether Tier 2 intervention should be initiated. Immediate Tier 2 intervention is recommended for students whose universal screening scores fall below the 10th percentile, while strategic monitoring (using the same measures) is recommended for students whose scores on universal screening measures fall at the "borderline" level (i.e., 10th–25th percentile). Conducted on a monthly or semi-monthly basis, strategic monitoring can reveal whether individual students are displaying adequate rates of growth; if growth rates are inadequate, Tier 2 intervention should be initiated. Without effective instruction or intervention, discrepant growth rates will continue, resulting in the ever-increasing gap between typical and struggling learners known as the "Matthew Effect" (Stanovich, 1986).

TIER 2

At Tier 2, problem identification has two applications: first, to specify the deficiencies that will be targeted by Tier 2 interventions; and, second, to interpret Tier 2 progress monitoring results to identify problems that require Tier 3 intervention. An important characteristic of Tier 2 interventions is that they are targeted to specific deficiencies in student performance. For example, some students may be deficient in acquiring a particular math skill, as revealed by a high error rate; others know how to perform the skill but have not yet mastered it, as revealed in a low fluency score (i.e., although the student makes very few mistakes, she works very slowly, earning a low "digits correct per minute" score). Still other students might have difficulty with literal or inferential reading comprehension. Interventions that fail to target deficiencies are unlikely to be successful, thereby demonstrating the need for problem identification at Tier 2 to include assessment of such deficiencies.

Haring and Eaton (1978) described the "instructional hierarchy" as a series of performance levels that are attained sequentially, wherein each level is a prerequisite for the level that follows. In this approach, problems can be analyzed to determine the level at which performance is deficient—acquisition (knowing how to perform the skill accurately), proficiency or fluency (being able to perform accurately and with speed), generalization (knowing how to use the skill in various situations), or adaptation (knowing how to use the skill in different ways suited to novel situations). Interventions based on the instructional hierarchy vary according to the specific level of deficiency. For example, an acquisition deficit should be addressed with interventions involving modeling, immediate performance feedback, and error correction.

Another way to target deficiencies is to determine specific subskills or aspects of performance that are problematic. The Subskill Mastery Measurement (SMM) model of assessment described in Chapter 2 (and associated task-analysis procedures discussed in Chapter 3) can be used for this purpose. Recall that this form of Curriculum-Based Measurement consists of a series of subskills measured one at a time, in the order they are taught. For example, a SMM of math might first evaluate student performance on a probe consisting solely of one-digit addition, sums to 10. If students display mastery (i.e., a score of 93%–97% correct), then the next subskill—one-digit addition, sums to 20—is evaluated, and so on. (Similarly, Skills-Based Measures, which combine the features of General-Outcome Measurement and SMM, can be used to identify specific subskills in which students are deficient.) In reading, assessment can reveal areas of weakness—decoding unfamiliar words, fluent oral reading, or comprehension of text. The identification of specific deficiencies enables planners to group children according to common needs and to provide appropriate interventions targeted to those needs.

For students receiving interventions at Tier 2, problem identification also is accomplished through a review of progress-monitoring results when results reveal unacceptably low scores and/or an inadequate rate of growth despite the provision of appropriate interventions. At Tier 2, the notion of a *dual discrepancy* (DD) becomes important for decision making. DD refers to progress monitoring results in which both the "end score" (i.e., most recent score) level and rate of growth over time (i.e., slope) are discrepant from expectations. For end scores, "discrepant performance" would be revealed in scores falling below the benchmark standard (e.g., 40 words read correctly per minute at the spring first-grade screening); for slope, discrepant performance is typically defined as one standard deviation below the slope defining average performance for the students' grade level (Burns & Gibbons, 2008).

The finding of a DD at Tier 2 should first result in changes that will intensify the intervention, perhaps by increasing its "dosage" or by adding new strategies to those interventions already being provided. Students who fail to make satisfactory progress even under intensified Tier 2 intervention (an estimated 5% of students) demonstrate problems that require a transition to Tier 3, where interventions will be tailored to the specific factors contributing to their performance problems.

TIER 3

At Tier 3, the focus of problem identification is three fold: First, data gathered at Tiers 1 and 2 are reviewed to confirm that a student's performance fails to meet expected levels and that inadequate progress has occurred even under intervention conditions; second, more in-depth assessment is conducted to certify the severity and significance of the problem, pinpoint actual skill levels, and determine appropriate goals; and, third, functional assessment is used to identify factors that may explain students' performance problems. The first of these applications is based on the results of assessment activities conducted at Tiers 1 and 2. The latter two applications of problem identification will be described in this chapter in more detail.

While some versions of RTI treat entry into Tier 3 as a referral for evaluation for a suspected disability, Tier 3 is described in this text in terms of a systematic problem-solving procedure (i.e., a case study) that is used to develop interventions addressing the specific needs of the referred student. Comprehensive evaluation to determine eligibility for special education need not occur at Tier 3 if the problem-solving consultation provided through the case study results in an effective intervention of low or moderate intensity. Some students will respond adequately only to interventions that are so specialized that they constitute "special education"; others may show a promising—though still inadequate—response to such interventions. In both instances, evaluation for special education eligibility, which we have designated as Tier 3b, would be warranted because evidence suggests that a disability may exist. Use of RTI data and case study data for purposes of special education eligibility determination are discussed in more detail in Chapter 9.

BEHAVIORAL DEFINITION OF THE PROBLEM

A problem definition may include both a description of a student's performance in comparison to that of peers or established standards ("There is, in fact, a problem") and indicators of the severity of the problem (" . . . and it is so severe that it requires intervention"). A problem definition should describe the behavior in observable and measurable terms (exemplified in the sample problem statements presented in Table 4.1). This is easily accomplished when the problem is academic in nature, since such problems are typically defined in terms of scores on Curriculum-Based Measures. In contrast, behavior problems have no common metric; they can be described across a number of dimensions (frequency, intensity, duration, topography, latency, etc.) requiring a variety of measurement techniques.

Table 4.1 Sample Problem Definitions

Andrew completed only four of ten assignments (40%) with a median accuracy score of 65%, compared with a peer average of 90% completion with 85% accuracy.

During a 40-minute instructional period, Emma was out of her seat, walking around the classroom, for 25 minutes, and she was actively engaged in academic tasks only 30% of the time, compared to a peer average of 5 minutes out-of-seat and active engagement 70% of the time.

Sometimes, the Stranger Test (described in Chapter 2) is helpful in judging whether a behavioral problem definition is appropriate (Kaplan, 1995). For purposes of problem identification, this is especially important as it sharpens the focus on the specific behavior that will be the target of intervention and lends itself to the selection of an appropriate behavior and method for baseline measurement and progress monitoring.

In addition to a quantified description of the problem behavior, the definition also might include a measure of the desired or goal behavior. For example, the problem description of a student who displays disruptive classroom behavior might read, "Jonathan calls out in class without raising his hand and waiting to be called on 70% of the time," or, "Emily fails to comply within 10 seconds with directives given by her teacher 80% of the time." Using language describing the student's current level of performance of a desired or goal behavior, the problem might be described, "Jonathan raises his hand and waits to be called on before speaking only 30% of the time," or, "Emily complies with directives given by her teacher within 10 seconds of the teacher's prompt only 20% of the time." In both cases, a "score" for the problem behavior or goal behavior will be derived from observation sessions, and these scores will then serve as baseline performance measures. It may be difficult to measure goal behaviors that do not typically occur, so that their frequency at baseline may be as low as zero; consequently, behavioral definitions typically describe quantities of problem behavior. However, the goal behavior also might be measured, with an expectation that it will increase upon implementation of an effective intervention. A graph depicting this practice is shown in Figure 4.1.

If Tiers 1 and 2 of the RTI model have been applied in an appropriate manner, all of the information needed for a behavioral definition of an academic problem should be available. A sample of the language that might be used in a definition of the reading problem of a student who has progressed through Tiers 1 and 2 follows:

At the fall universal screening, using Passage Reading Fluency (PRF) grade-level reading passages, Juan scored 20 words correct per minute (wcpm), compared to the class median score of 60 wcpm, and below the fall benchmark screening standard of 50 wcpm. Juan's score was less than half the peer median for his class and at the 19th percentile for his grade level, based on local norms. Strategic monitoring over a nine-week period with standard classroom accommodations confirmed Juan's risk status; the slope of his trend line was .15, below the benchmark improvement standard of +1.0.

At Tier 2, Juan received supplemental small-group services using a standard protocol intervention three times per week (30-minute sessions) for ten weeks. Weekly progress monitoring results showed a +.30 rate of improvement (below the standard of +.75) and a PRF score of 29 wcpm (below the standard of 70 wcpm).

This report specifies Juan's level of performance following ten weeks of Tier 2 intervention (29 wcpm in grade-level materials) and compares it to a benchmark standard (70 wcpm). Juan's rate of growth is also presented (+.30 slope of trend line) and compared to a published standard (+.75). Together, these data demonstrate a DD: Juan has not yet attained an adequate level of performance or rate of growth in reading skills. Unfortunately, few schools will be able to provide data of this nature, especially when RTI implementation lacks integrity or has not yet been brought to scale. Consequently, it may be necessary to collect relevant data

Figure 4.1 Progress-Monitoring Graph Showing Rates of Problem and Goal Behaviors

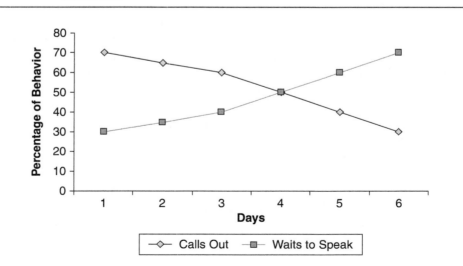

when a case study is initiated, typically through the administration of Curriculum-Based Measures, to quantify a student's academic problem.

Note that, while descriptions of academic performance problems are always framed in terms of the accuracy of performance on an academic measure (e.g., "Sam earned a score of only 18 wcpm on a third-grade level reading passage"), the number of errors committed by the student also might be recorded and tracked for both baseline- and progress-monitoring purposes. This practice would result in a graph similar to that depicted in Figure 4.1, with both the number of words read correctly and the number of errors plotted on the graph.

PROBLEM CERTIFICATION: ESTABLISHING THE SEVERITY OF THE DISCREPANCY BETWEEN ACTUAL AND EXPECTED PERFORMANCE

Academic problems. As discussed in Chapter 2, discrepancies between actual and expected levels of performance can be defined in terms of both peer comparisons (including local norms) and benchmark standards for academic performance. In Chapter 2, various methods for identifying discrepancies in levels of performance and rates of growth were described. For example, a school psychologist consulting with an individual classroom teacher might tentatively identify discrepant performance by halving the median score of the class and using the result as a cut score to establish possible risk for failure. Another method based on local norms uses the 25th percentile (or lowest 25% of the group) as a cut score for defining risk. Information and recommendations for values of Curriculum-Based Measurement (CBM) scores that correspond with risk for failure are available from the National Center on Response to Intervention (http:// www.rti4success.org) for both level of performance and rate of growth in skills. Apart from observing the degree to which a student's performance differs from that of his or her peers, or departs from benchmark standards for the student's grade level, how is the severity of an academic performance problem determined?

Shinn, Shinn, Hamilton, and Clarke (2002) suggest a method that can be used in schools where CBM universal assessments are conducted at multiple grade levels. Students whose performance on grade-level universal screening measures indicates risk for failure are administered CBM probes for the next lowest grade level. The student's score on that set of probes is compared with the performance of students at that grade level. The target student's problem would be considered severe if his or her score on the lower-level probes falls below the 16th percentile of scores earned by students at the lower grade level. For example, a fourth grader might earn a Passage Reading Fluency score of 38 wcpm on fourth-grade level materials—a score that is below the benchmark standard and below the 10th percentile (local norms) for the fourth grade. The student is then given third-grade–level materials and earns a score of 49 wcpm. However, inspection of local norms for the third grade reveals that a score of 49 wcpm falls at the 12th percentile for third graders. Thus, the target student's score, which falls below the 16th percentile when compared to the scores of third-grade students (i.e., students at a grade level one full year below the target student's grade placement), indicates a severe discrepancy between actual and expected levels of performance.

Another method, termed *survey-level assessment,* can not only be used to document the severity of the student's performance problem but also to pinpoint the level at which the student is performing adequately. This form of assessment is especially useful for a variety of reasons. First, it is preferable to the more common (albeit invalid) practice of describing students' "instructional levels" in terms of age- and grade-equivalent scores. The misuse of age- and grade-equivalent scores stems from a misunderstanding of the nature of these scores. A grade equivalent score of 4.5 represents the average score on the same measure of students currently placed at the 4.5 grade level. Many students at the 4.5 grade level (about 49%) will score higher on this measure; many (about 49%) will score lower, but the raw score corresponding to the 50th percentile (or median) is presented as the grade-equivalent score. In order to make the statement that a student "is reading at such-and-such a grade level," a performance measure that is actually drawn from the curriculum at that grade level would be administered to determine whether the student is able to perform adequately on that measure. Another advantage of survey-level assessment is its specification of an instructional level of student skill that not only can be used to plan intervention using materials with a suitable degree of difficulty but also for setting challenging but realistic performance goals.

To conduct a survey-level assessment, multiple probes are drawn from the curriculum at the student's own grade level as well as grade levels slightly above and below the student's current placement. First, probes from grade-level materials are administered to the student. If the student's score falls below the instructional standard for that grade level, probes are administered from the next lowest grade level, and so on, until the student's performance score falls within the instructional range for that grade level. Standards are available to define the quality of performance that is considered to be above expectations for each grade level (mastery or independent level), consistent with expectations (instructional level), and below expectations for each grade level (frustration level). Instructional standards for reading and math computation are presented in Shapiro (2004), and available from a variety of sources (Burns & Gibbons, 2008; Burns, VanDerHeyden, & Jiban, 2006; Gravois & Gickling, 2002).

Behavior problems. For concerns about students' behavior, establishing the severity of the problem is not as straightforward a process as it is with academic problems. The nature of the behavior problem might be considered, with certain kinds of problems regarded as inherently more serious and deserving of intervention. A list of factors indicating behaviors that probably warrant intervention follows:

- Behavior that is physically dangerous to the student him- or herself or to others (e.g., physical aggression; self-injury);
- Behavior that represents a significant departure from normative expectations (e.g., infantile speech mannerisms; an upper elementary student's crying when mother leaves);
- Behavior that is a "keystone" for the development of other important behaviors but is not in evidence (e.g., demanding that needs be met immediately rather than waiting one's turn; failing to follow the teacher's directives);
- Behavior that distinguishes the student from others in undesirable or counterproductive ways (e.g., inappropriate self-disclosures; very poor hygiene).

These criteria might be considered indices of "social validity," which refers to the significance of the problem and the importance of change relative to social and normative expectations. Care must be taken to ensure that judgments about the inappropriateness of a student's behavior are not the result of cultural bias, intolerance of differences, or a failure to consider unusual circumstances influencing the behavior. A useful index for determining whether a particular behavior warrants intervention is known as the "So What" test, which can be summarized in the following question: Does this behavior interfere with this child's (or another person's) physical, emotional, social, or academic well-being? If the answer is yes, then the So What test criterion has been met, and the case study and intervention should proceed (Kaplan, 1995).

Another general method for establishing the severity of a behavior problem uses peer comparisons obtained through interview and/or direct observation. An interview with a teacher or adult caregiver can provide an estimate of the severity of the problem behavior, in comparison with typical peer behavior, through questions such as, "About how often would you say that your typical student calls out without raising his or her hand first?" or, "Approximately how long does it typically take your students to begin work after you've finished giving directions?" The teacher's response would then be used to establish the standard for peer comparison.

To obtain more objective information, however, it is desirable to use direct observation (discussed in detail in Chapter 2), with reference to a specific performance standard. (A performance standard is important because, without it, it is impossible to know whether the measured behavior is within normal limits for a particular setting.) This requires the observer to alternate observation and recording of the behavior of the target student with observation and recording of the behavior of one or more peers. For example, an observation of "task-engaged" behavior (i.e., behavior that is directly relevant to the assigned task, such as looking at a textbook, writing answers on a worksheet, or asking questions related to the task) might use a momentary time sampling procedure over a 50-minute class period, in which, at 5-minute intervals, the observer glances at the student and marks whether the student is task-engaged or disengaged. At the end of each 5th minute, the observer glances first at the target student and records his or her behavior and then glances at a peer and records the peer's behavior using the same criteria. The observer might select three peers and alternate among them with each momentary recording event or randomly select a different peer for each recording event. By comparing the behavior of the target student with the behavior of typical peers, the observer can reach a data-based conclusion about the severity of the target student's problem. (Of course, if the rate of problem behavior observed in peers is similar to that of the target student, the observer would conclude that intervention at a classwide level is warranted.)

FORMULATING INTERVENTION GOALS

In Chapter 3, goal setting was discussed as part of the consultation process, noting that it is important to establish classwide goals that inform instruction and serve as a standard against which students' progress can be evaluated. Several methods for setting goals for *academic performance* were described. In general, classwide goals in the grade-level curriculum are used as the standard for performance of any student at Tiers 1 and 2. It is reasonable to expect, given appropriate instruction at Tier 1 and more intensive, research-based intervention at Tier 2, that students will demonstrate adequate growth in and eventual attainment of grade-level skills. If this does not occur, students proceed to Tier 3, which requires individualized intervention planning and, in some cases, performance goals that differ from grade-level expectations.

When a high-intensity intervention has been implemented at Tier 3 without success, a DD is observed. Inspection of progress monitoring data reveals that students are neither achieving at a satisfactory level (i.e., they have not closed the gap between their level of performance and the expected level), nor are they progressing at a satisfactory rate. In these cases, the students' current level of performance should be considered for purposes of modifying intervention goals based on the results of survey-level assessment, as described earlier. For example, for a fifth-grade student who is reading at a second-grade level and failing to make appropriate gains, it might be appropriate to set goals at the third-grade level of the curriculum. A general guideline recommends that, for students whose instructional level is two or more years below current grade placement, goals should be set in materials one year above the current instructional level (Burns & Gibbons, 2008).

It is important to specify the grade level of the curriculum at which goals will be set, as baseline measurement and progress monitoring will use goal-level assessment materials. Baseline measurement describes the student's current level of performance in goal materials and is used as a starting point from which progress is subsequently measured. If the student is expected to demonstrate satisfactory performance in grade-level materials as a result of intervention, benchmark standards or local norms can be used to define goals for performance. For example, to define the long-term math goal for a fifth-grade student whose current instructional level is at the fourth grade, and where the goal is to attain mastery of the fifth-grade level curriculum by year-end, the goal might be set at 30 digits correct per minute (dcpm), the year-end benchmark standard for the fifth grade.

If local norms have been generated for the fifth grade in math, the goal can be derived from the level of performance (i.e., a score that is at the 50th percentile) expected for the fifth-grade class on the universal screening conducted in the spring. This method is feasible if several years' worth of fifth-grade assessment results are available, so that an expectation for year-end performance can be established. (Otherwise, we would have no way of knowing, in advance, the average level of performance that will be attained at year-end by the current fifth-grade class.) (See Table 4.2.)

Table 4.2   Year-End Benchmark Scores for Goal Setting in Reading and Math

Grade Level	Reading (Using DIBELS Measures)	Math Computation (Digits Correct per Minute)
Kindergarten	Letter-Sound Fluency: 40 sounds correct/minute	—
One	Word Identification Fluency: 60 wcpm	20
Two	Passage Reading Fluency: 75 wcpm	20
Three	Passage Reading Fluency: 100 wcpm	30
Four	Maze Fluency: 20 correct replacements/2.5 minutes	40
Five	Maze Fluency: 25 correct replacements/2.5 minutes	30
Six	Maze Fluency: 30 correct replacements/2.5 minutes	35

Source: Adapted from the National Center on Student Progress Monitoring, retrieved April 16, 2009, from http://www.studentprogress.org

A third method of long-term academic goal setting uses national norms for weekly improvement. In this method, the expected weekly rate of improvement for the student's grade level is multiplied by the number of weeks left until year-end (see Table 4.3). The result is added to the median score obtained during baseline measurement. For example, if Lashawnda, a third-grade student, earned a baseline median score of 11 dcpm in math computation, and there are 18 weeks left in the school year, her goal score would be calculated as follows: .30 (expected rate of improvement) multiplied by 18 (weeks left in the school year) equals 5.40. Adding 5.40 to the baseline median score of 11, we set Lashawnda's year-end goal at 16 dcpm. For information about setting short-term intervention goals, the reader is referred to Chapter 8, where discussion of the changing criterion single-case design provides extensive information and examples of methods for goal setting based on benchmark scores and expected rates of improvement.

A final method for setting long-term goals for students at Tier 3 is to use high-stakes assessment data as the criterion for predictions using CBM scores (Burns & Gibbons, 2008). This method, which employs a logistical regression formula available in Burns and Gibbons (p. 27), identifies the level of CBM score that predicts successful performance on the high-stakes

Table 4.3   Slope for Goal Setting in Reading and Math Based on Weekly Rate of Improvement

Grade Level	Reading	Math Computation (Digits)	Math Concepts & Applications (Correct Responses)
One	Word Identification Fluency: 1.8 words	.35	No data available
Two	Passage Reading Fluency: 1.5 words	.30	.40
Three	Passage Reading Fluency: 1.0 words	.30	.60
Four	Maze Fluency: .40 replacements	.70	.70
Five	Maze Fluency: .40 replacements	.70	.70
Six	Maze Fluency: .40 replacements	.40	.70

Source: Adapted from the National Center on Student Progress Monitoring, retrieved April 16, 2009, from http://www.studentprogress.org

assessment. The scores of students who have completed both the CBM universal screening and high-stakes testing for their grade level are needed to perform this statistical analysis.

Unlike goal setting for academic problems, there are no formulas (or empirically derived cut scores) that can be used to set goals for behavior problems. However, *setting goals for behavior change* will be easier if several important factors are considered. First, what is the desired direction of the change in behavior—that is, should the behavior increase or decrease? Obviously, a desired increase in the behavior will mean that the goal level of the behavior will be of greater magnitude than the current (baseline) level of the behavior. Second, if the goal is to decrease the behavior, has a replacement behavior been identified? For example, for a student who calls out in class without raising her hand, the replacement behavior might be stipulated as "raising hand and waiting to be called on before speaking aloud in class." Third, what is a reasonable expectation for the goal level of the behavior, given information about the behavior of typical or "template" peers? If the typical first-grade student is able to maintain task engagement, without interruption, for an average of seven minutes, then "seven minutes" might be the goal for a first-grade student who currently sustains task engagement for an average of three minutes. And, fourth, what is the current (baseline) level of the problem behavior and of the replacement behavior? If the problem behavior occurs at a very high frequency (or the replacement behavior does not occur at all), the goal should be set lower than would be the case for low-frequency problem behaviors or replacement behaviors that already are in evidence. For example, although the classroom teacher might wish to eliminate a student's trips to the pencil sharpener completely, and peers show an average frequency of one trip per 50-minute class session, a reasonable goal for a student who currently makes eight trips to the pencil sharpener might be a reduction to two or three trips per class session. Of course, in the event of behavior that represents a danger to the target student or to others, the goal must be to eliminate the behavior; no minimal level of behavior (e.g., "throwing desks" or "punching peers") is acceptable!

PLANNING DATA-COLLECTION ACTIVITIES FOR BASELINE MEASUREMENT AND PROGRESS MONITORING

The final task of the problem identification phase is to plan data-collection activities for both baseline- and progress-monitoring measurement. Data-collection procedures include CBMs for academic problems and behavioral assessment techniques (typically, some form of direct observation) for behavior problems.

In the case of academic problems, CBM of the student's current level of skill may have occurred by this point in the process. For example, universal screening of reading in the fall of third grade will have yielded a performance score that can be used for baseline purposes, as long as (1) the score is a reliable indicator of the student's actual level of skill (i.e., reliability is adequate), (2) the baseline is stable, (3) changes in the student's skill have not occurred as a result of instruction since the score was obtained, and (4) the level of materials used in the universal screening is the same level in which the student's long-term performance goal has been set. In academic assessment (especially oral reading fluency), reliability can be enhanced by the use of the median score in a series of several measurements (e.g., the median score obtained from three administrations of reading fluency probes of equivalent difficulty). Stability of the baseline score is important whether the problem is of an academic or behavioral nature. The reader is referred to Chapter 8 for an in-depth discussion of variability/stability, level, and trend of the baseline.

For behavior problems, baseline- and progress-monitoring measures typically employ recording of operationally defined behaviors, using a method appropriate to the characteristics of the behavior to be measured as well as the resources available for measurement. These methods, which include recording the frequency, duration, latency, intensity, topography, or quality of a behavior, using techniques such as interval recording, time sampling or momentary recording, and direct-behavior ratings or performance-based recording, were discussed in detail in Chapter 2.

Permanent product recording is an appropriate method for behaviors that result in a product, such as completed assignments or attendance records. Often, an interview conducted during the problem identification stage of a case study results in an operational definition of the problem that differs somewhat from the problem initially described. For example, a teacher might describe a student's problem as one of inadequate homework completion (measured in terms of the number of assignments submitted), but further interviews of the teacher, parents, and student reveal that the more pressing problem is an overall lack of engagement in academic tasks and high error rates on assignments. In this case, more appropriate baseline and progress monitoring measures might consist of momentary recording by the teacher of the student's engagement in classroom activities as well as accuracy scores on both homework and in-class assignments. Thus, there may be a need to gather new data to define baseline levels of performance prior to the introduction of an intervention.

ASSESSMENT OF FACTORS RELATED TO THE PROBLEM

Recall the three purposes of problem identification at Tier 3: (1) to confirm that a student's performance falls short of expectations, (2) to certify the severity and significance of the problem and identify current instructional levels and goals, and (3) to identify factors that explain the student's performance problems. The first two purposes have been explored thus far in this chapter; the remainder of the chapter will be devoted to the third purpose, which is accomplished through a process known as *functional assessment*. Since a detailed examination of functional assessment is beyond the scope of this text, interested readers are referred to Watson and Steege (2003) or McDougal, Chafouleas, and Waterman (2006), which provide comprehensive information about the process.

The purpose of a functional assessment is to identify events that are functionally (i.e., causally) related to the occurrence of a problem; these events are classified as either *antecedents* (events occurring prior to the behavior) or *consequences* (events occurring subsequent to the behavior). The assessment is an attempt to identify antecedents and consequences and discern their relationship to the problem. Examples of antecedent conditions that might be relevant to an academic problem include the nature of instructions, the difficulty of the material, the type of task assigned, a directive given by the teacher, the number of people present, or the degree of structure and order in the setting. Antecedents that are further removed in time from the occurrence of the behavior (i.e., temporally distant setting events) might include the student's bedtime on the preceding evening, whether she ate breakfast that morning, or her parents' homework monitoring practices. Given these examples, it is easy to see why more immediate antecedents should be targeted for intervention: They are more accessible and amenable to change in the school setting.

Consequences that are functionally related to a problem might include the teacher's reaction to a behavior (praise, correction, ignoring, reprimand, etc.) or that of peers (laughter, praise, ignoring, disapproval, etc.). A more distant consequence would be the reaction of parents, or a reward to be delivered at the end of the week. (In many cases, more "distant" consequences tend to be less effective; this is especially true for younger children, which is the reason that "tokens" that can be exchanged for tangible rewards are sometimes used.)

Antecedents and consequences also can be "private events"—that is, conditions that are not immediately observable and are therefore more difficult to identify (feelings of anxiety, physical discomfort, relief from an itch, etc.). The role of sensory conditions as antecedents or consequences is typically revealed through interviews, which are discussed below. A list of antecedents and consequences that are often found to be functionally related to behavior is presented in Table 4.4.

The assumption underlying functional assessment is that every behavior has a function, or purpose, that can be discovered by studying the events that precede (antecedents) and follow (consequences) the behavior. These functions are generally understood to fall into two major categories,

Table 4.4   Examples of Common Antecedents and Consequences

Antecedents	Consequences
• **Distant (Removed in Time)** Learning history (past success/failure) Home structures/procedures related to school/learning (e.g., homework monitoring) Home bedtime Home responsibilities Home meal schedule/practices Medical conditions affecting behavior (e.g., medication, asthma) Home events prior to school day Events en route to school Daily schedule	Teacher attention (acknowledgment, calling on student) Teacher praise Teacher reprimand Teacher ignoring Teacher redirection (to another behavior) Teacher error correction Peer laughter Peer attention (acknowledgment, interaction) Peer ignoring Peer disapproval/rejection Obtain desired object
• **Setting (General Circumstances)** Type of activity Size of group Persons present Subject area (math, etc.) Classroom behavior management practices Degree of structure/transition times Time of day Emotional or physical sensation	Obtain/prolong desired activity Object taken away Activity terminated Negative feeling relieved (anxiety, anger, frustration) Positive sensation created (stimulation) Negative sensation relieved
• **Immediate** Teacher directive Teacher question Assigned task Difficulty of task Clarity of instructions Lack of attention	

as displayed in Figure 4.2: to get something or to avoid something. For example, a student whose disruptive behavior occurs only when a math assignment has been given (antecedent) and typically results in the teacher removing her from the classroom (consequence) is probably acting to avoid the math assignment, which she dislikes or finds too difficult. Further

Figure 4.2   Functions of Behavior

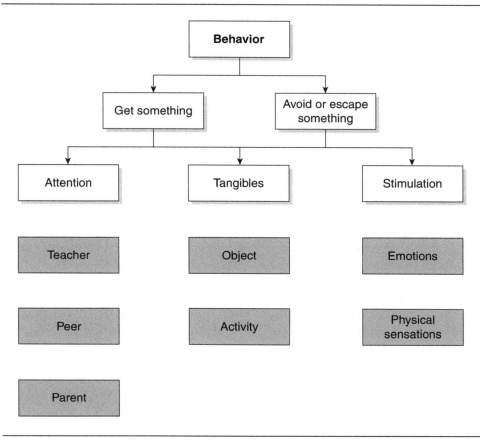

assessment, which might include testing her math skills, will reveal the reason she avoids math (e.g., she does not know how to perform the operation that appeared on her assignment; she makes frequent errors and has been teased by classmates). These explanations, termed *hypotheses,* are tested and used to develop interventions; this process is discussed in Chapters 5 and 7. Thus, the goal of the functional assessment that takes place in the problem-identification phase is to furnish information that will be used to generate and test hypotheses in the problem-analysis phase of the case study.

An additional purpose served by functional assessment is to gather information that can be used in interventions to promote replacement behaviors. A replacement behavior is a behavior that serves the same function as the original (undesirable) behavior but in a more positive, adaptive, and socially appropriate way. For example, a student who escapes disliked assignments by engaging in disruptive behavior might receive an intervention in which he can choose from among several assignments (thereby making the assignment more appealing, such that escape becomes unnecessary), or he might receive periodic work breaks contingent on having completed a specified amount of work. A well-executed functional assessment will provide sufficient information about circumstances prompting and following behavior, so those circumstances can be eliminated, modified, or managed in ways that discourage problem behavior and encourage positive behavior.

The behavioral-assessment methods discussed in Chapter 2 are used for functional assessment. Permanent product or record review involves the inspection of products resulting from behavior—attendance records, disciplinary notations, grades earned, standardized test results, medical history, work samples or portfolios, individual education plans, and so forth. Inspection of records might show a history of satisfactory achievement up until the fourth grade, at which point the student's grades declined and attendance problems began. Further assessment results (perhaps obtained through student and parent interviews) could help determine the reasons for the abrupt change in school performance. Attendance records can help to establish that a student's academic problems are not due to a lack of exposure to instruction, while materials contained in a portfolio might exemplify the degree of proficiency of which the student is capable.

Interviews are a rich source of information, but they must employ questions that elicit information that will be useful in a functional assessment. Rather than focusing on a student's developmental history, as in a classic "background" interview, questions should seek to identify specific events or circumstances that may help to explain current performance. As mentioned earlier, Kratochwill and Bergan (1990) present the Behavioral Consultation process as a series of interviews. In the problem-identification stage of consultation with a teacher, questions focus on circumstances in which the behavior is most and least likely to occur, the teacher's expectations for performance, comparisons with peers, skills that are emerging and those that have been mastered, events that seem to occur just before and after the behavior, and what interventions have been attempted. Similar questions might be posed in an interview with parents.

With students, functional-assessment interviews request information about the difficulty of assignments; whether and how the student seeks assistance; perceptions of the student's own competencies and skills; teacher, parent, and peer reactions to the student's behavior or academic work; and school-related likes and dislikes. Protocols for conducting functional-assessment interviews are widely available as commercially published instruments or surveys presented in texts and research articles. Suggested instruments include those developed by Shapiro (2004), Ysseldyke and Christenson (2002), O'Neill and colleagues (1997), and Watson and Steege (2003).

Behavioral observation in functional assessment. As discussed earlier in this chapter, problem identification employs behavioral measures to define problems in concrete terms, certify their severity or significance, and establish a baseline to which performance under intervention conditions can be compared. For these purposes, methods that quantify behavioral frequency, intensity, duration, latency, topography, or quality are appropriate. (Note that tests of academic skills, such as CBM, are a form of observation in which a student is prompted to engage in a behavior, such as solving a sheet of math problems or reading a passage aloud, and responses are evaluated for their accuracy.) Understanding the context in which the behavior occurs, however, may require additional or different assessment methods. For example, a frequency recording conducted to establish a baseline level of behavior might reveal that a behavior occurs more often when the student is in reading class and less often in math class. This information suggests that some aspect of the environmental condition of the reading class is functionally related to the problem behavior. Thus, observations should always be conducted in several settings (based on information from interviews suggesting settings in which the behavior is more or less likely to occur) and on several occasions (to enhance reliability), especially if being used in a functional assessment.

Observation techniques that are designed specifically for purposes of functional assessment include scatterplots and Antecedent-Behavior-Consequence (A-B-C) recording. A scatterplot provides a graphic display of days, times, and activities during which a behavior is most and least likely to occur. A sample scatterplot is presented in Figure 4.3.

Figure 4.3   Sample Scatterplot Displaying Occurrences of "Fighting and Provoking Peers" Behavior

Time of Day/Activity	Mon	Tues	Wed	Thurs	Fri
8:30 a.m.—Homeroom	X			X	
8:50 a.m.–9:40 a.m.—Social studies					
9:45 a.m.–10:35 a.m.—Physical education	X	X		X	X
10:40 a.m.–11:30 a.m.—Algebra					
11:35 a.m.–12:25 p.m.—Lunch & study	X	X	X	X	X

Note: X indicates behavior observed.

As portrayed in Figure 4.3, the results of the scatterplot demonstrate that the "fighting and provoking peers" behavior is most likely to occur in lunch and study hall, physical education, and, to a lesser extent, homeroom. The examiner might then ask what these settings have in common and discover that there is less structure and more opportunities for peer interaction in these settings. The scatterplot is a relatively simple device for recording occurrences of behavior, and it provides some information that may be useful in generating explanations (hypotheses) for the behavior in question; thus, it is often recommended for use by classroom teachers. However, more complete information about circumstances surrounding a behavior can be obtained using A-B-C recording. An example of A-B-C recording is presented in Figure 4.4. A third-party observer may be required if recording is continuous throughout a time period, but if information is recorded only when the behavior of interest occurs, it would be possible for the classroom teacher to conduct the observation. In Figure 4.4, the behavior of "calling out without prompting" occurs during homeroom period, so the observer begins to record the sequence of events prior to and following the behavior.

The role of antecedent and consequence conditions is clearly portrayed in Figure 4.4: Jill's calling out behavior occurs when she is in an "alone/no attention" condition; since the teacher responds to her, it is likely that Jill is calling out in order to obtain teacher attention.

Figure 4.4   Sample A-B-C Recording

Time/Setting/Activity	Antecedent	Behavior	Consequence
8:25 a.m.—Homeroom	T: Talking with group of students. S: Sitting alone	S: "Hey, Ms. Manty! Check out my new shoes!"	T: "Quiet, Jill."
	C*	S: "What? I just thought you'd like to see my shoes."	T: "Not now, Jill. I'm busy."
	C	S: "Well, alright, but you're missing something good."	T: "Maybe later."
	C	S: Takes out backpack and looks inside.	T: Continues talking with group of students.

*Note: The use of "C" in the Antecedent column indicates that the preceding consequence now serves as an antecedent.

While characteristics of students (e.g., medical conditions, temperament, measured intelligence) may contribute to some problems, educational interventions directly addressing those characteristics are seldom adequate, effective, or practical—except in the case of interventions to increase students' skill levels. Conducting a survey-level assessment represents a measurement of a student characteristic (i.e., skill in solving math computation problems), and intervention might seek to improve the student's skill through modeling, guided practice, and so forth.

Some behavior problems are (at least in part) a result of the student's lack of skill, knowledge, or ability to perform the desired behavior. These factors often are identified as *secondary dependent variables*, which are discussed in more detail in Chapter 5. For example, a student who has few friends might be found to have social skills deficiencies; this lack of capacity to perform a behavior must be addressed through an intervention to teach appropriate social skills. Apart from skill levels and the capacity to perform a behavior, the case study does not typically emphasize assessment and intervention targeting student characteristics. Diagnoses of attention deficit disorder (a student characteristic), for example, often result in a pharmacological intervention prescribed by a physician, but teachers find that medication doesn't fully remedy the behavior and learning problems observed in the classroom. While a student's intelligence (estimated as an IQ score) almost certainly contributes to rates of learning, it is impossible to increase intelligence and thereby enhance learning. While research has shown that a handful of "student characteristics" are indeed related to school outcomes, environmental conditions or events make up the vast majority of appropriate variables targeted for intervention; these are the focus of the case study method. (Readers interested in learning more about relevant student characteristics should explore the literature on academic enablers, such as motivation and goal orientation, summarized in a special issue of the *School Psychology Review*, edited by DiPerna and Elliott, 2002.)

Functional assessment of academic performance problems. Although this discussion of functional assessment has included references to academic performance problems, additional clarification of the functional assessment of academic problems, in contrast to behavior problems, may be helpful to the reader. The functional assessment of academic problems rests on the same principles as those underlying the assessment of behavior problems; that is, assessment seeks to identify environmental variables (antecedents and consequences) that are functionally related to performance problems. In the case of academic problems, variables considered in a functional assessment consist primarily of instructional practices and materials. Antecedents to academic problems include the nature of learning tasks, difficulty of instructional materials, use of modeling and demonstration by the teacher, amount of time allotted for instruction, instructional grouping of students, availability of choices, and effectiveness of classroom management. Consequences that may be functionally related to academic performance include the timing and quality of feedback, error correction, and meaningful incentives. Functional assessment is offered as an alternative to diagnostic or structural assessment, which focuses instead on the characteristics of students to explain problems (e.g., learning disabilities, neurological processing deficits). Functional assessment is the approach recommended in this text because structural factors, while they influence learning, are not amenable to change, nor is there adequate evidence of a causal relationship with academic performance.

Structural-equation modeling has identified student engagement as a first-order predictor of academic performance, while teacher behavior and instructional materials and activities serve as second-order factors composing the variable of "instruction" (DiPerna & Elliott, 2002). In other words, the nature of instruction influences the degree to which students are engaged in academic tasks, which, in turn, predicts academic outcomes. Changes in engagement are made possible by changes in antecedent conditions—for example, instruction—that are functionally related to engagement. More specifically, interventions should increase "opportunities to respond" by employing tasks that are motivating and prompt high response rates (Greenwood, Horton, & Utley, 2002). Changes in engagement also can be achieved by changing the consequences arising from engagement behaviors, including feedback, praise, and rewards for successful performance.

Several useful interview and observation instruments have been designed for use in functional assessment of academic problems, including interview and observation materials created by Shapiro (2004), the Functional Assessment of Academic Behavior (Ysseldyke & Christenson, 2002), interview and observation protocols developed by Witt, Daly, and Noell (2000), and the Instructional Validity Checklist (Olson, Daly, Andersen, Turner, & LeClair, 2007). The BOSS protocol for behavioral observation (Shapiro, 1996) focuses on active and passive student engagement in academic activities and allows for peer comparisons and notation of the teacher's instructional behaviors.

How can assessment uncover the hypothesis that explains a particular student's academic performance problem? As noted earlier, methods used for behavioral assessment also can be used in the assessment of academic-performance problems. If insufficient motivation is suspected as the cause of a student's problem, inspection of completed assignments and the teacher's record book (i.e., permanent product inspection), as well as interviews of the teacher, parents, and student, might reveal that the student sometimes completes work with a high degree of accuracy, but there is an erratic pattern of performance, and the student finds tasks to be "boring" and unchallenging. Direct observation might reveal that when classroom activities are stimulating and engaging, the student participates enthusiastically and responds favorably to competitive tasks. Alternatively, a hypothesis that cites the difficulty of instructional materials as the factor impeding a student's performance would require the administration of measures to identify the student's instructional level. This is best accomplished through the use of survey-level assessment with CBM or Mastery Measurement materials. As described earlier, survey-level assessment begins with materials at the student's current grade placement and moves upward or downward to materials at other grade levels until the instructional level is identified.

SUMMARY

The school psychologist, in collaboration with the teacher, has now accomplished several important goals: A working relationship has been created, a sense of the teacher's expectations for class performance has been attained, the behavior that will be the focus of intervention has been clearly defined, the severity and significance of the student's problem has been certified, tentative goals for improvement have been identified, and a plan for data collection has been formulated and implemented. Data collected through functional assessment procedures have revealed a number of variables (environmental events or circumstances as well as student characteristics) that appear to be functionally (causally) related to the problem. In Chapter 5, the generation and testing of hypotheses explaining performance problems will be discussed, along with their relevance to intervention planning.

5

Problem Analysis

Problem analysis is a crucial component for assisting students who have not been responsive to interventions implemented at the first two tiers of the RTI process. Information gathered during the problem identification stage is used to generate logical reasons for the problem, which are then translated into hypotheses. In the problem-analysis stage, hypotheses are tested to determine whether they actually reflect the cause of the problem. Accurate hypotheses provide the focus for interventions. The benefits of hypothesis testing are that it (1) ensures an accurate target for remediation, (2) reduces biased decision making, (3) eliminates inappropriate intervention options, and (4) increases the likelihood that interventions will have the desired impact on behavior.

Interventions at Tiers 1 and 2 of the RTI process are chosen based on their efficacy, which is established through research showing a replicated beneficial impact on the targeted problem. A comprehensive investigation of the cause of the problem for an individual child is generally not conducted at the first two tiers. Students who reach Tier 3 are assumed to have made little improvement in the preceding tiers either because they require a more intense application of the intervention or because an incorrect cause of the problem was targeted for intervention. Occasionally, in some very complex or urgent cases, Tiers 1, 2, and 3 may be conducted concurrently (e.g., Barnett et al., 2006).

As shown in the diagram in Chapter 1 (Figure 1.2), a comprehensive individualized case study is conducted in Tier 3 to identify the cause of a problem, find the most appropriate intervention, and determine the intervention intensity that is needed to have a positive impact for the student. At Tier 3b, high-intensity interventions are evaluated to determine special education eligibility, but this is not a necessary component of Tier 3.

GENERATING HYPOTHESES

Hypotheses have three parts: (1) the dependent variable (target problem), (2) the explanation, and (3) a linking word that establishes the relationship between the two (Batsche, Castillo, Dixon, & Forde, 2008). The *dependent variable* is the behavior targeted for improvement. The main dependent variable is typically identified prior to the initiation of the individualized case study. However, data gathering and hypothesis testing may lead to a secondary dependent variable that requires intervention in order for the primary dependent variable to improve, as explained in the next section of this chapter. The explanation clarifies the reason for and/or the conditions under which the target behavior is suspected to occur. For example, a student who frequently yells out and disrupts the class may be suspected to do so as an attention-getting behavior resulting from boredom. Further investigation reveals that this inappropriate behavior occurs primarily during physical education class, when the student is unable to perform required tasks at a high level of proficiency. In this instance, two hypotheses could be developed.

> *Primary hypothesis:* The student yells out and disrupts the class (dependent variable) when (linking word) he is bored (explanation).

> *Secondary hypothesis:* The student yells out and disrupts the class (dependent variable) because (linking word) he wants to distract others from the fact that he lacks the skills to perform at a high level (explanation).

Hypotheses are restated as prediction statements to establish a format for hypothesis testing. In addition, prediction statements replace the suspected cause of the problem with an intervention that is likely to have an effect on the dependent variable, if the hypothesis is true.

Interventions cited in prediction statements should have empirical support for their efficacy in remediating the problem under consideration. Two prediction statements are created for each hypothesis: a *confirmatory* prediction statement, and a *rejection* prediction statement. Confirmatory prediction statements are structured to validate the hypothesis, while rejection prediction statements are structured to invalidate the hypothesis. A five-step process is used to set up the format for hypothesis testing. Consider a simplified version of the situation of Kim, who is experiencing a problem with reading.

Step 1: Restate the problem situation.

> Kim's reading fluency of 25 words per minute (wpm) is below the 10th percentile in relation to class norms (mean of 90 wpm in grade-level text).

Step 2: Establish the relationship between the problem situation and the cause of the behavior by using the word *because.*

Step 3: Provide the logical explanation.

> Skill deficit: She has not mastered the vowel sounds (*e, o,* and *u*).
>
> Skill deficit: She does not practice reading.
>
> Performance deficit: She is distracted during reading.
>
> Performance deficit: She does not like to read.

Step 4: Combine elements to form complete hypothesis statements.

> Kim's reading fluency of 25 wpm is below the 10th percentile in relation to the class norms (mean of 90 wpm in grade-level text) because she has not mastered the vowel sounds (*e, o,* and *u*).
>
> Kim's reading fluency of 25 wpm is below the 10th percentile in relation to the class norms (mean of 90 wpm in grade-level text) because she has not had enough practice in reading.
>
> Kim's reading fluency of 25 wpm is below the 10th percentile in relation to the class norms (mean of 90 wpm in grade-level text) because she is distracted during reading.
>
> Kim's reading fluency of 25 wpm is below the 10th percentile in relation to the class norms (mean of 90 wpm in grade-level text) because she does not like to read.

Step 5: Create confirmatory and rejection prediction statements for each hypothesis.

> Confirmatory Prediction 1: Kim's reading fluency will improve as a result of instruction and practice in the vowel sounds of *e, o,* and *u.*
>
> Rejection Prediction 1: Kim's reading fluency will not improve as a result of instruction and practice in the vowel sounds of *e, o,* and *u.*
>
> Confirmatory Prediction 2: Kim's reading fluency will improve as a result of increased reading practice.
>
> Rejection Prediction 2: Kim's reading fluency will not improve as a result of increased reading practice.
>
> Confirmatory Prediction 3: Kim's reading fluency will improve when she is in an isolated setting free of distractions.
>
> Rejection Prediction 3: Kim's reading fluency will not improve when she is in an isolated setting free of distractions.

Confirmatory Prediction 4: Kim's reading fluency will improve when she reads text that is interesting to her.

Rejection Prediction 4: Kim's reading fluency will not improve when she reads text that is interesting to her.

PRIMARY AND SECONDARY DEPENDENT VARIABLES

Well-developed hypotheses and prediction statements lead logically into testing scenarios. Careful designation of the variables is critical for unbiased hypothesis selection. Recall that Tier 3 differs from Tiers 1 and 2 in that the first two tiers provide interventions that research has suggested will have a positive impact on the dependent variable. At Tier 3, the assumption is that the complexity of the problem and its causes requires a different approach. In many cases, the primary dependent variable is supplemented with a secondary dependent variable, and both should be targeted for intervention.

For Kim, reading fluency was determined to be the problem at both Tiers 1 and 2. Reading fluency is the primary dependent variable; however, as a result of further investigation into Kim's problem, it appeared that mastery of the vowel sounds (*e, o,* and *u*) might be the underlying cause of the reading fluency problem. Therefore, there are two dependent variables: (1) oral reading fluency (primary) and (2) mastery of the specific vowel sounds (secondary).

Hypothesis testing for primary and secondary dependent variables occurs in two steps. First, the secondary dependent variable is tested by investigating the impact of an intervention. Next, the relationship between the primary and secondary dependent variables is examined by comparing outcome data for both. In the case of Kim, a positive correlation between vowel-sound knowledge and reading-fluency data provides proof that vowel-sound mastery is a cause of low reading fluency, as noted in Figure 5.1. In other words, as vowel-sound mastery (secondary dependent variable) increases, reading fluency (primary dependent variable) increases.

There are four general types of dependent variables: academic, cognitive or metacognitive, social/behavioral, and adaptive (Knoff, 2002). *Academic* outcomes are related to the demonstration of knowledge and skill. For example, a commonly addressed academic outcome is reading fluency, but there are a variety of academic outcomes ranging from simple math skills to complex scientific procedures. *Cognitive* or *metacognitive* outcomes include strategies for learning and problem-solving skills. Study skills and organizational strategies are examples of this type of dependent variable. *Social/behavioral* outcomes refer to interpersonal and

Figure 5.1   Relationship Between Primary and Secondary Dependent Variables

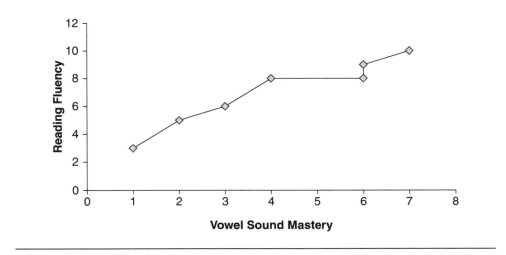

intrapersonal skills and performance. Attending behaviors and prosocial behaviors, such as turn taking and helping others, are a few of the many social/behavioral dependent variables that are important in schools. *Adaptive* behavior concerns basic survival skills, particularly for low functioning students, but also for students who must adapt to adverse environmental conditions. For example, appropriate responses to unsafe conditions (e.g., telling an adult when approached by a stranger) could be a dependent variable of concern. All of these domains include potential primary and secondary dependent variables that could contribute to the complexity of the problem.

TYPES OF HYPOTHESES

Examining problems in a collaborative manner encourages multiple perspectives, and, by extension, a variety of hypotheses. Enough hypotheses should be generated so that at least one hypothesis is accepted and at least one hypothesis is rejected. One or more of the four types of dependent variables (academic, cognitive or metacognitive, social/behavioral, and adaptive) can be the target for the chosen intervention. When there is more than one target for intervention, it is prudent to develop a set of hypotheses for each concern. For each targeted problem, hypotheses are generated to answer the question: Why is this situation happening? As a rule, for all types of problems, both *skill* and *performance* hypotheses are considered in order to avoid hypothesis bias. The goal of hypothesis generation is to ensure that appropriate hypotheses can be verified, inappropriate hypotheses can be eliminated, and bias in these decisions is minimized. Accepted hypotheses lead directly into intervention implementation. If multiple hypotheses are accepted, then the intervention plan should include components to address each one.

Skill-based hypotheses. Skill-based hypotheses are needed when a student does not know how to do something, and problems are due to lack of instruction or practice. Hypothesis testing incorporates brief instructional and/or practice interventions to determine their impact on the dependent variable. For example, Deborah's poor scores on math measures may be hypothesized to be the result of a lack of instruction in calculation procedures. This hypothesis could be tested in several sessions involving direct instruction, modeling, practice, and error correction. If Deborah's score improves, the hypothesis is supported, and a more comprehensive intervention plan incorporating these strategies can be initiated. Direct instruction interventions include the implementation of instructional programs and techniques, and it may incorporate materials at different skill levels. Practice interventions are tested to verify the amount and type of activities that yield the greatest impact.

Performance-based hypotheses. Performance-based hypotheses are employed when a student does not demonstrate a skill that has been learned. Hypothesis testing occurs by manipulating the environment through a functional behavior analysis (Chandler & Dahlquist, 2002; Knoster & McCurdy, 2002) to determine the impact of the identified independent variable on the dependent variable (e.g., see Mueller, Sterling-Turner, & Moore, 2005). For example, a reward might be offered as a consequence of an increase in the student's score on a math measure. In this example, the dependent variable (math score) changes as a result of the manipulated independent variable (reward). If the student is successful in raising the score, the "won't do" (performance-based) hypothesis is supported.

Distant setting events, often termed *slow triggers,* are typically more difficult to address through brief experimental hypothesis testing because they cannot be manipulated in the school setting. Instead, immediate antecedents are often the intervention targets (Knoster & McCurdy, 2002) because they are perceived to be the conditions that encourage or exacerbate the problem behavior.

Level of inference. Hypotheses can be placed on a continuum of low- to high-inference based on the relationship between the data and the hypothesized cause of the problem. Low-inference hypotheses are developed directly from data and require few assumptions about the relationship between the problem and the cause. High-inference hypotheses are those that are inferred from an unmeasured condition or from an indirect measure of a behavior assumed to correlate with the problem behavior. High-inference hypotheses are more likely to suffer from hypothesis bias and have a greater chance of rejection. As much as possible, hypothesis generation should be low inference and data based; however, some high-inference hypotheses can be reconfigured into low-inference data-based hypotheses. The following scenarios provide examples of low-inference, unmeasured-condition, and high-inference hypotheses.

Low-inference hypothesis: A student's noncompliant behavior is defined by the length of time between an oral prompt given by the teacher and the appropriate response by the student. Observations in the classroom reveal that the student responds within five seconds to teacher direction 30% of the time compared with his peers who respond to teacher direction within five seconds 80% of the time. The poor response time is hypothesized to be caused by a hearing problem because the student has had six ear infections this year, has failed the hearing screening, does not react to a question when the questioner is standing immediately behind him, and has been observed to look at other students prior to following teacher instructions 90% of the time. This hypothesis is data based and can easily be converted into a testing scenario to determine validity.

Hypothesis inferred from an unmeasured condition: A student's failure to memorize addition facts is hypothesized to be due to the lack of sufficient structured homework practice. Although the completed math homework can be measured, the "lack of sufficient structured homework practice" may be based on conclusions drawn from interviews, and it may not actually be confirmed. In this case, the dependent variable is the specific math skill, and the assumed cause of the problem is lack of homework practice. Practice can occur anywhere, so the importance of the practice setting should be minimized. This moderately inferential hypothesis can be converted into a data-based, low-inference hypothesis by redefining the independent variable (unmeasured condition) of "homework practice" to practice in an observable setting, such as school.

High-inference hypothesis inferred from an assumed correlated behavior: A student's reading difficulties may be assumed to be the result of a low level of intelligence as measured by a standardized instrument. The low score on an intelligence measure represents an "assumed correlated behavior," and while it suggests that the student will have difficulty learning, it does not lend itself to hypothesis testing or intervention. This hypothesis is discarded due to its high level of inference and lack of practical application.

INTERVENTION SELECTION

Prediction statements are used to restate the hypothesized cause of the problem into intervention terms. Intervention terms define the *independent variable* as the condition that is expected to cause a change in the dependent variable. Hypothesis testing verifies that the independent variable is appropriate by demonstrating a favorable, measurable change in the dependent variable as a result of the intervention. For example, if the hypothesis is that inappropriate behavior (dependent variable) is caused by the student's need for attention, the independent variable includes an intervention that establishes an acceptable way for the student to gain attention. The expectation is that the acceptable behavior will substitute for the unacceptable behavior, thus accomplishing the goal of reducing inappropriate behavior.

When interventions do not work, it is usually because the real problem was not targeted, the intervention was not sufficiently powerful or directly related to the problem, or the intervention was not implemented with integrity (Marolt & Telzrow, 2007). Hypothesis bias occurs when any of these conditions occur during hypothesis testing. The result of hypothesis bias is that the problem is not adequately addressed through intervention, and the problem of interest will not be solved.

If the intervention did not target the real problem, a false dependent variable is created. This often occurs when the search for the cause of the problem is limited to the primary dependent variable and investigation into secondary dependent variables has not been sufficiently conducted. Consider the case of a student who has a low homework-completion rate, and the chosen intervention is to have the student stay after school to complete the work. The assumption for choosing this intervention is that the student is able to complete the work, but for some reason did not do it. The intervention is unlikely to yield success if the real reason for the problem is that the student lacks the knowledge to complete the work. Thus the false dependent variable (deliberate failure to complete the assignment) triggers an intervention (staying after school) that does not target the real reason for the problem (lack of knowledge).

If inappropriate intervention choices lead to unsuccessful problem solving, alternatives should be investigated. Interventions are selected based on the logical relationship between the intervention and the reason for the problem, historical information about what has and has not worked with this student, and the research literature linking the chosen intervention to the targeted problem. Intervention methods that have been used previously may be considered if there is reason to believe that they were not implemented with integrity or that they could work if modified. However, in most cases, interventions that have not worked in the past will not be chosen. Research literature should be consulted to identify other interventions that have worked for this type of problem. It is likely that an empirically validated, successful intervention will generalize to most students. However, a "research base" only increases the *probability* that the intervention will have the desired impact: There is no guarantee that it will work. For Kim, the independent variable is the intervention method used to help her master the vowel sounds (*e, o,* and *u*) and skill-based problems are typically resolved through instruction and practice interventions.

HYPOTHESIS TESTING

Hypothesis testing verifies the cause of the problem and quantifies the impact of the intervention toward the desired outcome. This occurs through the execution of a set of brief experimental or observational procedures (Daly, Persampieri, McCurdy, & Gortmaker, 2005). Experimental procedures are created by setting up or manipulating the condition that is expected to improve the target behavior. For example, if a desire for teacher attention has been hypothesized as the cause of a student's disruptive classroom behavior, then "teacher attention" can be provided or withheld in the hypothesis-testing procedure. Observational hypothesis testing does not involve a manipulation of conditions; it is conducted by observing the student in different settings or under different preexisting conditions. Settings and conditions are chosen based on their association with occurrence or nonoccurrence of the behavior of concern. For example, if disruptive behavior is hypothesized to be prompted by chaotic, unstructured situations, the hypothesis test would involve observations of the student in unstructured (e.g., transitions in the hallway) versus structured (e.g., planned classroom activity with teacher monitoring) settings to assess whether disruptive behavior occurs more often in the unstructured setting. If so, the hypothesis would be confirmed. Hypotheses are accepted or rejected based on data trends. Accepted hypotheses validate the link between the intervention and the targeted problem, and they increase the likelihood for student success. Data to demonstrate the impact of an intervention are gathered on a single-case design schedule chosen from among those described in Chapter 6.

Strategies for hypothesis testing can be built around various single-case designs. In most cases, hypothesis testing is conducted using a brief A-B design. For the A-B design, baseline data that are gathered prior to the intervention are represented by A, while data gathered during intervention are represented by B. Hypothesis testing can often be completed in one session with the student; however, continued data gathering is needed to monitor the impact of the intervention over time. In Kim's case, the process begins by testing the skills-based hypotheses.

Step 1: For each dependent variable, a baseline must be established.

> Oral reading fluency: Kim's oral reading fluency baseline was previously determined and included in the hypothesis statement: "25 words correct per minute in grade-level text."

> Vowel sound knowledge: A baseline is determined for vowel sound knowledge. This can be done by looking at error analyses from oral reading CBMs or by administering CBMs. For Kim, the baseline indicates that the vowel sounds *e, o,* and *u* are read correctly 10% of the time.

Step 2: The intervention is implemented.

> Although there are two dependent variables for Kim, the intervention targets the secondary dependent variable (vowel sound knowledge), which is expected to yield a correlated change in the primary dependent variable (oral reading fluency). In this case, a review of the results of previously implemented interventions and the research literature indicate that an intervention that combines instruction with practice should target the skill-based problem adequately.

Step 3: Data are gathered to determine the impact of the intervention on both the primary and the secondary independent variables using the same methods used for gathering baseline data. For example, if fourth-grade level CBM probes were used for baseline measurement, alternative versions of the same types of probes would be used to determine the impact of the intervention on the primary dependent variable (oral reading fluency). In addition, alternative forms of probes that measure knowledge of the targeted vowel sounds (secondary dependent variable) could be administered; for this purpose, a form of Mastery Measurement would be appropriate.

Step 4: Data are evaluated. A simple method for determining whether the intervention has had the desired effect is to graph the data and conduct a visual examination. See both Figures 5.1 and 5.2 for examples of data graphing.

The results of the hypothesis test using an A-B design are demonstrated in Figure 5.2. Recall that this session with Kim is designed to determine whether or not improved knowledge in vowel sound skills correlates with improvement in reading fluency. Hypothesis testing occurred over the course of two weeks and yielded one data point for each dependent variable per day. A comparison of baseline (A) with progress-monitoring (B) data shows that Kim's vowel sound knowledge and reading fluency improved after the intervention was introduced. Intervention data demonstrate progress in the desired direction, and the conclusion is that the hypothesis is correct and can be accepted.

Figure 5.2   Comparison of Baseline With Progress-Monitoring Data for Primary and Secondary Dependent Variables

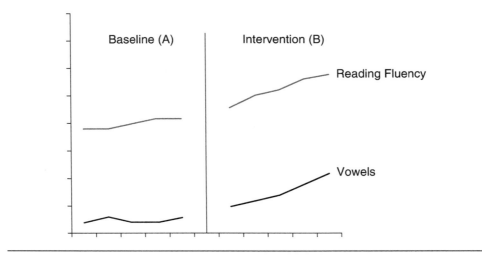

SUMMARY

This chapter described a step-by-step process for creating and testing hypotheses generated from information collected in the problem identification stage. Hypothesis testing is the foundation for the RTI process in the case study. It reflects the principles of the RTI model in that the child's response to the intervention is used to identify the best solution to the problem. The hypothesis is tested through application of a brief single-case design, such as the commonly used A-B design described here. A positive response to the intervention indicates that the intervention has a high probability for success if applied over time. Chapter 6 will discuss additional single-case designs that can be useful in hypothesis testing.

6

Single-Case Design

Recall that Tier 3 comprises the entire case study, resulting in an intervention, which—if of high intensity—is evaluated at Tier 3b for purposes of determining special education eligibility. There are three separate but related purposes for using single-case design research methods at Tier 3 of the RTI process. First, as discussed in Chapter 5, hypothesis testing uses a brief, single-case-design experiment to confirm or discard hypotheses before an intervention is selected for extended use. Second, single-case designs are used to interpret the results of progress monitoring in order to guide decision making. Finally, data from single-case designs reveal discrepancies between expected and actual performance that can be used for special education eligibility decisions at Tier 3b, as discussed in Chapter 9.

There are four types of single-case designs: (1) ABAB, (2) multielement, (3) changing criterion, and (4) multiple baseline. Designs differ according to the pattern used to implement and evaluate interventions. For example, the A-B design discussed in Chapter 5 is a simple version of the ABAB design in which the experimental manipulation of the independent variable is not replicated. In each method, data are gathered across phases, and trends are monitored, to determine the direction and degree of change in the dependent variable. The impact of the independent variable on the dependent variable is evaluated through visual analysis and through procedures such as goal attainment scaling, and effect size. (These procedures are described in detail in Chapter 8.)

SINGLE-CASE DESIGN
AND HYPOTHESIS TESTING

As explained in Chapter 5, hypothesis testing is conducted by manipulating or observing the independent variable to determine its impact on the dependent variable. In school settings, hypothesis testing must be a rapid, relevant, and effective procedure. Hypothesis testing can be completed in one session if the experimental question (i.e., hypothesis and associated prediction statements) is well constructed, a clear plan for manipulating the independent variable and for measuring the dependent variable has been established, and the results are analyzed with methods appropriate to the single-case design that has been selected for use.

For instance, the administration and analysis of one math test suggest that problems with division computation are caused by a student's failure to have memorized multiplication facts. The hypothesis is then tested through brief practice activities with multiplication flash cards (manipulation of independent variable) and a second administration of a math probe (dependent variable). The hypothesis is tentatively accepted, and the intervention begins. If a brief hypothesis-testing method is used (i.e., completed in one session), then continued data monitoring during intervention is used to validate the decision. However, hypothesis testing may occur as frequently as is necessary to determine functional relationships as well as components and characteristics of an effective intervention.

In determining the method that will be used for hypothesis testing, it is important to consider measurement issues such as student reaction to assessment or observation, observer bias, and ceiling or floor effects of tests or other instruments. If one of these factors appears to be related to the dependent variable, the factor should be controlled by neutralizing it (e.g., correcting measurement problems), incorporating it into the brief experiment as an independent variable, or by acknowledging the issue as a limitation to the brief experimental procedure. Failure to thoroughly consider a broad range of factors can result in threats to the validity of the brief experiment (Campbell & Stanley, 1967), resulting in an incorrect conclusion about the cause of the problem.

SINGLE-CASE DESIGN AND
PROGRESS MONITORING

A single-case design detects functional relationships between dependent and independent variables. When a relationship is found, the single-case design may be retained for progress monitoring, or it can be altered to answer related research questions. Progress-monitoring data indicate whether to continue, discontinue, or alter the intervention so that it will have maximum impact on the dependent variable. The strength of the single-case design is that it is sensitive to changes in data trends, suggesting the need for revision in an intervention. For instance, if the intervention is no longer having a substantial beneficial impact, the intervention can be modified, or hypothesis testing can be conducted again to find a more appropriate intervention.

Dependent variable. For both hypothesis testing and progress monitoring, the method for recording data must be appropriate for the problem being addressed. As discussed in Chapter 4, frequency counts, duration recordings, response latency recordings, and interval recording are methods that are frequently used to measure behavior. The reliability of observational data is improved when there is more than one observer and the rate of interobserver agreement is high. In addition, observations across various settings validate the existence and nature of the problem behavior. For example, a student who demonstrates argumentative behavior with one teacher in one classroom, but not with teachers in two other classrooms, may be reacting to a specific environmental mismatch rather than demonstrating a behavior disorder.

Dependent variable measures for academic problems include Curriculum-Based Measurement (CBM), percent correct, and error analysis. CBM can be employed for repeated brief assessments of basic academic skills over time (i.e., reading, math, and writing). Alternate forms of CBM probes containing items of the same difficulty level are useful for this purpose. Classwide, schoolwide, or individual CBM results can be analyzed in comparison to local norms to determine relative skill levels.

Academic problems that are content specific (e.g., science) are measured by the percent correct. This is a commonly used technique in most classrooms, but it suffers from a lack of consistency in the content being tested. In most cases, each test is unique and alternate forms of the test are not available. The most appropriate way to use percent correct is to compare scores earned by the target student with the scores of peers across multiple testing occasions.

Consider the student who attained an average score of 50% correct on each of the last five tests, which are the same tests on which her peers attained an average score of 85% correct. The data are not content specific (i.e., the knowledge being tested changes from one testing event to another), but the consistency of performance and the discrepancy between her average score and that of her peers suggests that a process-oriented problem (e.g., study skills) exists, and perhaps instruction in study skills would be the remedy.

Error analysis is used to identify specific academic problems when there are multiple dependent variables targeted for improvement or when a lack of subskills underlying a poorly performed primary skill is suspected. The purpose is to select intervention targets that show a pattern of consistent errors. An error analysis is conducted through review of work samples or observations of task performance. For example, a writing sample can be analyzed for numbers of errors in capitalization, punctuation, and spelling. Because writing samples are permanent products, performance on several samples can be compared over time.

Independent variable. The process of selecting an independent variable (intervention) for use in a single-case design is described in Chapter 5. Regardless of the intervention chosen, adherence to the implementation plan is critical to the integrity of the single-case design. Interventions that are implemented in precisely the same way during each intervention session increase the likelihood that changes in the dependent variable are due to the intervention (independent variable), and not to some other factor. Improperly or inconsistently implemented interventions contribute to unreliable results, making it impossible to draw conclusions about the relationship between the dependent and independent variables. As discussed in Chapter 7, one way to ensure intervention integrity is to develop a script or checklist to be followed each time the intervention is implemented. The script or checklist serves as a set of guidelines for implementation and as a method for collecting data on the integrity of the intervention.

CHOOSING A SINGLE-CASE DESIGN

The experimental question is the basis for selecting a single-case design, and six types of experimental questions are used to make the choice. These questions are presented in Table 6.1. The answer to the first question determines whether there is a functional relationship between the dependent and independent variables. Once this relationship has been established, the single-case design can be used for more detailed analysis to determine optimal characteristics of the intervention.

ABAB design. The ABAB design is the most frequently used brief experimental design; it answers the question, Will the independent variable alter the dependent variable? A functional relationship between the variables is demonstrated by alternating baseline (A) and treatment (B) phases. For example, the ABAB pattern begins with a no-treatment, baseline phase, is followed by a treatment phase, another no-treatment phase, and finally the reintroduction of the treatment phase. When the data consistently change in the same direction each time an intervention is applied and return to the baseline level when the intervention is withdrawn, the answer to the question is yes, there is a functional relationship between the independent and dependent variables.

Table 6.1 Experimental Questions and Corresponding Single-Case Designs

Experimental Question	Single-Case Design
Will the independent variable alter the dependent variable (i.e., will the intervention alter the target behavior)? (Kennedy, 2005)	ABAB, multielement, changing criterion, multiple baseline
Will Intervention 1 alter the dependent variable to a greater degree than Intervention 2 (i.e., which intervention is best)? (Kennedy, 2005)	Multielement
What characteristics of the intervention are most powerful (e.g., amount, intensity, or frequency of exposure)? (Kennedy, 2005)	Multielement
Is each component of the intervention necessary to have the desired effect? (Kennedy, 2005)	Multielement
What is the optimal amount of improvement that can be obtained with this intervention (through gradual systematic increase or decrease of the intervention)? (Richards, Taylor, Ramasamy, & Richards, 1999)	Changing criterion
Does the intervention generalize across behaviors, settings, or people? (Kennedy, 2005)	Multiple baseline

A brief A-B experiment may suggest that there is a functional relationship between assignment completion (dependent variable) and a teacher-administered reward (independent variable). However, the increase in assignment completion may have been caused by something else, such as peer competition. Repeated administrations of the baseline and intervention conditions (ABAB), yielding similar data, are required to confirm that the teacher-administered reward is causing the improvement in behavior.

When an intervention is already in place, a modified version of the ABAB design (known as a BAB design) can be used to demonstrate a functional relationship between the dependent and independent variables. The BAB design acknowledges the absence of a baseline condition, but it allows for an analysis of the relationship by removing and then reinstating the intervention. This design is particularly useful when the impact of a current intervention is in question, especially if hypothesis testing regarding the cause of the behavior has not occurred.

When deciding whether to use the ABAB design as opposed to another single-case design, consider the requirement that the target behavior must be reversible. That is, the target behavior can be turned off and on by introducing an independent variable, such as those cited in performance-based (i.e., "won't do") hypotheses. The ABAB design would not be used to test a skill-based hypothesis because learning is cumulative and not generally reversible (i.e., a student cannot "unlearn" reading skills). Nor is it appropriate to use when it is ethically inappropriate to withdraw an independent variable (e.g., when there are risks to safety or health, as when self-injurious behavior is the target of intervention). Figure 6.1 presents an example of the ABAB single-case design.

Figure 6.1   ABAB Single-Case Design Example

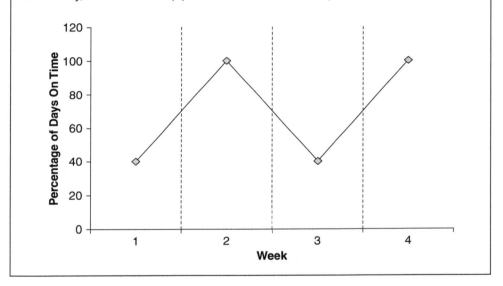

Timothy is a ninth-grade student who arrives on time to class only 40% of the time (baseline—A). He has agreed to be on time to class 100% of the time, and the teacher has agreed to allow him to work on a computer program that he enjoys at the beginning of each class when he is on time or early (intervention phase—B). After one week of 100% on-time arrival, the intervention is removed, and Timothy is again on time only 40% of the time. Finally, the intervention (B) is reintroduced and Timothy is on time 100% of the time.

Multielements design. The multielements design is used to answer the question: Will intervention 1 alter the dependent variable to a greater degree than intervention 2? Variations of this design can be constructed to determine the optimal intensity or frequency of exposure to the intervention and to investigate what combination of components in a multicomponent intervention is critical to the success of the intervention. The independent variables (interventions) are alternated, and the optimal intervention is the one that consistently yields a higher rate of response in the preferred direction.

This design can be used for both brief experiments for hypothesis testing and to monitor the effects of various interventions over longer time periods. It is particularly helpful with interventions that tend to lose their potency with repeated use (e.g., reinforcement methods). In addition, the multielement design can be constructed with or without a baseline, so it can be used in situations that do not allow for removal of an intervention (e.g., self-injurious behavior). However, students must be able to discriminate between the interventions and react accordingly.

Most often the multielement design is used for performance-based ("won't do") deficits. A rule of thumb is that the multielement design should be used to determine which intervention is most effective when the dependent variable is able to be reversed. Consider the case of a student who self-mutilates through cutting. Reversibility in this instance is judged by the notion that the dependent variable would be "turned on or off" or is increased or reduced by the various interventions. For skills-based ("can't do") deficits, a combined multielement–changing-criterion design may be used to use to determine which intervention results in the greatest rate of improvement.

A multielement design can incorporate more than two interventions. Consider a research question that seeks to ascertain the differential impact of three interventions on reducing the number of cigarettes that a high school student smokes in a day. Intervention B is "self-monitoring on a chart." Intervention C is "loss of privilege to use the restroom without supervision." Intervention D is "replacement of cigarettes with gum." The construction of this design is critical for obtaining accurate information about the functional relationship between the dependent variable (number of cigarettes smoked) and independent variables (interventions B, C, and D).

A poorly constructed multielement design could lead to false conclusions about the functional relationship between the dependent and independent variables. In the cigarette-smoking case, it is possible to create several different designs: BCD, BDC, CDB, CBD, DBC, or DCB. Should the BCD design be chosen, self-monitoring would occur first, followed by restroom supervision, and finally by the provision of gum. By virtue of the order alone or interaction effects, the third condition, gum, is likely to appear to have the greatest impact on smoking. Should the order be reversed (DCB), the third element would be the self-monitoring intervention, and the data would suggest that it was the most effective intervention. Consequently, a well-constructed design must address the potential problems of interaction effects (Barlow & Hensen, 1984; Kennedy, 2005) caused by the sequencing of the independent variable conditions. Planned counterbalancing of condition sequences decreases potential interaction effects. Counterbalancing occurs by equally distributing the possible interaction effects across conditions. In the smoking example, the Latin Square counterbalancing technique (Reese, 1997) is used to create the design in Figure 6.2, in which each condition precedes and follows all other conditions once (i.e., BCDBDCB).

Figure 6.2   Counterbalancing Example

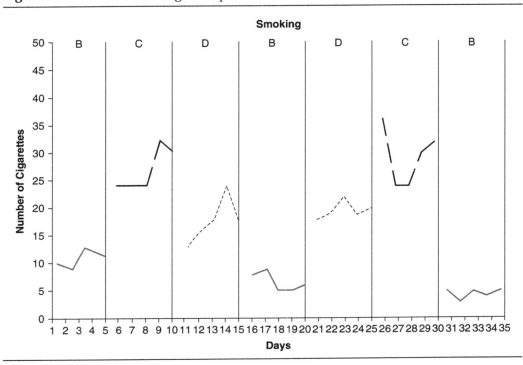

Figure 6.2 reveals that the self-monitoring chart (Intervention B) was the most effective method for reducing cigarette smoking for this student. Note that we did not begin with a baseline (A). A baseline was not necessary because we were only interested in identifying the most effective intervention. The heavy solid line (intervention B) indicates that each of the three 5-day periods of self-monitoring resulted in fewer cigarettes smoked than both the loss of unsupervised restroom periods (intervention C—dashed line) and the gum chewing periods (intervention D—dotted lines). These data warrant a high level of confidence that the relationships between the dependent and independent variables are not significantly affected by external factors or by order effects. Thus, it is clear that the self-monitoring intervention is the most appropriate choice for long-term implementation.

An *alternating treatments* design (Figure 6.3) is the simplest version of a multielement design, which requires rapid alternation of two or more interventions. When a consistent pattern of results is observed across a greater number of phase changes, the reliability of (or confidence in) the results is enhanced.

Changing-criterion design. The changing-criterion design evaluates the gradual effects of the independent variable (intervention) on the dependent variable by monitoring the accumulated change in the dependent variable over repeated application of the intervention. The goal is to increase or decrease the rate and/or level of the dependent variable over time. The

Figure 6.3   Alternating Treatments Design Example

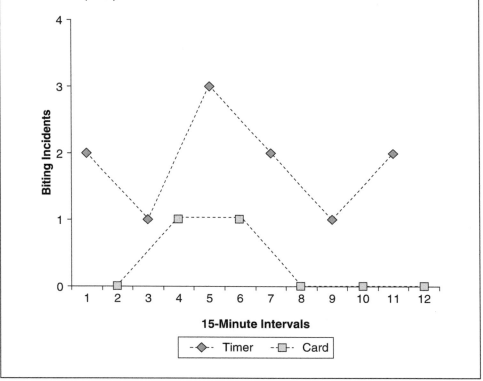

To reduce the frequent number of biting incidents with a preschooler who is hypothesized to bite in order to receive attention, two interventions are introduced alternately over the course of a three-hour class session. Intervention B, "timer paired with a reward for nonbiting," is alternated with intervention C, "teacher praise for displaying a card to get the teacher's attention." Alternations are on a 15-minute schedule according to the following pattern: BCBCBCBCBCBC. In this case, the baseline is not used because the biting is an injurious behavior that needs to be eliminated as soon as possible. Note that the graph shows that intervention C (card) has a stronger impact on the behavior than does intervention B (timer).

changing-criterion design answers the question: What is the optimal amount of improvement that can be obtained with this intervention?

The changing-criterion design is particularly useful with nonreversible dependent variables because there is no need to withdraw the intervention. In addition, it can be used to monitor both improvements in performance and increases in skill acquisition (i.e., learning). In order for the changing criterion design to be executed, the targeted dependent variables must be present, at least at a minimal level, in the student's repertoire of behavior. Although various time periods can be used for phase changes in this design, a week is recommended as the period of time for each phase. However, the appropriate phase length would depend on the particular dependent variable being considered.

The changing criterion design is more complex than the previously described designs, but it is often the best choice for addressing skills that need to be improved gradually over time (i.e., learning). The key to successful use of this design is to make educated predictions about the degree of change that will occur. Figure 6.4 presents data graphed in a changing-criterion design.

There are three methods that can be used to make predictions: weekly gain criteria, calculated individual increase criteria, and calculated norm-based criteria. The *weekly gain* and *calculated individual increase* methods use a two-step cumulative process to construct the design: (1) establish baseline, and (2) determine criterion levels for subphases. These methods can be used regardless of the number of weeks planned for intervention implementation because there is no inherent long-term goal. The dependent variable is expected to continue to change at approximately the same rate each week for a total cumulative score at the conclusion of the intervention period.

The weekly gain criteria method uses established local or national norms to set the expected weekly rate of improvement. Even though the target weekly gain rate is higher than the student's baseline rate of gain, the student is not necessarily expected to catch up with peers in the same grade. The purpose of this method is to increase the rate of performance based on the average rate of gain for same-grade peers. For example, a student is expected to increase his rate of weekly gain in oral reading fluency to a rate that parallels that of his peers, but that does not result in a final outcome similar to theirs. According to the second-grade classwide

Figure 6.4   Example of a Changing-Criterion Single-Case Design

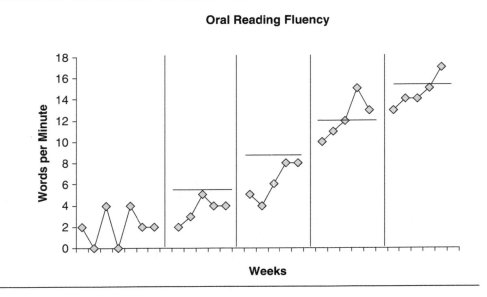

Oral Reading Fluency

average scores for oral reading fluency from fall, winter, and spring DIBELS administrations from the previous year, students, on average, gain 3 correctly read words per minute (cwpm) per week. The target second-grade student shows a baseline increase of 1.5 cwpm. With appropriate intervention, the target student is expected to gain 3 cwpm per week.

The calculated individual increase method sets the rate of student improvement as the average baseline rate of improvement plus 50%. This method is solely dependent on baseline scores for the target student and can be used when peer comparison data are not available. For example, a high school student wanted to see if she could increase her scores on timed practice tests in preparation for the year-end schoolwide examination. Each time she took alternate forms of the practice tests, she increased her score by an average of 5 points. She was concerned that her rate of improvement was not sufficient to pass the end-of-year examination at the level she desired, so she enrolled in a study seminar with the expectation that it would increase her rate of improvement. She established a goal to increase her rate gain to 7.5 points per practice test ($50\% \times 5 = 2.5, 5 + 2.5 = 7.5$), based on the calculated individual increase criteria.

The *calculated norm-based criteria* method uses a three-step reductive process to construct the design: (1) establish baseline, (2) determine final measurable goal, and (3) reduce the final goal into criterion levels for sub-phases. Long-term goals include both measurable criteria and designated points of time in the future for accomplishing the goal. The rate of weekly change is calculated by dividing the overall expected amount of change by the number of weeks of intervention implementation. In the calculated norm-based criteria method, long-term predictions are stated as final measurable goals and are generally set according to established norms. This design is based on the expectation that the appropriate intervention will allow the student to catch up with the performance levels of classroom peers. It requires long-term predictions for both the class and the target student.

Weekly gains are calculated by subtracting the target student's current level of performance from the student's final goal (which is the same goal as that established for the class) and dividing by the number of weeks of intervention. In the case of oral reading fluency (ORF), local or national norms for CBM or DIBELS measures provide goals in the form of expected ORF rates (measured in wcpm) for fall, winter, and spring testing events.

A student who is performing below the 10th percentile (22 wcpm), in relation to norms for expected performance, has a long-term goal stating that, in four weeks, this student will read at a wcpm rate consistent with the 25th percentile (34 wcpm) for the norm group. Thus, the long-term goal is to increase the wcpm by 12 wcpm (34 − 22) over the four-week intervention period. This translates to an approximate increase of 3 wcpm per week.

Multiple-baseline design. The multiple-baseline design consists of a series of A-B designs that are replicated across behaviors, setting, or participants. It answers the question: Does the intervention generalize? The functional relationship between the dependent and independent variables is demonstrated by implementing the same intervention across different people, settings, or behaviors at different points in time. See Figure 6.5 for a depiction of a multiple-baseline design. The graphed data show that prior to intervention, each student's level of "talking out" was greater than it is after implementation, regardless of the point in time at which the intervention was initiated.

Figure 6.5 Example of a Multiple-Baseline Design Across Students

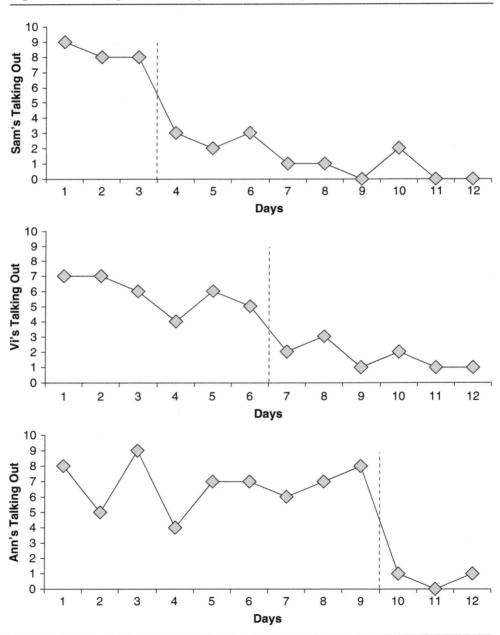

The multiple-baseline design across behaviors establishes relationships between the independent variable (intervention) and multiple dependent variables when there are several versions of a behavior that are similar in function. For example, a child with autism may struggle with three different social interactions with adults: greeting a person who comes into a room, maintaining appropriate physical distance from another person, and looking at the person who is speaking. The dependent variable, "social interactions with adults," is demonstrated in three measurable variations. Because the target behaviors are similar in function (poor social skills), one intervention (e.g., social stories) can be used across all three behaviors.

The multiple-baseline design also can be used when the target behavior (dependent variable) is the same but needs to be addressed with one student across multiple settings or in the same setting across multiple students. For instance, in Figure 6.5, when several students in class tend to talk out excessively, the same intervention was initiated with each student at different points in time to determine whether it works to reduce each student's inappropriate behavior. The relationship between the dependent and independent variable is clear. Visual analysis reveals a pattern that confirms that, each time the intervention was begun, a decrease in the dependent variable occurred. The key to a well-constructed multiple-baseline design is to gather baseline data and begin the intervention across conditions (behaviors, settings, or students) at different times, while continuing to gather baseline data for those conditions in which the intervention has not yet been introduced.

SUMMARY

This chapter described four single-case designs to use for hypothesis testing and intervention monitoring. Although each of these designs is useful for a variety of purposes, each design has a characteristic function. A brief administration of the ABAB design is often conducted for hypothesis testing in order to rapidly detect a functional relationship between the targeted problem and various interventions. The multielement design is particularly useful for distinguishing between interventions of varying levels of intensity. Students who only respond to high-intensity interventions are considered for special education services, as explained in Chapter 9. The changing-criterion design is predominantly used for monitoring rate of change in learning. This design has implications for predicting whether the student will be expected to catch up with peers, or if improvement will be slow and require long-term intervention. The multiple-baseline design is considered a design of generalization across behaviors, students, or settings. It is particularly relevant for behavior problems that have a common cause, but interventions will need to be implemented across settings or across different forms of the same behavior.

Confidence in drawing conclusions based on the results of the brief experiment can be increased by using a combination of single-case designs for hypothesis testing. For example, Daly, Martens, Hamler, Dool, and Eckert (1999) were interested in determining the best approach from among five reading intervention strategies: reward, repeated readings, listening passage preview, sequential modification, and easier materials. A multielement single-case design was used to establish the extent of the functional relationship between each intervention component and reading skill. A withdrawal (BA) design then confirmed the relationship through a brief withdrawal of the intervention. Daly and colleagues recommended progress monitoring to confirm the long-term effectiveness of the intervention. This approach also can be used to determine whether high-intensity interventions are required for the student to show improvement.

The single-case design reflects the scientist-practitioner aspect of the RTI model, as it serves as a framework for hypothesis-testing and progress-monitoring procedures that lead to confident, data-based decision making.

7

Intervention

The goal of the case study is to eliminate or reduce the discrepancy between a student's actual and expected performance; intervention is the vehicle through which this is accomplished. At Tiers 1 and 2, students' needs were accommodated through instruction and interventions whose efficacy has been established through research. Students who reach Tier 3 have failed to respond adequately to Tiers 1 and 2, thereby indicating a need for assessment to identify variables that are functionally related to the identified problem. Application of the case study method enables planners to determine variables that should be targeted for intervention; this occurs during problem analysis, discussed in Chapter 5. This chapter will describe factors that are associated with successful intervention and offer recommendations for planning and implementing them effectively.

SELECTING RESEARCH-BASED INTERVENTIONS

There are two general approaches to intervention selection: empirical and functional. In the empirical approach, which is used at Tiers 1 and 2, interventions are selected because research has supported their efficacy, but they are selected without reference to the specific causes of a problem for a given student. For example, an intervention team might decide to use the strategy of "repeated readings" (RR) with third-grade students demonstrating fluency problems without first having identified a lack of practice (which RR is designed to remediate) as the basis for the targeted students' reading problem. The RR intervention is selected simply because research has shown it to be successful in improving the reading fluency of many students; that is, it is considered to be an *efficacious* intervention (O'Shea, Sindelar, & O'Shea, 1985).

The functional approach employed at Tier 3, in contrast, matches research-based intervention to factors that have been shown to be functionally related to the performance problem. In the above example, the RR intervention would be selected precisely because it corrects the lack of practice that has been identified as the cause of the problem. If data indicate that RR is successful, it is considered to be an *effective* intervention because its use has resulted in success for a particular student.

The key to successful use of an empirical approach at Tiers 1 and 2 is the ability to access intervention strategies that have an acceptable research base; unfortunately, many practitioners do not know how to identify an "acceptable research base." It is important to evaluate the quality of research on interventions being considered for adoption, as the current emphasis on research-based practice will likely result in an increased number of commercially available interventions citing studies conducted to document their efficacy.

Fortunately, a number of resources are available to assist practitioners in determining whether specific interventions have an adequate research base; they offer judgments on intervention efficacy based on a comprehensive review of the research literature. In the absence of such guidance, however, practitioners need to evaluate studies to assess their validity before concluding that an intervention has an adequate research base. A publication of the U.S. Department of Education (2003), entitled *Identifying and Implementing Educational Practices Supported by Rigorous Evidence: A User-Friendly Guide*, is an excellent guide that individuals can use to evaluate research on the efficacy of interventions. In this guide, standards for designating an intervention as "research-based" are summarized as follows:

1. The intervention must be supported by "strong" evidence of its efficacy, exemplified by research of acceptable quality (i.e., randomized, controlled trials that are well designed and implemented) and quantity (i.e., more than one study in typical settings appropriate to the population with which the intervention will be used).

or

2. Though not supported by "strong" evidence of its efficacy, the intervention is supported by "possible" evidence of efficacy (i.e., there were some flaws in the randomized controlled trial designs, but the intervention is supported by research using several well-designed and implemented, but non-randomized, designs).

Among the criteria for "well-designed and implemented" studies are a clear description of the intervention; an absence of systematic differences between experimental and control/comparison groups prior to the intervention; valid short- and long-term outcome measures; findings of effectiveness accompanied by evidence of the strength of the effect, as well as statistical significance; and reporting of data on all outcome measures, not just those for which a significant effect was found. The criteria explicitly rule out studies using a "pre-post" design without a control or comparison group; comparison group studies in which the intervention and comparison groups were not well-matched; and meta-analyses that combine individual studies that themselves do not meet the criteria for "possible" evidence of efficacy.

In addition, Kratochwill, Clements, and Kalymon (2007) offer a comprehensive listing of resources that identify and evaluate research-based interventions. Practitioners are encouraged to consult this and other resources; a partial list of resources categorized by target domain (academic, social-behavioral, and mental health) is presented in Table 7.1.

Table 7.1   Sources of Information About Research-Based Interventions

Source	Domain	Where to Find It
What Works Clearinghouse	Academic	www.whatworks.ed.gov
Florida Center for Reading Research	Academic (reading)	www.fcrr.org
Oregon Reading First Center	Academic (reading)	reading.uoregon.edu
Social Programs That Work	Mental health	www.evidencebasedprograms.org
Collaborative for Academic, Social, and Emotional Learning (CASEL)	Social-behavioral Mental health Academic	www.casel.org
Promising Practices Network	Social-behavioral Mental health Academic	www.promisingpractices.net
Center for the Study and Prevention of Violence, University of Colorado	Mental health	www.colorado.edu/cspv/blueprints

When considering scientific, research-based interventions for implementation at Tier 2—where the deficits of students who are at risk are addressed, typically, through targeted, small-group interventions—educators should consider whether interventions satisfy the following criteria:

1. Appropriate for use with small groups of students;

2. Based on research showing a relationship between the intervention and improvement in the skills being remedied;

3. Able to be intensified or strengthened (e.g., by adding incentives or increasing frequency or duration of sessions);

4. Flexible with respect to appropriate ages and skill areas with which intervention can be used; and

5. Feasible for use in general education settings because they can be used with an entire class, or because they will not disrupt existing instructional routines.

The last two of these criteria (4 and 5) are desirable, but not essential. Peer-assisted learning strategies meet all of the criteria outlined above and might be considered for adoption on a schoolwide basis as a model for Tier 2 interventions. Readers interested in learning more about peer-assisted learning are encouraged to consult a number of excellent references, including Ginsburg-Block, Rohrbeck, Fantuzzo, and Lavigne (2006), McMaster, Fuchs, and Fuchs (2006), and Topping and Ehly (1998).

As noted earlier, the functional approach to intervention selection seeks to identify the specific factors that are contributing to the academic or behavior problems of a targeted student. It is the method that should be used at Tier 3. In this text, the case study approach incorporates functional assessment practices, which were discussed in more detail in Chapters 4 and 5. Factors revealed by functional assessment as potential explanations of students' performance problems might include the nature of assigned tasks or their difficulty level, adequacy of the student's social skills repertoire, or the availability of sufficient opportunities for practice of the deficient skill. In other words, this approach is designed to identify variables that are functionally (causally) related to the identified problem. Interventions that address those variables are then selected; of course, the interventions must have an acceptable evidence base, as described above.

Figure 7.1 depicts the empirical and functional approaches to intervention selection, as they might occur in the hypothetical case of Bryce. In both approaches, Bryce displays an oral reading fluency problem. In the functional approach (employed in context of the Tier 3 case study), factors that might contribute to Bryce's nonfluent reading are explored through a record review, interviews with him, his teacher, and his parents, a classroom observation during reading instruction, and testing to more closely evaluate his decoding and fluency skills. A consistent theme suggesting that Bryce avoids reading emerges during this functional assessment. Coupled with test results showing that Bryce possesses adequate decoding skills, these findings suggest that his nonfluent reading is due to a lack of sufficient practice. Consequently, interventions are designed to increase practice opportunities and make reading more attractive to Bryce, so he will engage in reading on a more frequent basis.

In the empirical approach, there is no problem analysis to test hypotheses that might explain Bryce's reading problem; the process moves immediately to the identification of reading intervention strategies that might improve his reading performance. The empirical approach, characteristic of Tier 2, is employed because Bryce's reading problem places him in the "at-risk" category (i.e., his oral reading fluency scores places him at the 18th percentile relative to grade-level peers, a level at which Tier 2 is typically recommended). While both the empirical and functional approaches require that research-based strategies be used, the functional approach recommends only those strategies that provide increased opportunities for reading practice in order to enhance fluency, based on the accepted hypothesis for Bryce's reading problem. The empirical approach, on the other hand, results in interventions using flashcards to increase Bryce's sight word vocabulary, and modeling accurate reading with listening passage preview. (Note that, despite the research base supporting these interventions as generally efficacious, they won't improve Bryce's reading performance because they incorrectly target word recognition skills.) Only the third intervention—offering incentives for engaging in reading, which will enhance fluency—is common to both approaches.

To summarize, in this text, the functional approach is recommended for use at Tier 3, reserving the use of an empirical approach for the design of effective instruction and intervention at Tiers 1 and 2. Using a functional approach, practitioners can select interventions that will target factors that the assessment has shown to be a cause of the student's performance problem. A functional approach focuses on a limited, manageable number of high-probability hypotheses, thereby making the process of intervention selection more efficient and more likely to succeed.

INTERVENTION INTEGRITY

Gansle and Noell (2007) use the term *treatment plan implementation* to refer to "the degree to which a treatment plan developed for remediation of referral concerns is implemented as designed" (p. 244). Gresham (1989) observed long ago that intervention integrity is a key determinant of success and a critical focus of consultant attention.

The acceptability of an intervention is commonly regarded as a key element in treatment plan implementation (Roach & Elliott, 2008; Telzrow &

Figure 7.1   Empirical and Functional Approaches to Intervention Selection

Empirical Approach	Functional Approach
Identify the problem: Bryce reads only 23 words correct per minute (wcpm), compared to peers, who read 42 wcpm. Tier 1 screening showed that Bryce's score is at the 18th percentile for his grade, well below the benchmark of 40 wcpm. Bryce is included in the Tier 2 group for supplemental intervention.	**Identify the problem:** Bryce reads only 16 wcpm, compared to peers, who read 42 wcpm. Tier 1 screening showed that Bryce's score is at the 5th percentile for his grade, well below the benchmark of 40 wcpm. Bryce's problem becomes the subject of a Tier 3 case study.
Interventions: Use flashcard drill to improve sight-word vocabulary; model fluent reading by using listening passage preview; provide incentives for reading aloud for a set period of time at home.	**Analyze the problem:** Bryce misses school frequently, misbehaves and is sent to timeout during reading, and complains that he doesn't like to read. Frustrated, his teacher rarely calls on him to read. He is able to decode nonsense words, though his reading fluency is poor. **Hypothesis:** Bryce reads only 16 wcpm because he avoids reading and has had insufficient practice to develop fluency.
	Objective: Increase practice opportunities; provide incentives for practice. **Interventions:** In daily sessions, use repeated readings; assign Bryce to read to a younger student; provide incentives for reading aloud for a set period of time at home.

Beebe, 2002). *Acceptability* refers to judgments about interventions across dimensions such as appropriateness, fairness, reasonableness, likely effectiveness, and outcome importance. Interventions regarded as impractical, resource intensive, or inequitable (with respect to other students) are less likely to be viewed as acceptable to those responsible for providing them. In these instances, according to conventional wisdom, interventions are less likely to be implemented as planned.

According to Gansle and Noell (2007), however, "intervention acceptability" may be less important than the presence of environmental contingencies favoring intervention implementation. For example, Noell, Witt, LaFleur, Mortenson, Ranier, and LeVelle (2000) found that teachers improved treatment plan implementation when presented with prompts, praise, performance feedback, negative reinforcement, and reminders of accountability to administrators and parents. Further research conducted by Noell and colleagues (2005) indicated that while acceptability contributes to initial implementation, it is inadequate to support implementation integrity on a long-term basis.

When teachers are asked to implement interventions in the classroom, a number of factors interfere with their doing so in a manner that conforms to original plans. Roach and Elliott (2008) cite research showing that integrity of implementation is degraded by increased intervention complexity and time required for implementation and as the need for multiple resources increases. If students are poorly motivated or resistant to interventions, integrity of implementation will undoubtedly suffer. Characteristics of interventionists also influence integrity, with higher levels of training, education, and motivation exerting a favorable impact. In contrast, interventionist resistance, familiarity with other potential interventions, and demographic characteristics of students (i.e., membership in nonmajority ethnic or cultural groups) tend to decrease intervention adherence.

Gansle and Noell (2007) suggest that a number of variables might influence or moderate interventionists' treatment-plan implementation, including interventionist stress, perceived importance and salience of the referral concern, and, for teachers, the degree of interest shown by parents and administrators.

Apart from establishing a positive consultative relationship with teachers (as discussed in Chapter 3 of this text), school psychologists and other planners can use the principles of social influence to enhance adherence to an intervention plan. Social-influence-focused consultation includes a conversation with teachers in which the tendency to depart from initial commitments to interventions is acknowledged and discussed along with the importance of intervention to various parties, the possible loss of teacher credibility and harm to students if the intervention is not implemented, and steps that might support implementation efforts, such as goal setting, self-rewards, and so on (Roach & Elliott, 2008).

Research has examined the effectiveness of efforts to change the behavior of interventionists—that is, to increase the integrity with which they implement intervention plans. Often, problems with integrity of implementation are attributed to a lack of knowledge or skill on the part of the interventionist. Consequently, planners assume that the interventionist requires additional information and didactic training, but research shows that this solution often fails (Taylor & Miller, 1997). A comparison of didactic training and "direct" training (guided rehearsal and feedback) demonstrated that direct training was more effective in improving implementation integrity (Sterling-Turner, Watson, & Moore, 2002), suggesting that, at minimum, interventionists should be provided with the opportunity to practice interventions and receive corrective feedback.

A promising line of research initiated by Noell and colleagues (2000) suggests that performance feedback is far more important than treatment acceptability, and more effective than training, in enhancing treatment plan implementation. Gansle and Noell (2007) point out that performance feedback is different from (and does not require) follow-up meetings and "checking in" with teachers, although it might occur in those contexts. Performance feedback "consists of reviewing implementation data with the treatment agent" (Gansle & Noell, 2007, p. 248) and might include review of checklists of intervention steps completed by the teacher, inspection of permanent products generated by the intervention, records of observations of teacher implementation behavior, and the presentation of graphs depicting implementation behavior. When direct observation of the teacher's implementation behavior is employed, it is important to clarify the reasons for the observation (i.e., to give feedback and support rather than to evaluate performance) and to appoint observers whose presence in the classroom will not be a threat to the teacher. School psychologists are an ideal resource for this purpose, given their training in observation techniques and their lack of administrative authority over teachers.

Intervention scripts have been cited as a means to enhance intervention integrity (Ehrhardt, Barnett, Lentz, Stollar, & Reifin, 1996; Telzrow & Beebe, 2002). Standard protocol interventions, which consist of packaged "kits" containing materials needed for an intervention, typically include a manual, lesson plans, and/or scripts. A script presents a step-by-step outline of the intervention procedure; a sample of an intervention script for precision requests (Rhode, Jenson, & Reavis, 1993) is presented in Table 7.2.

In addition to accurate plan implementation, Gansle and Noell (2007) describe other intervention-related factors that influence student-performance outcomes, including treatment fit (interventions suited to the referral concern) and treatment strength, also known as "dosage" (sufficient intervention frequency, intensity, and duration). Clearly, intervention plans devised in context of the functional-assessment process described in this text are likely to "fit" referral concerns (i.e., are likely to target factors that are causally related to problematic performance). Similarly, appropriate dosage is more likely to be attained when interventions are tested during problem analysis and monitored (for effectiveness) during plan implementation, as described in Chapters 5 and 8 of this text, respectively.

Table 7.2   Sample Script for Precision Requests

1. Advance preparation: Determine a hierarchy of negative consequences, ranging from the least severe (e.g., warning) to the most severe (e.g., full-day office or in-class suspension); there should be no more than four negative consequences.

2. Describe the hierarchy of negative consequences to the class:

   When a rule is broken or students fail to do something I've asked them to do, there will be negative consequences, starting with the first one on the list (e.g., verbal warning). If the problem continues, I will go to the next consequence on the list (e.g., loss of five minutes of recess time), and so on.

3. Explain the precision request procedure and its consequences to the class:

   When asking a student to do something, I will first say "please." For example, I might say, "Andrew, please put your books in your desk." If Andrew puts his books in his desk, I won't need to say anything more. But, if he doesn't, I'll say, "Andrew, please put your books in your desk" . . . (etc.)

4. Begin the precision requests procedure: If a student does not comply with a directive, stand near the student, make eye contact, and make a "please" request in a nonquestion format (e.g., "Andrew, please put your books in your desk.")

5. Wait 5 to 10 seconds. Do not interact with the student further.

6. If student begins to comply, reinforce verbally (e.g., "Thank you, Andrew.").

7. If student does not comply, give the request a second time, using the word *need* (e.g., "Andrew, I need you to put your books away.").

8. If student starts to comply, reinforce verbally.

9. If student does not comply, implement preplanned consequence (e.g., "Andrew, this is your warning.").

10. After stating the negative consequence, repeat the request using the word *need,* as above. If student complies, reinforce; if not, implement the next consequence from the preplanned hierarchy (e.g., "Andrew, you have lost five minutes of your recess time."). (Do not continue this process beyond two preplanned consequences.)

Source: Derived from Rhode, Jenson, and Reavis (1993)

LINKING INTERVENTIONS TO HYPOTHESES

Having developed and tested several hypotheses that described relationships between situational variables (antecedents, consequences) and the problem behavior—as well as the functions served by the behavior—planners are now ready to design specific intervention strategies. Research shows that school teams have difficulty linking interventions to hypotheses developed during problem analysis, but this may be due, at least in part, to the fact that team members often don't understand how to conduct an appropriate and comprehensive functional assessment (Burns, Vanderwood, & Ruby, 2005; Telzrow, McNamara, & Hollinger, 2000). Clearly, this indicates a need for training and consultation with a school psychologist or other person knowledgeable about functional assessment, so teams can successfully identify antecedents and consequences associated with interfering behaviors.

Once one or more high-probability hypotheses have been identified, interventions must target variables implicated in the hypotheses. For example, if poor writing skills are hypothesized to be a result of inadequate instruction in grammar and punctuation, an appropriate intervention would provide such instruction (rather than simply require more practice in writing, which would likely reinforce inadequate writing skills).

Academic problems. Daly, Witt, Martens, and Dool (1997) proposed a series of five general hypotheses that should be considered in a functional assessment of academic problems (see Table 7.3). These hypotheses might serve as categories within which specific factors or events can be classified. For example, an interview and record review conducted during the problem identification phase of a case study might reveal that a student has been absent from school frequently, she complains of not understanding how to solve math problems, and her completed assignments contain a significant number of errors. These findings might be consistent with (and therefore classified under) the general hypothesis, "hasn't had enough help to do it." Alternatively, behavioral observation, interviews, and a review of work products might reveal that a student is frequently out of her seat during activities involving practice of newly learned skills, is actively engaged only 20% of the time (compared to a peer average of 80%), and rarely completes homework assignments. These findings are consistent with the hypothesis, "hasn't spent enough time doing it." Hypothesis statements developed in the case study would likely refer to the specific conditions implicated in the "not enough practice" explanation, such as disengagement and noncompletion of assignments that were revealed in the assessment process.

To illustrate the manner in which intervention strategies are linked to hypotheses, Table 7.3 presents Daly and colleagues' (1997) hypotheses, with corresponding intervention recommendations. Note that, while relevant in a case study at Tier 3, these hypotheses also are useful for planning instruction and interventions at Tiers 1 and 2. Hypotheses are ordered hierarchically; that is, the possibility that the student's poor academic performance is due to the fact that the student "does not want to do it" is the first hypothesis that should be considered. Daly and colleagues (1997) offer a series of brief experiments that can be used to test each of these general hypotheses.

Table 7.3 Hypotheses for Academic Problems With Corresponding Intervention Strategies

Hypothesis	Intervention Objective	Sample Intervention
1. They do not want to do it.	• Provide incentives. • Provide choices to enhance motivation.	• Use contingency contract for specified success level; lottery tickets for accuracy, to be entered in a reward drawing. • Give choice of working alone or with a partner. • Student completes set number of items on assignment and additional items as student wishes.
2. They haven't spent enough time doing it.	• For acquisition (accuracy) problems, provide structured tasks with immediate feedback. • For fluency problems, provide tasks with high success rates to increase responding.	• Use team-assisted individualization (Slavin, Leavey, & Madden, 1984) with peer-corrected worksheets and immediate feedback. • Use end-of-lesson drills (Jenkins & Larson, 1979) for incorrectly read words. • Intersperse easy items with more difficult items (Calderhead, Filter, & Albin, 2006). • Use flashcard technique that presents unknown items to known items at a 3:7 ratio, to maintain response momentum.
3. They have not had enough help to do it.	• For acquisition problems, increase learning trials with training, modeling, and error correction. • For fluency problems, increase practice, drills, and incentives.	• Use "think-aloud" procedure while modeling correct performance, then have student think aloud while performing task. • Create practice opportunities that include error correction, such as cover-copy-compare (Stading, Williams, & McLaughlin, 1996). • Use peer-assisted learning as motivating context for drill and practice. • Create teams with performance objectives and graphing for improved scores on flashcard drills.

(Continued)

Table 7.3 (Continued)

Hypothesis	Intervention Objective	Sample Intervention
4. They have not had to do it that way before.	• Match instructional practices to intended topography of student responses. • Match instructional practices to "real-world" application of skills.	• Change materials so that activities require student responses of the type intended to be taught (e.g., if teaching spelling, have students spell words, not color worksheets that display correctly spelled words). • Teach student self-management strategies for independent work, and teach how to recognize (discriminate) situations in which to use them.
5. It is too hard.	• Make instructional materials more accessible. • Use materials that are at the student's instructional level.	• Create study guides for content-area readings and study sessions. • Teach student how to use visual aids and formatting that appear in textbooks. • Involve student in cross-age teaching (with younger student). • Drop back to lower level of the curriculum for instruction.

Source: Adapted from Daly, Witt, Martens, and Dool (1997)

For example, the first hypothesis, which cites issues of motivation, can be tested by offering a reward if the student is able to increase his or her oral reading fluency score to a criterion level on a Curriculum-Based Measure (CBM) (e.g., improve score by 20%). If the student's score reaches the criterion level, the hypothesis would be supported, and a longer-term intervention should be developed to provide incentives for fluent performance. The second hypothesis suggests that the academic performance problem is occurring because there have been insufficient displays of accurate responses by the student to have resulted in satisfactory acquisition or mastery of the skill in question. (Recall that "opportunities to respond" is a key predictor of successful learning outcomes.) The third hypothesis addresses instructional issues, suggesting the need for interventions that provide additional prompts and practice (if the skill already has been acquired) or models and error correction (if the skill has not yet been acquired), including complete learning trials consisting of a prompt (e.g., "What is twelve times three?"), response ("36"), and consequence ("Correct."). The fourth hypothesis cites factors related to discrimination, transfer, and generalization of skills, while the fifth and final hypothesis, "it is too hard," posits a mismatch between the material used for instruction and the instructional level of the student.

In the RTI model, the goal of instruction and intervention should be the attainment of skills at levels appropriate to a student's current grade placement, as discussed in Chapter 3. Unless a modification in the presentation of instructional materials is sufficient (e.g., study aids such as outlines, highlighted text, audiotaped presentation), interventions addressing this hypothesis are typically intensive and individualized, involving the selection of instructional materials at a level different from that employed with other students. It is only when high-quality intervention (typically, intensive intervention at Tier 3) has failed to elicit satisfactory performance that a lowering of goals (and corresponding change in curriculum) should be considered; this is the condition to which the fifth hypothesis refers.

Behavior problems. Witt, Daly, and Noell (2000) offer general hypotheses that might be generated through functional assessment of behavior problems. These hypotheses are presented in Table 7.4, along with intervention objectives and examples of corresponding interventions. Note that these hypotheses are grouped by the nature of the problem (behavioral excess versus behavioral deficit) and that the reasons for behavioral excess problems correspond with the "functions of behavior" discussed in Chapter 4; that is, behaviors are performed in order to obtain or avoid attention, tangibles, or stimulation. Behavioral deficits, on the other hand, are attributed to either an inability to perform (skill deficit) or an unwillingness to perform (performance deficit). As was suggested in relation to the general hypotheses proposed by Daly and colleagues (1997) for academic problems, specific circumstances or events that appear to be functionally related to the problem behavior would be identified through assessment and cited in hypotheses generated in a case study. The behavioral hypotheses presented by Witt and colleagues (2000) are useful for guiding the process of hypothesis development, suggesting categories of explanations that should be considered as problem-identification data are reviewed.

CHARACTERISTICS OF EFFECTIVE ACADEMIC INTERVENTIONS

Numerous researchers have identified features that are characteristic of effective interventions, notably Lentz, Allen, and Ehrhardt (1996). Academic interventions are regarded as "strong" interventions to the extent that they possess one or more of the features outlined by Lentz and colleagues: opportunities to respond; immediate postwork feedback about accuracy, with error correction; positive post-work contingencies for independent, accurate performance; appropriate pacing and instructional strategies; and progress monitoring.

Table 7.4   Hypotheses for Behavior Problems With Corresponding Intervention Strategies

Hypothesis	Intervention Objective	Sample Intervention
For Behavior Excesses		
1. Situational factors prompt the behavior.	• Reduce problem behavior. • Remove/change factors (antecedents, such as transitions, teacher directives, peer provocation). • Teach replacement behavior.	• Structure transition periods: Remind students of expectations and rules; assign "bell work"; offer incentives for orderly transition to new activity; shorten time allowed for transitions. • Assign leadership role to student during class transition periods.
2. They want to escape/avoid something.	• Eliminate opportunity for escape/avoidance. • Offer relief contingent on work completion.	• Use precision requests (Rhode, Jenson, & Reavis, 1993) to give directives. • Use timeout sparingly, and require original task completion during timeout period. • When specified amount of work is completed, give passes that students can use to eliminate portions of homework or items on assignments.
3. They want to get something.	• Withhold desired consequence when problem behavior occurs. • Teach replacement behavior.	• Ignore attention-getting behaviors; do not provide desired object or activity in response to problem behaviors. • Contract for desired outcome (attention, object, activity) contingent on display of alternative behavior.

Hypothesis	Intervention Objective	Sample Intervention
	For Behavior Deficits	
1. They lack the necessary skill.	• Teach the skill. • Teach when to use the skill (generalization and discrimination). • Build support for use of new skill.	• Provide social-skills training. • Use role-plays to anticipate future situations calling for skill use (and "not-use"). • Teach self-instruction for using skills in new or unfamiliar situations. • Arrange for "real-world" situations (e.g., teachers, parents) to provide appropriate antecedents (opportunities, prompts) and consequences for skill use.
2. They possess the skill, but don't use it consistently.	• Discourage competing behaviors. • Alter circumstances to motivate students to use skill.	• Use differential reinforcement to extinguish problem behaviors while promoting replacement behaviors. • Provide opportunity for involvement in leadership and service activities requiring student to use skill (McNamara, 2000).

Source: Adapted from Witt, Daly, and Noell (2000)

Opportunities to respond to tasks requiring the behaviors targeted for improvement. The principle of direct intervention (Shapiro, 2004) asserts that the best way to improve performance of a skill is to engage in activities requiring the use of that skill. In other words, if the goal is to improve a student's math computation skills, interventions should require the student to compute math problems. If the goal is to improve a student's ability to engage in appropriate peer interactions, interventions should provide numerous opportunities for the student to interact with peers.

Although this may seem to be an obvious feature of effective interventions, it is not uncommon for intervention tasks to target constructs that are assumed to underlie or enable successful performance of the skill to be learned rather than require performance of the skill itself. For example, children who are struggling with beginning reading skills may receive interventions targeting auditory perception. This practice is based on the notion of aptitude-treatment interactions (ATIs), which refers to the expectation that skills will improve if a specific aptitude underlying academic skills is identified and remedied. (Note that ATIs and secondary dependent variables are not the same; a secondary dependent variable, typically a deficient requisite subskill, as discussed in Chapter 5, can be tested, and its relationship to the primary dependent variable can be demonstrated through a brief experiment.)

Although it is beyond the scope of this text, the debate over ATIs has been raging for years and, with the increasing popularity of neuropsychological and cognitive explanations for children's academic problems, is likely to continue into the foreseeable future. At present, there is little evidence to support ATIs as a valid basis for effective intervention (Arter & Jenkins, 1979; Reschly, 2008), although refinements in the ATI approach (based on recent developments in the study of cognitive processing) hold some promise (Kavale & Flanagan, 2007). Even in cases where ATI-based interventions result in improved performance, arguments for their value typically violate the principle of parsimony: Was the ATI construct really needed to explain the problem or develop an intervention? Thus far, the research on academic interventions suggests that the answer is "no," and that, when ATI is used in an intervention that works, the effectiveness of the intervention was just as likely due to other characteristics of the intervention—such as opportunities to practice the targeted skill.

Opportunities to respond is a phrase that refers to antecedents of academic engagement, which research has shown to be a predictor of academic performance (Greenwood, Horton, & Utley, 2002; Shapiro, 2004). Such antecedents consist primarily of tasks that elicit active student responding, such as peer-assisted learning, choral responding, and oral reading. The presentation of an assignment or directing a question to the class—which many educators regard as "opportunities to respond"—are insufficient to draw some students into the learning process. Like reinforcement, an opportunity to respond is a true "opportunity to respond" only if it is successful in eliciting an appropriate academic response. The challenge for educators, then, is to design interventions that effectively engage students in activities to practice the skill that is being targeted for remediation.

Immediate postwork feedback with error correction. Students should receive feedback about their responses as quickly as possible, and the feedback should provide information about the accuracy of the response. In this way, errors in performance can be corrected rather than repeated. This doesn't mean that students' written assignments must be immediately corrected and returned to them; instead, it encourages the use of tasks that have "built-in" feedback mechanisms.

For example, the intervention strategy of cover-copy-compare (Stading, Williams, & McLaughlin, 1996) presents a model of accurate performance of an item (e.g., an addition problem showing the correct answer), which is then covered while the student responds (e.g., calculates an answer to the problem). Then, the student uncovers the original model and compares his or her answer to the model. If the student's answer is incorrect, the correct answer is written several times to reinforce it instead of the incorrect response produced previously. Similar interventions use taped models (e.g., the correct spelling of a word following its dictation; accurate reading of unfamiliar text) for improving spelling or reading skills. Peer-assisted learning activities offer similar opportunities for immediate feedback and error correction.

Positive postwork contingencies. Students are more likely to engage in activities and work toward a goal if they know that a reward is available, contingent on their performance. Incentives are often recommended as a primary intervention for students who lack motivation to perform (i.e., performance deficits, in which they can but don't want to do the work). However, they also are useful with students who have skill deficits (i.e., they can't do the work) as a means to elicit effort and engagement in remedial activities. When incentives are offered, it is important to set performance criteria based on the accuracy of students' work rather than the amount of work completed. Increased rates of accurate responding are associated with improved performance; therefore, accuracy should be the focus of intervention strategies, and it should be the outcome that is measured as an indicator of effectiveness (Shapiro, 2004). (Note that measures of performance recommended for use in an RTI model, such as CBM, use fluency as a standard, since fluency requires both accuracy and rapid rates of responding.)

Pacing and instructional strategies. For interventions that teach students how to use a skill or strategy, appropriate pacing of instruction, immediate error correction, use of models and prompts, and an appropriate criterion for success are critical. Although it is commonly believed that learning is best accomplished when the pace of instruction is slow—allowing every student time to "digest" newly presented information—research suggests that rapidly paced instruction may be more effective, especially when fact-based information is being presented. For example, Carnine (1976) found that students responded correctly 80% of the time in a fast-paced instructional condition (i.e., 12 questions per minute) but only 30% of the time in a slow-paced condition (in which questions were asked at a rate of 5 per minute).

The direct instruction approach (Engelmann & Carnine, 1982), which has extensive research support, incorporates rapid responding as one of its principal features. A teaching sequence using rapid presentation of information might proceed from the teacher's brief introduction of a new skill, through demonstration of the skill using one or two examples, followed by a task requiring students to use the skill before a model portraying accurate performance is presented. Students who are not able to use the skill correctly might be directed to compare their work with that of their seatmates, and, if they are still unable to perform the skill accurately, to request the teacher's help. In this way, the pace of instruction is neither too slow for students who quickly grasp the new skill nor too fast for those who require additional modeling of the skill.

The need for immediate error correction has already been discussed; it is especially important when students are working to achieve accurate use of a new skill. As noted earlier, immediate correction of errors avoids the counterproductive practice of allowing students to repeat their erroneous responses. After all, if learning occurs as a result of repeated practice, students who repeatedly practice an erroneous response will learn that response.

Initially, students may require modeling so they can achieve accuracy, but the ultimate objective of intervention is to foster skills that allow students to perform independently. When it is clear that students have learned how to perform the skill being taught (e.g., subtraction with regrouping, initiating conversations with peers), interventionists should replace models of correct performance with prompts to elicit correct use of the skill. For example, an interventionist might first demonstrate how to regroup numbers to solve a subtraction problem and explain the procedure aloud to a student who makes frequent errors (i.e., hasn't yet achieved accuracy) on problems requiring this skill. Once the student's error rate has dropped to an acceptable level, the interventionist might offer occasional prompts, such as "Are the top numbers bigger than the bottom numbers?" Eventually, the student will no longer need to be prompted to execute the skill successfully; at this point, the interventionist should fade, or gradually eliminate, the use of prompts.

Although accuracy of responses is an important goal of intervention (and the measure of its effectiveness), some students display fluency problems, in which accuracy—but not speed—of responding has been attained. Accuracy problems can be ruled out if students are able to execute a skill correctly, with a minimum of errors. A fluency problem reflects inadequate mastery of the skill, such that performance, while largely accurate, is slow and uneven. In such cases, goals and incentives should emphasize both accuracy and rate of responding. For example, a student who knows his multiplication facts but is slow in responding to problems presented on flashcards might be rewarded if the number of flashcard problems answered correctly during a one-minute drill exceeds a specified criterion.

Similarly, attainment of both accuracy and fluency goals can be measured by the rate at which students improve their performance, as reflected in, for example, the percentage increase from week to week in the number of words read correctly per minute.

Progress monitoring. A data-collection plan to monitor progress will serve as the basis for decision making. Chapter 2 reviewed data-collection methods appropriate for use in an RTI model, such as CBM and direct behavioral observation. Here, the need is to incorporate these methods in a plan for routine, systematic measurement of the academic skill or behavior that the intervention is designed to improve. Research shows that monitoring student progress results in improved performance, and this effect is enhanced when the data are used to modify instruction (Fuchs & Fuchs, 1986). The latter point deserves special emphasis: Decisions about the effectiveness of interventions must be data based. Too often, conclusions about an intervention's success are based on a perfunctory review of student worksheets, tests, or grades, or they are based on the teacher's opinion as to whether significant improvement has occurred. This approach to judging intervention effectiveness is fraught with difficulties, including nonstandard and unreliable evaluation practices and the subjectivity of teacher judgments. Fortunately, there are ample resources available that present "decision rules" that can be used to analyze data to judge intervention effectiveness; this topic will be discussed in greater detail in Chapter 8.

CHARACTERISTICS OF EFFECTIVE BEHAVIORAL INTERVENTIONS

There also are characteristics of behavioral interventions that should be incorporated to make interventions more effective; some of these characteristics pertain to *replacement behaviors*. The functional-assessment approach to behavioral intervention emphasizes the importance of identifying and promoting desirable behaviors as a replacement for problematic, interfering behavior; this emphasis is reflected in several of the characteristics of strong behavioral interventions, as outlined by Lentz, Allen, & Ehrhardt (1996): reduction of problem behavior accompanied by promotion of equivalent desirable behavior, prompting, positive contingencies for desired behaviors, practice opportunities, transfer of control to the natural environment, response to inappropriate behavior, and clear goals and data-based decision making.

Reduction of problem behavior with promotion of equivalent desirable behavior. As noted above, functional assessment recommends positive behavioral support in the form of a plan to promote more desirable behavior. For example, a functional assessment might reveal that a student engages in disruptive behavior when the teacher presents tasks that she dislikes (antecedent) and that the disruptive behavior typically ends with her being sent to timeout (consequence). In this case, our hypothesis would be, "When presented with a task that she dislikes, Jane calls out and disturbs others in order to avoid having to complete the task." By sending Jane to timeout, the teacher is (unknowingly) rewarding or reinforcing the disruptive behavior by providing a means of escape. Not surprisingly, the disruptive behavior continues, as Jane has found an effective means to accomplish her goal.

In a functional approach to intervention, efforts would be made to identify more appropriate behaviors that Jane might use in place of disruptive behavior to accomplish the same purpose: escape from a disliked task. She might be permitted to take breaks periodically and contingent on having completed a portion of the task, allowed to select a subset of the task to complete, taught a signal to use to let the teacher know that she'd like a break, allowed to work with a seatmate to increase the appeal of the task, and so on. At the same time, Jane would always be expected to complete the assigned task, thereby "blocking" her escape. By refusing to allow Jane to escape or avoid the assigned task, reinforcement is withheld, thereby extinguishing the disruptive behavior. Note that, in this example, not only is the undesirable disruptive behavior being eliminated but also it is being replaced with more appropriate ways of obtaining relief from the task.

Prompting (and fading of prompts) for new behaviors. Consistent with the emphasis on replacement behaviors, this feature represents an effective teaching strategy: When a new behavior is being taught, prompts will help the student (1) remember how to perform the new behavior, and (2) know when it is appropriate to perform this behavior. In this way, the correct use of a newly taught behavior is facilitated, and generalization of the behavior to similar settings is promoted. Fading is characterized by gradual reduction of prompts; it begins after the target behavior and the prompts show a consistent link. The goal of fading is to unlink the prompts from the target behavior so that the student will perform the appropriate behavior under naturally occurring conditions.

Positive contingencies for desired behaviors. In efforts to persuade students that new behaviors are preferable to the old, interfering behaviors they are meant to replace, incentives are often needed. As students practice a replacement behavior and learn that it results in the outcome desired by the student (e.g., relief from a disliked task; attention from the teacher), incentives can be removed, albeit gradually. Until the student has made this connection, however, motivation to perform the new behavior must be supplied in the form of rewards or incentives.

Many incentive plans fail because the incentives (1) are not motivating to the student, either because they are poorly defined or of insufficient value to the student; (2) are not provided consistently, as soon as possible after the behavior is performed; or (3) are not provided in sufficient quantity, or dosage. Here, the basic principles of behavior change must be observed. Students are unlikely to respond to a reward that is viewed as insignificant or that only the teacher (and not the student) values, such as a "good grade." Similarly, requiring the student to wait a week or more for a reward is counterproductive, especially since the old behavior delivered a rewarding consequence more promptly. In cases where it is not practical to provide rewards immediately following the behavior, tokens (to be exchanged for a reward later) can be used as a form of secondary reinforcement.

Opportunities to practice newly learned behaviors. As discussed earlier with respect to academic interventions, new responses are unlikely to be learned if there are insufficient opportunities for practice. For behavioral interventions, this requires awareness of circumstances in which the replacement behavior would be useful and appropriate and the incorporation of such circumstances into the intervention plan. For example, disruptive behavior may be used to obtain peer attention, and it is generalized to many circumstances, including recess play, conduct on the school bus, physical education class, and lunch periods.

Consequently, intervention planners should address all of these circumstances by training relevant personnel, including playground and lunch supervisors, bus drivers, and physical education teachers in how to "cue" and provide incentives for more appropriate attention-getting behavior. In addition, planners might incorporate a provision for "previewing" such circumstances with the target student in the form of role-plays and discussion.

Transfer of control to the natural environment. This principle is a companion to practice opportunities; it acknowledges the critical importance of transferring and generalizing newly learned behaviors to real-world settings. In fact, it has been noted that transfer and generalization are perhaps the greatest challenge to successful social-skills training interventions (DuPaul & Eckert, 1994).

Response to inappropriate behavior. While functional assessment focuses on identifying and promoting replacement behaviors, it also is important to eliminate undesired, interfering behaviors. A class of intervention strategies that accomplish both of these purposes is known as *differential reinforcement*, in which only desired behaviors are reinforced while undesired behaviors are extinguished. There are four types of differential reinforcement:

1. Differential reinforcement of incompatible behavior (DRI): Reinforce only those behaviors that cannot be performed at the same time as the interfering behavior (e.g., praise for being in seat, when out-of-seat behavior is being addressed as the problem).

2. Differential reinforcement of alternative behavior (DRA): Reinforce behavior that is being promoted as a replacement for the interfering behavior (e.g., acknowledge "good leadership" of a student by placing him at the head of the recess line to serve as line leader, in place of the hitting and poking he'd been using to gain peer attention during transition times).

3. Differential reinforcement for the omission of behavior (DRO): Reinforce behavior wherein the student in not engaging in the interfering behavior for a period of time (e.g., provide a lottery ticket for a weekly drawing to a student who has not gotten out of her seat or talked with others during an independent work session, when past behavior during independent work included several instances of getting out of her seat and talking with others).

4. Differential reinforcement of low rates of behavior (DRL): For students who have engaged in high-frequency interfering behaviors, provide reinforcement when the student significantly reduces the frequency of the behavior (e.g., tell a student who frequently leaves his seat to sharpen pencils that he will be rewarded for getting out his seat without permission no more than three times per day). The standard for determining whether the behavior occurs at a sufficiently low rate will be based on several factors, including its initial (baseline) frequency and the extent to which any occurrence of the behavior disrupts the student's (or others') learning.

Clear goals and data-based decision making. In a statewide study of schools' intervention practices, the quality indicator of "clearly defined goal" was found to be a significant predictor of intervention outcomes (Telzrow, McNamara, & Hollinger, 2000). That is, the success of interventions could be predicted by the extent to which planning teams defined goals in clear, behavioral terms. In addition, as discussed earlier with respect to academic interventions, it is important to implement a system for collecting behavioral data that can be used to monitor progress toward intervention goals and to use these data as the basis for making decisions.

TARGETS OF INTERVENTION

The functional-assessment methods employed in the case study approach yield information about antecedents and consequences that are functionally related to problem behavior. Witt and colleagues (2000) offer a description of "usual suspects," or common antecedents and consequences for problem behavior grouped according to grade levels. For example, for grades three to five, they describe typical behavior problems as talking, making noises, moving around, attention seeking, noncompliance, and fighting. Witt and colleagues suggest that common antecedents for these problems include teacher demand, confrontation, task difficulty, lack of supervision, lack of classroom rules, little structure, no preplanned consequences, and transitions; common consequences include teacher attention, peer attention, and escape from work. One or more of these antecedents or consequences could thus serve as targets for intervention. For example, a "demand" condition could be modified by offering students choices of tasks, "transitions" can be structured by creating time limits and routines, and "no preplanned consequences" can be remedied by creating a hierarchy of consequences and explaining them to students. Relative to consequences, an intervention targeting "escape from work" might involve the specification of a quota of expected behavior; upon reaching the agreed-upon quota, students would be permitted to take a break.

According to Witt and colleagues (2000), there are two options for interventions when antecedent conditions account for problem behaviors:

1. Eliminate undesirable or unnecessary antecedents, or change antecedents that cannot or should not be eliminated (as in above examples); or

2. Teach the student a different response to the antecedent (e.g., instead of throwing papers to the floor when presented with a difficult task, teach the student to raise her hand to request assistance).

When consequence conditions are hypothesized to be functionally related to problem behavior, Witt and colleagues (2000) suggest three general strategies:

1. Stop the problem behavior from producing the consequence that maintains it (e.g., withhold teacher attention when the student interrupts instruction).

2. Change the situation so that an appropriate behavior leads to the consequence that was maintaining the problem behavior (e.g., provide immediate teacher attention when the student raises a hand and waits to be called on rather than when the student interrupts instruction). The authors caution that this strategy is feasible only when the student knows how to perform the appropriate "replacement" behavior.

3. Change the situation so that the student will lose interest in the consequence that was maintaining the problem behavior (i.e., prevent the problem behavior from occurring by providing the desired

consequence, such as teacher attention, before the student displays the behavior, a strategy known as *noncontingent* attention; or make the consequence less attractive by reducing or eliminating its rewarding properties, such as the stimulation and task escape afforded by "timeout" served in a neighboring classroom).

Of course, when a student's problem behavior is a result of his or her lack of knowledge about an appropriate behavior, or a deficiency in the skills needed for the behavior (i.e., a "can't do" hypothesis), interventions must target these deficiencies by providing needed instruction (e.g., social-skills training).

SUMMARY

This chapter described two general models for selecting interventions, based either on an *empirical* or a *functional* approach, noting that the empirical approach is typically applied at Tiers 1 and 2 while the functional model serves as the framework for the Tier 3 case study. Factors affecting intervention integrity (application of the intervention as designed) were explored along with recommendations for enhancing integrity.

At Tier 3, interventions are matched to specific factors that were identified through problem analysis as functionally related to students' performance problems. Two sets of likely hypotheses for problems were presented, based on research in academic and behavior problems, and examples of corresponding interventions were described. Finally, characteristics contributing to the strength of interventions were discussed, including opportunities to respond, feedback and error correction, contingencies for accurate responding, and data-based progress monitoring.

In the next chapter, detailed information about methods for evaluating case study outcomes is provided. Progress monitoring yields data describing the impact of interventions, and, in Chapter 8, the reader will become familiar with several research-based methods for analyzing and making decisions based on those data.

8

Evaluating Case Study Outcomes

Outcome evaluation is a critical element in the case study procedure. At Tier 3 of the RTI model, data from brief single-case designs are used to test hypotheses so that interventions can accurately target variables contributing to students' problems. When the single-case design and corresponding data analysis are extended over a longer period of time, more details can be obtained about the functional relationship between independent (intervention) and dependent variables (target behavior). Decisions about whether to continue, modify, or replace an intervention all depend on evaluation of the data from these monitoring procedures.

Accountability issues that can be addressed using case study data include special education eligibility determination and individualized education plan (IEP) development, evaluation of the skills of case study facilitators, and program evaluation. For example, a student's responsiveness to high-intensity interventions, revealed in progress monitoring results, is regarded as evidence supporting eligibility for special education. Student outcome data also can be used to assess the impact of school psychological services, and data from universal screenings can be used to predict scores on high-stakes testing (leading to the introduction of appropriate early intervening services). Administrators can plan appropriate professional-development activities for facilitators and interventionists when data indicate that the quality of case studies or intervention integrity are less than adequate.

Selecting an appropriate case study evaluation procedure is a complex process; this is illustrated in the extensive research literature regarding techniques and decision rules used in statistical and visual analyses of data generated in single-case designs. Three criteria guided the selection of the methods recommended in this chapter. First, practitioners must be able to understand and use the method with ease. Methods that require complicated statistical analysis, lengthy time periods for data gathering, or costly software were excluded as impractical for use in daily practice. Second, methods in which advantages outweighed disadvantages were chosen. Finally, methods tending to lead to biased results were eliminated, or their limitations are explained.

On the basis of these criteria, three methods will be described for use in hypothesis testing, decision making, and accountability: (1) visual analysis, (2) magnitude of change or effect size (ES), and (3) goal-attainment scaling (GAS). Each of these methods offers a different perspective of the evaluation process. Visual analyses are used to identify general patterns in the data across time. ES calculations provide descriptive statistics verifying the magnitude of change across various phases of intervention. GAS is both a qualitative measure of the degree of success of an intervention and an indicator of realistic goal setting. Each method has advantages and disadvantages, and as a general rule, it is advisable to use multiple evaluation methods for decision making in order to minimize the effects of measurement bias or error.

VISUAL ANALYSIS

Visual analysis is conducted by examining graphed data to determine whether the intervention evoked improvement, deterioration, or no change in the target behavior. In a case study conducted at Tier 3, the goal is to increase, decrease, stabilize, or maintain a behavior. Effective interventions are those that meet the goals for improvement in the dependent variable. Visual analysis enables the observer to view patterns in the data that develop over time. As a result, functional relationships between the intervention and the target behavior can be determined. When a functional relationship exists, graphed data will fluctuate in reaction to changes in the independent variable (i.e., implementing, withdrawing, or modifying an intervention). Visual analysis provides a general picture of a fluid process that is not as easily captured through statistical methods.

Visual analysis is an important method that can be used by practitioners for immediate and direct feedback. However, it should be supplemented with other analyses to ensure the validity of interpretations and data-based decisions because agreement among raters reviewing the same graphed data using visual analysis is not high (Bloom, Fischer, & Orme, 2003; Park, Marascuilo, & Gaylord-Ross, 1990). Judgments about the impact of an intervention on a target variable differ based on contextual factors as well as methods used in the analysis.

Unfortunately, certain attributes that are characteristic of visual analysis can lead to false conclusions about the data. The serious problem of serial dependency, or autocorrelation, refers to the fact that scores within a time series tend to be related to or predictive of one another (Jones, Vaught, & Weinrott, 1977). Autocorrelation increases the possibility of concluding (erroneously) that an intervention has had an effect when, in fact, it has not. To address this problem, caution in interpreting data is recommended, supplementation of visual analyses with other measures is needed.

Visual analysis of graphed data also can be influenced by the scales used to define points on the graph's horizontal (x) and vertical (y) axes. To minimize this effect, graphs should be scaled consistently by using approximately the same intervals between points on both the x and y axes.

Many visual analysis methods are available; unfortunately, a "best practice" standard has yet to be determined. One example is the method used to calculate the mean shift in data from baseline to intervention phases. Three different methods are common: (1) simple mean difference; (2) mean difference controlling for the overall data trend; and (3) mean difference controlling only for the baseline trend. Standardization of terms is a similar issue. In a review of the literature, different definitions and applications were found for "reliable," "level," "magnitude," and other similar terms. Confusion resulting from the variety of available methods and multiple definitions of terms leads to difficulty in making judgments from the data.

Judgments about improvement, regression, or no change in performance are often described in relative degrees. The notion of "degree of change" and cut-off points are rarely defined in specific terms. These issues are particularly important when data generated throughout the RTI process are being used to make decisions about special education eligibility based on the intensity of needed interventions. There are no generally accepted standards or decision rules. The type and characteristics of the data being examined must be considered, so that appropriate judgments, standards, and decision rules can be applied. This chapter defines and explains many of these problematic terms, calculations, and decision issues.

CONDUCTING VISUAL ANALYSES

Graphic properties are considered in concert, rather than individually, in visual analysis. Three properties of graphed data are relevant: (1) stability or variability, (2) level and gross magnitude of change, and (3) trend and specific rate of change. These properties are influenced by the goals of the case study and the characteristics of the data. Some properties are relevant (and their associated steps are applied) only under certain circumstances.

Stability and variability. Data that clearly predict future levels of the target behavior from a prior period are considered to be stable. Although stable baseline data are preferred, variable baseline data are common in single-case studies. It is generally accepted that no fewer than three data points are necessary to establish a baseline, but seven or more points are preferred. Sometimes, additional data are collected to determine whether variability in baseline data is an anomaly and will stabilize. As the number of data points increases, so does confidence in the conclusions generated through visual analysis. A greater number of data points more clearly distinguishes patterns that lead to specific conclusions. See Figure 8.1 for examples of stable and variable data.

Faced with a high degree of variability in the data, school psychologists might conclude that these unpredictable patterns should not be interpreted using visual analysis. On the other hand, instability of data can be interpreted as relevant information for generating hypotheses or setting goals. Variable data may indicate that the underlying cause of the problem has not been adequately identified. For example, it is hypothesized that Elias demonstrates emotions ranging from controlled (1) to highly uncontrolled (10) during math class because he dislikes math. If this hypothesis is accepted, and the resulting intervention targets aspects of math class, the goal would be to reduce the range of emotional reactions by eliminating the aversion to math. However, further analysis of the graphed data reveals that even though these emotional reactions only occur during math class, they do not occur every day and to a predictable degree. A second hypothesis is that Elias has irregular sleeping patterns at home, and when he does not go to bed early enough,

Figure 8.1   Stable and Variable Data

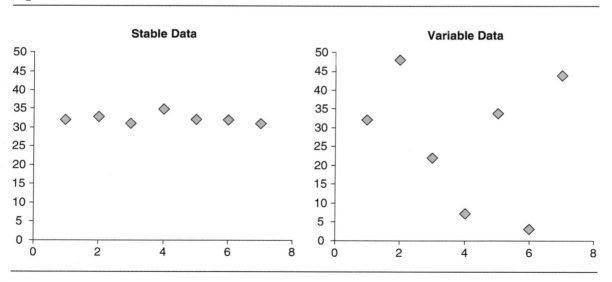

extreme emotional reactions occur during math, the first class of the day. If the data are reworked to detect the relationship between sleeping patterns and Elias' emotional displays, the second hypothesis might be found to be correct. In this case, the data will be stable in relation to each of the sleeping conditions. In Figure 8.2, the upper broken line represents behavior following nights with less than eight hours of sleep, and the lower line represents behavior following nights with eight or more hours of sleep.

Another issue may be the actual instability of the behavior. For example, the goal for Marco, who exhibits extreme emotional responses ("withdrawn" rated as "1," and "agitated" rated as "10" on a scale of 1–10), due to poor coping skills, throughout the day, is to reduce the variability of responses. In this case, a highly variable baseline followed by an intervention phase with a narrow range of the target behavior (relatively moderate emotional responses, with values ranging from 4–6) is viewed as a success. See Figure 8.3 for case study data that show the change from variable to stable data as a measure of success.

Figure 8.2   Graphed Data for Math Hypothesis Versus Sleep Hypothesis

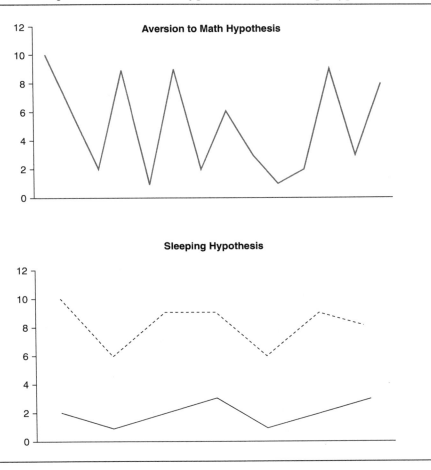

Figure 8.3   Graphed Data Showing Change From Variable to Stable Data

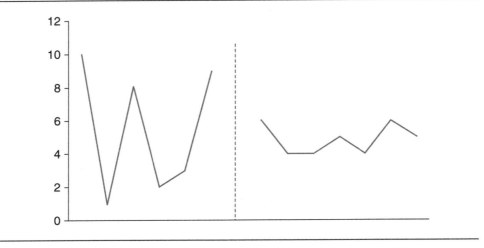

Three questions can be used to guide judgments about the variability of baseline data. First, have enough data been gathered to find a stable pattern if it exists? Second, is the variable pattern due to an inappropriate hypothesis about the cause of the behavior (as in the above example of disliked math versus inadequate sleep)? Third, would the problem be solved by stabilizing the dependent variable?

If the goal is to stabilize the data during the intervention phase, failure to do so leads to one of the following conclusions: The intervention needs to be extended in order for the impact to be detected; the intervention does not work to solve this problem; or the intervention does not have a consistent impact and may need to be modified.

Level and magnitude of change. Interventions that are intended to increase target behaviors are expected to have an overall lower level of scores in the baseline phase and a higher level in the intervention phase. The reverse is true for interventions intended to reduce problem behaviors. Baseline and intervention phases in which data are at the same level suggest that the intervention did not have an impact on the targeted behavior, or the intervention was not intended to result in an increase or decrease. Figure 8.4 includes examples of all three patterns.

Level is determined by the mean or median score on the dependent variable for each phase. Because a middle score is used to summarize data, the level (mean or median score) is not useful when there is a trend in the data (i.e., when data show a systematic pattern of change in a given direction). A mean level score is calculated by adding all scores within a phase and dividing by the number of scores within the phase. Interpreting the mean score for a phase is appropriate when there are no widely divergent scores, called *outliers*. When there are outliers, a more appropriate technique is to

Figure 8.4   Graphic Displays Demonstrating Increase, Decrease, or No Change
in Data

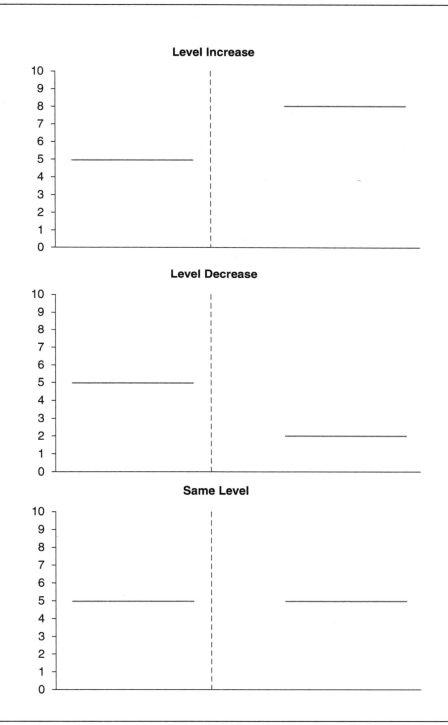

use a trimmed mean score, in which the extreme scores are removed from the equation. In addition, a mean score may not be representative of scores when there are fewer than seven data points in a phase or when there is a large amount of variation in the scores.

In the case of a limited number of data points, or when there are outliers in the baseline phase, readers should consider using the median score because it will be less affected by extreme scores. The median score is determined by arranging all scores within a phase in numerical order, from lowest to highest score, and then locating the point that would divide the scores at the midpoint. For example, when the baseline scores 6, 9, 4, 7, 11, 5, and 8 are arranged in order (4, 5, 6, 7, 8, 9, 11), the median score is 7.

The level of each phase is displayed as a horizontal line drawn through the set of graphed data. A visual comparison of levels across phases reveals the relative magnitude of change. Visual analysis of change in level is a gross estimate of change. The magnitude of change is analyzed relative to the goals of the intervention and variability of the data. Note that a small change for a very intractable problem may signify success, while a very large change for an easily corrected problem may be viewed as the appropriate outcome. Visual analysis of the magnitude of change should be supplemented by calculating the *d*-index and percent of nonoverlapping data points (PND), discussed later in this chapter.

Trend and specific rate of change. A trend is demonstrated when graphed data show systematic directionality. Trends are expected to slant in an upward direction when the goal is to increase a targeted behavior, while a downward trend is desired when the goal is to reduce unwanted behaviors. Flat or no trends indicate that there is neither an increase nor a decrease apparent in the data. See Figure 8.5 for examples of the three trends.

Figure 8.5   Upward, Downward, and Flat Trends in Graphed Data

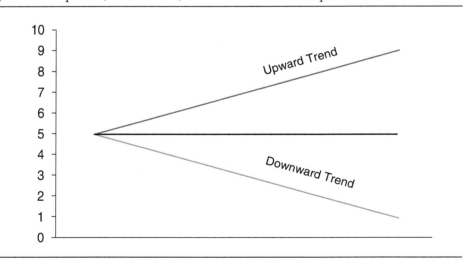

As a prediction method, a trend line is created for the baseline phase and extended into the intervention phase before intervention data are entered. The line predicts the trend in data that would be expected during the second phase if the intervention were not implemented. When the actual intervention data are entered, a new trend line is created for the intervention-phase data only, and the original prediction trend line is compared with the new intervention trend line to visually reveal the difference between the predicted and actual scores. See Figure 8.6 for an example of a successful improvement in learning rate.

There are two qualities of trend lines that should be considered in visual analyses. The first quality is the *direction of the slant.* Slant direction reveals whether the data indicate progress, deterioration, or no change in the dependent variable. In school settings involving academic problems, the most common data trends are upward trends in learning.

The second quality of trend lines is the *specific rate of change* (slope), which is measured in time increments. Specific rate of change is relevant when both the baseline and intervention phases show trend lines that slant in the same direction. For example, a student may be improving scores on "words read correctly per minute" (wcpm) at a rate of .5 wcpm per week, but this rate is considered inadequate, so an intervention might be introduced to increase the rate of improvement to 1.0 wcpm per week. When the rate of change is the same for baseline and intervention phases (indicated by parallel lines on the graph), the conclusion is that the intervention did not have an impact because it is likely that the improvement would have occurred even without the intervention. A rule of thumb is that a small rate of change in the desired direction during baseline followed by a larger rate of change in the desired direction during the intervention phase indicates that an intervention has had an impact on the target behavior.

Figure 8.6   Comparison of Predicted and Intervention Trend Lines

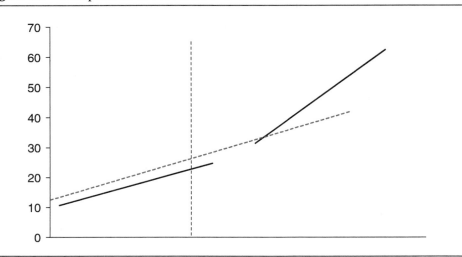

Trend lines are drawn on the data graph for both baseline and intervention phases. There are two common ways to draw a trend line: The Tukey method and the *regression line* approach. The Tukey method can be applied by hand. A line connects the means or medians of the first and second halves of each phase. However, this approach has been replaced by readily available technology that constructs graphs for which trend lines are automatically generated.

The regression line approach involves using computer software programs such as Microsoft Excel or SPSS or programs available from the Intervention Central (http://www.interventioncentral.org) and AIMSweb Web sites (http://www.aimsweb.com/) to calculate and insert the line into each phase of the single-case design. AIMSweb and SPSS are flexible tools; however, there are costs associated with their adoption. Microsoft Excel is readily available at low cost, and Intervention Central provides free graphing options to consider. (For an excellent step-by-step procedure for creating graphs and inserting the trend line using Microsoft Excel, see http://wps.prenhall.com/wps/media/objects/2028/2077456/Volume_medialib/BOOK.PDF.) Intervention Central offers graphing options that include the creation of graphs for progress monitoring as well as automatic insertion of trend lines.

Specific rate of change (slope) can be compared across baseline and intervention phases for the individual student or in relation to a norm group. The specific rate of change is easily calculated for data generated through Curriculum-Based Measurement (CBM). For example, periodic administrations of three-minute CBM oral reading fluency probes allow for an estimate of specific rate of change. The specific rate of change concept is integral to data-based decision making in the RTI model. Students move from Tiers 1 and 2 to Tier 3 as a result of a lack of progress in relation to their peers in local (or national) norm groups. Consider a class with a mean oral reading fluency rate of 22 words read correctly per minute (wcpm) that improves to an average of 42 wcpm in a ten-week period.

The class has a change rate of 2 words per minute per week. In contrast, a student in the class who has improved during that same ten-week period from 22 to 31 wcpm has a change rate that is less than 1 word per minute per week, which is below the expected rate of growth observed for peers.

A step-by-step procedure is used to address the properties of (1) stability or variability, (2) level and gross magnitude of change, and (3) trend and specific rate of change. The following steps are followed for an AB single-case design:

1. Graph data and identify phase changes with a dotted vertical line.

2. Visually analyze data in each phase for stability or variability.

3. Determine whether variability has increased, decreased, or remained the same across phases.

4. Calculate the level (i.e., mean or median) for each phase, and plot representative horizontal lines for each phase if appropriate.

5. Calculate the gross magnitude of change across phases.

6. Plot a trend line for the baseline phase if appropriate. Extend the baseline trend line into the intervention phase.

7. Plot a trend line for the intervention phase.

8. Visually compare the slope of the baseline trend line with the slope of the intervention trend line.

9. Calculate the specific rate of change (slope) for baseline and intervention phases if the trends for baseline and intervention phases are slanting in the same direction toward the goal.

10. Compare specific rates of change.

MAGNITUDE OF CHANGE

Effect size (ES) is a generic term for descriptive statistics that summarize behavior change across phases in research studies. There are approximately 40 different ways to calculate ES (Kirk, 1996), and a substantial body of literature has addressed the usability of the ES for single-case designs. The ES methods discussed in this text were selected based on a review of their advantages and disadvantages, their relevance to single-case design, and the criterion of ease of understanding and use.

The ES is useful for summarizing the magnitude of the change in the dependent variable in relation to the independent variable. By assigning a quantitative value to the preintervention and postintervention implementation phases, ES allows for specific comparisons and judgments that are not possible with visual analysis alone. Another benefit of the ES calculation is that it is not greatly affected by small sample sizes, and it can therefore be used in single-case designs with relatively few data points.

Unfortunately, the use of effect size as an indicator of change suffers from some of the same limitations as visual analysis (Kirk, 1996). These issues are beyond the scope of this text; however, Cohen (1988) and Kline (2004) provide a thorough review for interested readers. In brief, the most salient concerns include lack of interpretation standards, problems with autocorrelation and other statistical issues, and lack of conclusion validity.

For example, there has been much debate about the interpretation of ES in single-case designs. In addition, data from single-case research often suffers from problems of autocorrelation, failure to meet the assumption of normality, and issues arising from homogeneity of variance. Finally, ES does not establish a functional (cause-effect) relationship between variables; it simply provides a measure of the amount of change in the dependent variable across conditions. Therefore, ES statistics should be interpreted with caution and in conjunction with other measures of outcome effectiveness.

CHOOSING, CALCULATING, AND INTERPRETING EFFECT SIZES

ES methods are chosen based on the goal of the intervention and the characteristics of the graphed data. Four measures are included in this chapter: (1) effect size (ES_{var}), (2) d-index, (3) percentage of nonoverlapping data points (PND), and (4) g-index. An ES_{var} is used to measure change in variability of the data (Kromrey & Foster-Johnson, 1996). The d-index determines the magnitude of effect across baseline and intervention levels when there is no trend in the data (Bloom, Fischer, & Orme, 2003). The PND is also useful for gauging the extent of change across phases when there is no trend (Scruggs & Mastropieri, 1998). Finally, the g-index provides a rough estimate when there is a trend in the data (Bloom, Fischer, & Orme, 2003; Cohen, 1988).

Change in variability. An ES_{var} can be used to summarize the magnitude of change in variability (Kromrey & Foster-Johnson, 1996). The ES_{var} supplements visual analysis to determine the magnitude of the change. ES_{var} interpretation for changes in variability recommended by D. A. Cohen (1988) and J. Cohen (1992) are values of 0.02, 0.15, and 0.35, representing small, medium, and large effects, respectively.

The ES_{var} is calculated in three steps:

1. Calculate the variance of each phase.

2. Divide the larger of the variances by the smaller variance to obtain the variance ratio.

3. Compute ES_{var} using the following equation:

$$ES_{var} = \frac{(\text{Number of data points in phase with largest variance} -1)\,(\text{Variance ratio})}{\text{Total observations}}$$

Returning to the case of Marco, the student who received training in coping skills to stabilize extreme emotions, calculation of ES_{var} provides a useful means for interpreting data. Baseline scores were 10, 1, 8, 2, 3, 6, and 9, and intervention phase scores were 6, 4, 4, 5, 4, 6, and 5. Visual analysis of the graph in Figure 8.3 suggests that Marco's behavior was quite variable during baseline but became more stable during intervention. Using the following steps, an ES_{var} score supplements the visual analysis to show the magnitude of the change:

1. The baseline variance for Marco is 12.95, and the intervention variance is .81. (Standard deviation is easily calculated using the statistical calculator on any PC. The variance is the standard deviation squared.)

2. The variance ratio is calculated: 12.95 / .81 = 15.99. This result indicates that the variance in Marco's behavior was nearly 16 times greater during baseline than during intervention.

3. $ES_{var} = \dfrac{(7-1)(15.99)}{14} = 6.85$

Both ES_{var} (6.85) and measures of baseline (12.95) and intervention variances (.81) must be evaluated to detect the magnitude of change and the relative direction of change. In the case of Marco, there was a large magnitude of change in the desired direction, moving from variable to stable behavior.

Change in level. The magnitude of a change in level when the data do not reveal a trend can be calculated using the *d*-index or the PND. The methods differ in that the former method takes into account the actual score for each data point, and the latter does not. Both should be calculated when possible.

The *d*-index calculates the standard mean difference in scores across phases. A larger difference in the desired direction indicates a greater impact. If the data have changed in the desired direction from baseline to intervention phases (either upward or downward, depending on the goal), the effect size is reported as a positive change. Interpretation of effect size for this method is based on Cohen's (1988) recommendation to use .2, .5, and .8, as rough guidelines for estimating a small, moderate, and large impact. ES interpretation based on Cohen's recommendation has been challenged in recent years. We suggest that the *d*-index be considered with caution and in conjunction with visual analysis.

Four steps are required to calculate the *d*-index:

1. Calculate the means for each phase, and insert level lines on the graph.

2. Determine whether levels represent change in the desired direction.

3. Calculate the standard deviation for all data.

4. Compute the ES using the following formula:

$$d\text{-index} = \dfrac{\text{Intervention mean} - \text{Baseline mean}}{\text{Standard deviation of all data}}$$

The PND is based on the notion that the smaller the percentage of overlap in data across phases, the greater the impact of the intervention. An advantage of PND lies in the fact that it is not influenced by autocorrelation and other problems that may be inherent in the data. However, judgments based on PND can be affected by the fact that the procedure ignores all baseline data except the most extreme point in the desired direction. This point, because of its extremity, is likely to be the most unreliable. The PND cannot be calculated when there is a basal or ceiling point in the baseline in the desired direction. In addition, PND lacks sensitivity for highly successful interventions (i.e., 100% PND). As with all other methods, PND should be interpreted with caution and in conjunction with visual analysis. The suggested criteria for judging PND (Scruggs, Mastropieri, Cook, & Escobar, 1986) are 90% PND = highly effective; 70%–89% PND = moderately effective; 50%–69% PND = questionably effective; and below 50% PND = ineffective.

The goal specified for Charisse is to decrease her aggression in the classroom. Aggression has been defined as hitting, tripping, and yelling at other students. To calculate the PND, the number of nonoverlapping data points is divided by the total number of data points. Figure 8.7 provides a graphic representation of the PND method. The process begins with identification of the most extreme baseline data point in the desired direction. (*Desired direction* is determined by the goal of the case study; for a desired increase in behavior, the highest data point would be employed.) Charisse's most extreme data point in the baseline in the desired direction is 6. (Note that this is the lowest data point, since the goal is to decrease her aggressive behavior.) Draw a horizontal line from that data point through both the intervention and the baseline phases (indicated by the lower line). Next, identify the most extreme point in the intervention phase in the undesired direction. The most extreme point in the intervention phase in the undesired direction is 8. Draw a horizontal line from that data point through both phases (indicated by the upper line in Figure 8.7). Data points on or between these lines are overlapping (6 points).

Figure 8.7 Graph Displaying Percentage of Nonoverlapping Data Points

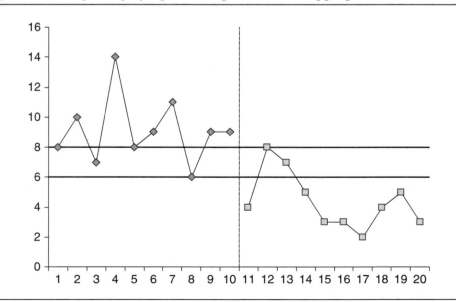

Count the number of nonoverlapping data points (NDP) across both phases, above the upper line and below the lower line (14). Count the total number of data points in both phases. There are a total of 20 data points. Compute PND using this formula:

$$PND = \frac{\text{Number of NDP} \times 100}{\text{Total number of data points}}$$

$$PND = \frac{14 \times 100}{20} = 70$$

The resulting PND of 70% is interpreted as questionably to moderately effective.

Change in trend. The g-index summarizes the magnitude of change across phases when there is a trend in the data. This ES method uses the baseline trend line to determine the proportion of scores above or below the line in each of the phases. If the goal is to increase the behavior, the proportion of the scores above the trend line is the focus of analysis. The reverse is true when the goal is to reduce the problem behavior. The g-index does not take into account the numeric values of the scores. Like the PND, it considers only whether scores are above or below the line.

Interpretation of the g-index is based on the concept that a greater amount of change in the desired direction during intervention than during baseline is an indication of success. A larger g-index indicates a larger magnitude of effect. The literature does not provide any cutoff points indicating the specific magnitude of change (e.g., large versus small). Instead, the direction of the change as determined by the sign of the g-index (positive or negative) reveals whether improvement or deterioration occurred from baseline to intervention phases. A positive g-index indicates improvement, and a negative g-index indicates deterioration.

The data depicted in Figure 8.8 suggest that Charlie is making progress in correctly calculating multiplication problems with increased fluency. Visual analysis of the graph for both baseline (first 7 data points) and intervention phases reveals upward trends. It is not clear whether math calculation was positively impacted by the intervention, since Charlie's scores were improving during the baseline phase. A calculation of the magnitude of improvement using a g-index will reveal whether the intervention is needed.

The g-index is calculated using the following procedure:

1. Plot the baseline trend line on the graph and extend it into the intervention phase. (See Figure 8.9 for the resulting graph.)
2. Calculate the proportion of scores in the baseline phase that are located on the side of the trend line consistent with the desired change. In this case, the proportion of baseline scores above the trend line is calculated because the goal is to increase behavior.

$$PB = \frac{\text{Number of baseline scores above trend line}}{\text{Total number of baseline scores}}$$

$$PB = \frac{4}{7} = .57$$

3. Calculate the proportion of scores in the intervention phase that are located on the side of the trend line consistent with the desired change.

$$PI = \frac{\text{Number of intervention scores above trend line}}{\text{Total number of baseline scores}}$$

$$PI = \frac{1}{7} = .14$$

4. Compute the *g*-index using the following formula:

g-index = PI − PB

g-index = .14 − .57 = −.43

The *g*-index value (−.43) indicates, although Charlie's math scores continue to increase, there is deterioration in the intervention phase. The intervention should either be modified or eliminated because it has not improved the rate of increase in Charlie's math scores beyond the rate predicted by baseline data prior to intervention.

Figure 8.8 Graph of Charlie's Baseline and Intervention Phase Data

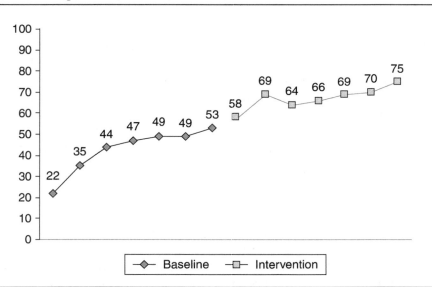

Figure 8.9   Graph Displaying the *g*-index

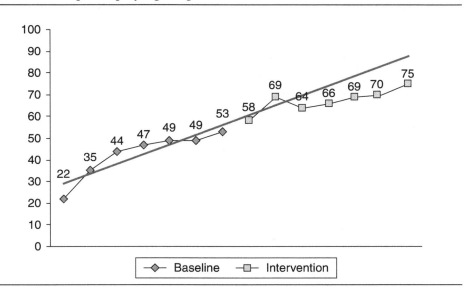

QUALITY OF THE OUTCOME: GOAL-ATTAINMENT SCALING

GAS is a method for predicting the amount of change expected in a case study and then generating a quality rating for the actual outcome (Kiresuk, Smith, & Cardillo, 1994). As a criterion-referenced approach for describing behavior change and documenting treatment outcomes, GAS standardizes ratings of outcomes across cases. The five-point rating scale ranks the quality of the outcome from +2 (greatly improved) to 0 (no improvement), to −2 (greatly deteriorated). The key to using GAS appropriately is to make educated predictions of the magnitude of change over time.

Successful case study outcomes are rated with easily understood GAS scores of +1 or +2, and those that are not successful are rated with scores of −1 or −2. These summary ratings require expertise on the part of the developer to create an appropriate scale prior to implementing an intervention. The scale links anticipated case study outcomes with patterns apparent in the baseline phase.

The qualitative nature of the scale allows each case to be individualized, and it is a versatile tool for use in school settings. But these same advantages raise questions of validity and reliability. Validity of the GAS scale requires appropriate representation of the target behavior. For example, ratings can be nominal scores (e.g., "improvement") that do not require equal intervals on the GAS scale. A range of scores can be equivalent to a rating of +1 (improvement), while a specific score is equivalent to a rating of 0 (no change). Though this type of scale is acceptable, approaches to scale development can vary widely. The absence of standardized guidelines for the creation of the GAS creates problems of scale validity. In this chapter, a set of guidelines for developing quantitative GAS is recommended to remedy this problem.

Reliability of scoring also is an issue in the use of qualitative GAS. Case study outcomes defined in purely qualitative terms are exemplified in Figure 8.10. This GAS was developed based on the practitioner's knowledge of the student and the context of the problem. There are no specific guidelines for qualitative GAS development except to use logic and best practices to establish goals for improvement and to rate outcomes with as much objectivity as possible.

Figure 8.10   Example of a Qualitative Goal-Attainment Scale

−2	−1	0	+1	+2
Unable to discuss the death of his mother.	Able to discuss the death of his mother, but does not accept the relationship between the grief process and his circumstances.	Generally aware of the grief process as it relates to the death of his mother.	Can identify his own feelings as they relate to his loss.	Able to discuss grief reaction with significant family members and friends.

Construction of a quantitative GAS begins with a prediction about the level of target behavior that would be expected to occur without intervention. This prediction is based on baseline data and the goal of the case study. The next step is to formalize the ±2 ratings using a specific technique. GAS ratings of ±1 are then developed based on the score difference between ratings of 0 and ±2. The last step requires an objective review of the scale by individuals who are familiar with the student's abilities. If the GAS is not realistic, then it should be altered as necessary.

There are two basic strategies for operationalizing the GAS. One strategy is to project a long-term goal that includes both measurable criteria and designated points in the future for accomplishing the goal. An alternate strategy is to generate short-term progress monitoring goals. For GAS, a four-week period is typically considered to be long term, and a one-week period is considered to be short term. These time periods were established on an arbitrary basis because they are convenient for monthly monitoring in the school setting and can be adjusted as needed.

Long-term goals have the advantage of minimizing the impact of scores that depart from the student's typical response pattern. When most scores are within the general range of the prediction, it is easy to identify an extreme score as an anomaly. For example, if a student's outcomes over a four-week period generate GAS ratings of +2, −1, +2, and +2, the −1 rating is clearly an anomaly and would likely be dismissed as an inaccurate reflection of the student's actual progress. On the other hand, short-term GAS monitoring is not so forgiving, and may lead to false conclusions influenced by unusual scores.

An advantage of short-term goals is that frequent monitoring allows for rapid modification of ineffective interventions. Although it is possible to establish short-term and long-term GAS measures for the same case study, short-term GAS results cannot be compared to long-term GAS outcomes.

Short-term monitoring is likely to produce an irregular pattern of success, while long-term measurement tends to smooth the variability of responses over time.

Variability and stability. When the goal of the case study is to reduce or increase variability, baseline data are used exclusively to construct the scale. The standard deviation of the baseline (SDb) scores is the predicted outcome (no change) without intervention and is therefore assigned a GAS rating of 0. For example, Adam rarely shows emotion; the standard deviation of his baseline scores (SDb = .6) is assigned a GAS rating of 0. Adam's goal is to increase his range of appropriate emotional responses. See Figure 8.11 for an example of this scale.

The *absolute score technique* can be used to establish the best and worst possible outcomes (depending on the goal). The worst possible outcome for Adam would be an absolute elimination of all variability, such that SD = 0. The *percent of change technique* is used to create the +2 GAS rating. For Adam, a 100% increase in variability (SD = 1.2) is set as the +2 GAS rating. The GAS scale is completed by filling in the ± 1 rating descriptions as the difference between the 0 rating and the ± 2 ratings.

Figure 8.11   Goal-Attainment Scale for Evaluating Adam's Range of Emotional Responses Using the Percent of Change Technique

−2	−1	0	+1	+2
0	>0 to <.6	.6	>.6 to <1.2	1.2

As a short-term GAS, the intent could be to incrementally increase the SD by the same amount (e.g., 100% each week) to measure gradual expansion of the student's repertoire of demonstrated emotions. However, if the problem is intractable, the GAS +2 rating may be set for a longer period of time to allow for smaller incremental changes (e.g., 100% increase is expected in four weeks).

Level. When the goal of the case study is to change the level of performance, construction of the GAS begins with a rating of 0, representing the level observed during the student's baseline. Techniques for developing the scale depend on the availability of comparison norms. When no norms are available, the GAS ratings of ±2 are constructed using the percent of change, the absolute score, or the *extreme data point technique*. The extreme data point technique is similar to the absolute score technique, except that, instead of using the absolute score of 0, the lowest or highest score in the baseline in the desired direction is adopted for the +2 rating. Each of these techniques is based on the notion that the specified score becomes the target level (mean or median) for the +2 GAS rating.

The GAS for a change in level based on local norms is constructed by using either the *standard deviation technique* or the *percentile rank technique*. When the mean is used to establish the level of performance, the standard deviation technique is used to create the GAS. Evette has a problem with submitting assignments (baseline mean = 40%). A GAS rating of 0 = 40% predicts no change in the level of assignment submission during the intervention phase. Evette's classroom peers submit assignments, on average, 90% of the time with a standard deviation (SD) of 5; that is, the majority of students submit their assignments between 85% and 95% of the time. A +2 GAS rating of 1 SD below the class mean (85%) was set as a realistic goal for Evette. A GAS rating of −2 reflects the worst possible scenario for submitting assignments. See Figure 8.12 for Evette's GAS based on the SD technique.

Figure 8.12   Goal-Attainment Scale for Evaluating Evette's Assignment Submission Using the Standard Deviation Technique

−2	−1	0	+1	+2
0	>0 to <40%	40%	>40% to <85%	>85%

When the median is used to establish the level of performance, the percentile rank technique is used to develop the GAS. Consider Sundra, who displays a high rate of bullying behavior. Bullying behavior is defined as making negative comments to others. The problem is so severe that collection of baseline data was limited to one day because of the urgent need for an intervention. Sundra's baseline score of 16 incidents per day is used as the GAS rating of 0.

The frequency of bullying behavior for all students in the class that day ranged from 0–16. Frequencies are ranked in order from smallest to largest to identify the percentiles associated with specific scores: 25th percentile = 0, 50th percentile = 2, and 75th percentile = 4. Sundra's bullying score was greater than the scores of 99% of the students in her class. Her ultimate long-term goal is acknowledged to be 0 incidents of negative comments per day, but a more realistic +2 GAS rating is set for Sundra at the 75th percentile of the class (4 times per day) as a short-term goal. Since the problem is already severe, a frequency of more than 16 incidents per day is rated −1. The −2 rating is quantitatively the same, but a qualitative component ("plus other bullying behaviors") is added. See Figure 8.13 for Sundra's GAS based on the percentile rank technique.

Figure 8.13   Goal-Attainment Scale for Evaluating Sundra's Bullying Behavior Using the Percentile Rank Technique

−2	−1	0	+1	+2
>16 negative comments; plus other bullying behaviors	>16	16	<16 to >4	4

Trend. Similar to the procedure for creating a GAS for level of performance, a trend-based GAS is based on the availability of norms for comparison. Most often, an upward trend is associated with learning, and the evaluator is interested in an increase in the rate of change. Construction of the GAS begins with a rating of 0 representing the target student's baseline rate of change. When no norms are available, the GAS is constructed using the percent of change technique. Sean's rate of improvement for oral reading fluency during baseline is one word per minute per week. The +2 GAS rating is calculated by adding 50% of the baseline rate of change to the baseline rate of change (1 + .5 = 1.5).

When norms are available, the GAS is developed using the rate of change or the benchmark technique. The *rate of change technique* is used when the goal specifies a short-term rate of improvement. The student's long-term progress will parallel that of peers, but there is no expectation that the student will attain the same level of performance. For example, norms indicate that, on average, students' oral reading fluency (ORF) improves by two words per minute per week. So the +2 GAS rating is 2, which is an improvement over the student's baseline rate of improvement (.75). See Figure 8.14 for a GAS developed using the rate of change technique.

Figure 8.14   Goal-Attainment Scale for Evaluating Improvement in ORF Using the Rate of Change Technique

	−2	−1	0	+1	+2
Rate of weekly improvement	0	>0 to <.75	.75 wpm	>.75 to >2	2 wpm

The *benchmark technique* uses fall, winter, and spring norms to determine long-term performance criteria. The expectation is that the student will earn scores similar to those of peers during the next CBM administration. Once again, construction of the scale begins with the 0 column. The final data point in the target student's baseline (30) is used to anchor the 0 rating. The rating of 0 is calculated by multiplying the number of weeks remaining before the next CBM administration by the baseline rate of change and adding the anchor score (4 weeks × .75 rate of change + 30 = 33). The anchor score (30) represents no change in the four-week period and is rated −2.

Assume, for example, that last year's norms are used to predict that current students will attain an oral reading fluency benchmark score of 55 (50th percentile) in the upcoming winter assessment. A score of 55 wcpm is unrealistic for the target student; a more realistic goal is to increase the ORF to the 25th percentile (38 wcpm). Figure 8.15 is an example of a GAS constructed using the benchmark technique.

Figure 8.15   Goal-Attainment Scale for Evaluating ORF Using the Benchmark Technique

	−2	−1	0	+1	+2
Winter benchmark goals in four weeks in wcpm	≤30	>30 to <33	33	>30 to <38	38

CHOOSING EVALUATION METHODS AND JUDGING OUTCOMES

This chapter offers a set of guidelines selected for their ease and efficiency of use for analyzing case study outcomes. However, other guidelines considered to be more relevant to specific settings can be adopted. Whatever methods are chosen, it is important for all data analysts to apply a consistent decision frame so that users of the data will have clear reference points for understanding results. Once criteria are chosen, they must be applied whenever the impact of an intervention is evaluated.

Evaluation methods are chosen based on the characteristics of the data and the goals of the case study. Multiple evaluation methods should be used for every case study so that methodological limitations can be overcome and to verify judgments of the results. Table 8.1 provides a summary of evaluation methods that can be used as a selection guide.

Table 8.1   Evaluation Methods

Goal	Visual Analysis	Descriptive Statistics	Magnitude of Change	Quality of Change GAS Development Technique
Variability/ Stability	Variability/ Stability	Standard Deviation	ES_{var}	Absolute Score Percent of Change
Level	Increase Decrease Maintain	Mean/ Median Difference	d-index Percent of Nonoverlapping Data Points	No Norms • Percent of Change • Absolute Score • Extreme Data Point Norms • Mean • Standard Deviation • Median • Percentile Rank
Trend	Slant Direction	Rate of Change	g-index	No norms • Percent of change Norms • Rate of change • Benchmark

Evaluation of outcome data alone is insufficient to ensure that the case study is responsible for the results of an intervention. A measure of case study fidelity is needed to ascertain whether the cause of the problem has been correctly identified and remedied as intended. Adherence to the case study model increases the potential for successful problem solving. Evaluation of case study fidelity is particularly important when expected improvement is not reflected in actual outcomes. Measures of intervention integrity are also needed to determine the degree to which the intervention was implemented as planned.

It is not uncommon for results to appear incongruent at first glance. In-depth analysis of the data increases the value and quality of the interpretation. See Table 8.2 for examples of case study interpretation incorporating case study fidelity, goals, intervention integrity, and outcome data. Note that the goal of the case study (i.e., change in data variability, level, or trend) is the organizing element. This format is useful for interpreting and comparing data patterns across multiple case studies.

In Table 8.2, cases 2, 3, 7, 10, and 11 suffer from poor case study fidelity, preventing valid interpretation of results. For example, the lack of responsiveness to intervention may be due to the failure to correctly identify the underlying problem, failure to develop the most appropriate intervention, or some other methodological problem. When outcome data suggest that improvement has occurred in a case study implemented with poor fidelity, it is impossible to know whether the outcome is a product of the case study or another factor. It is important to reemphasize that this model represents a "rule-in" procedure to identify what works to remedy a problem, not a "rule-out" effort to learn what doesn't work. Therefore, hypothesis testing continues until the actual cause of the problem and appropriate interventions are identified. Case study fidelity is discussed in detail in Chapter 10.

Cases 3, 7, 8, and 12 in Table 8.2 are characterized by poor intervention integrity. Although the cause of the problem may have been detected through an appropriate case study procedure, the absence of intervention integrity makes it impossible to link changes in the target behavior to the intervention.

It is always desirable to document the quality of success achieved in all case studies. GAS and statistics expressing the magnitude of change are useful for evaluating the quality and quantity of change. However, GAS ratings must be interpreted with caution. Since GAS also monitors the adequacy of predictions for goal attainment, data interpretation will be affected by patterns of inadequate predictions across cases, such as under- or overestimation of expected levels of change. For example, in Table 8.2, cases 1, 6, and 14 display GAS scores that are inconsistent with the amount of change indicated by the effect size. Consistent underestimation of predicted outcomes could result in high GAS scores (+2) but may not reflect a strong impact of the intervention on the target behavior. Similarly, consistent

Table 8.2   Case Study Interpretation Data

Case	Case Study Fidelity	Goal of Intervention	Intervention Integrity	Magnitude of Change	GAS	Evaluation
		Stabilize Variable Data		ES_{var}		Small = .02 Moderate = .15 Large = .35
1	5/5		95%	$ES_{var} = 2.01$	0	Overestimated goal
2	3/5		95%	$ES_{var} = .01$	0	May be incorrect target; check hypothesis
3	2/5		40%	$ES_{var} = 1.35$	+2	Change may be due to an external factor, not case study or intervention
4	5/5		100%	$ES_{var} = .17$	+1	Effective intervention for difficult problem or need to modify intervention
5	4/5		98%	$ES_{var} = 3.29$	+2	Effective intervention
		Change Level	ES (*d*-index) PND			ES (*d*-index) • Small = .2 • Moderate = .5 • Large = .8 PND • Ineffective = 49% • Questionably Effective = 50%–69% • Moderately Effective = 70%–90% • Highly Effective = 90%

Case	Case Study Fidelity	Goal of Intervention	Intervention Integrity	Magnitude of Change	GAS	Evaluation
6	4/5	Decrease	97%	ES = .2 PND = 54%	+2	Underestimated goal
7	2/5	Decrease	65%	ES = 3.1 PND = 70%	+1	Change may be due to an external factor, not case study or intervention
8	5/5	Increase	0	ES = .1 PND = 40%	1	Failure to implement intervention; target behavior deteriorated
9	5/5	Decrease	89%	ES = 1.5 PND = 95%	+2	Effective intervention
10	2/5	Increase	100%	ES = .4 PND = 61%	0	Inappropriate target; check hypothesis
		Improve Trend		ES (g-index)		positive g-index = improvement negative g-index = deterioration
11	3/5	Increase	91%	ES = .02	0	Inappropriate target; check hypothesis
12	5/5	Increase	50%	ES = .58	−2	Failure to implement intervention with integrity; target behavior deteriorated
13	4/5	Decrease	90%	ES = +.35	+1	Effective intervention
14	5/5	Increase	100%	ES = +.99	0	Overestimated goal
15	5/5	Increase	100%	ES = +1.77	+2	Effective intervention

overestimation of expected change in the target behavior would result in low GAS scores (−2) but may be a reflection of inappropriate goals rather than actual failure to accomplish the goals.

SUMMARY

Several techniques for evaluating the effectiveness of interventions were presented in this chapter, including those analyzing patterns in the data, magnitude of change, and the quality of performance. The data interpretation methods proposed in this chapter should be employed in a holistic manner, taking into consideration visual analysis, historical information, and the nature of the referral question. In this way, the case study will be anchored in a meaningful context that will aid in decision making. Finally, interpretations of case study results should take into consideration the fidelity with which the process was applied as well as the integrity of interventions, so that valid judgments can be made.

9

Using the Case Study to Determine Special Education Eligibility

Special education eligibility decisions traditionally have depended on the categorization of students according to their individual characteristics (e.g., ability measured using an individual IQ test; measured achievement using a published, norm-referenced measure; and, for behavior, type, and severity of problems). In particular, the IQ score has been treated as an index of what could be expected of a student, and, in the case of specific learning disabilities (SLD), it served as a standard for establishing the "significant discrepancy" that has been a consistent feature of SLD definitions over the past several decades. Judgments about service delivery options for identified students focused on the least restrictive environment (LRE), as required by law, but were largely the result of a "rule-out" procedure establishing the inadequacy of student performance in a less restrictive environment, such as the general education classroom. Individualized education plans (IEPs) were developed after decisions about special education eligibility were made, and they were built around the identified deficit. Long- and short-term goals and objectives in the IEP were set on the basis of expert opinions about reasonable expectations for rates of growth. Instructional and intervention methods for accomplishing goals were rarely included in IEPs, and decisions about the success of special education services made at annual reviews were typically not based on progress-monitoring data gathered on a frequent basis during the intervention.

These features of traditional eligibility determination have been criticized by many experts, especially in recent years, when legislative mandates have placed greater emphasis on accountability for student outcomes. Meta-analytic research conducted by Kavale and Forness (1999) made it painfully clear that special education, in itself, offers no guarantee of improved performance; indeed, their research suggested that some students would have demonstrated better outcomes had they not been placed in special education programs. Moreover, the No Child Left Behind Act directs schools to document "adequate yearly progress" for all students, including those with disabilities, and many have been unable to do so (U.S. Department of Education, 2006).

Near-universal agreement on the shortcomings of existing disability identification and progress-monitoring practices led the U.S. Congress to make significant changes in the Individuals with Disabilities Education Act of 2004 (IDEA), emphasizing the importance of adequate instruction and early intervention and modifying procedures for identifying children with SLDs. Although the RTI approach is cited in the law as an acceptable method for identifying only SLDs, its assessment and intervention provisions offer significant advantages for identifying and addressing the needs of children with a variety of disabilities.

This chapter discusses the use of the case study—in context of the RTI process—to make special education eligibility decisions consistent with provisions of the revised law. Two major principles frame the content of this chapter: First, there is a distinction between what disabilities are and how the law requires practitioners to identify them for funding entitlement; and second, special education eligibility determination is secondary to the goal of identifying effective interventions.

DISABILITY VERSUS ELIGIBILITY DETERMINATION

The law and its regulations are essentially mechanisms through which funding entitlement is established; they are not repositories of scientifically derived knowledge about the nature and characteristics of disability conditions. The controversy over the exclusion of attention deficit hyperactivity disorder (ADHD) from the disability categories enumerated in IDEA reflects this distinction. Although ADHD is not included as a disability category eligible for funding under IDEA, this does not mean that ADHD does not exist; rather, policymakers determined that, for various reasons it should not be included as a separate category. Similarly, while there is no doubt that emotional disturbance (ED—a disability category under IDEA) occurs, it is not a unitary phenomenon: ED appears in many disorders, including schizophrenia, bipolar disorder, depression, and anxiety disorders, as long as they adversely affect educational performance. The "disconnect" between definitions of disabilities under IDEA and definitions derived from empirical and clinical sources is nowhere more clearly revealed than in the bewilderment of parents who have been advised by a physician that a child has a particular disabling condition while the school asserts that the child is ineligible for special education services.

Federal regulations explicitly cite "inadequate instruction" in reading and math as exclusionary criteria for any disability category (see Box 9.1). Historically, the requirement for adequate instruction has been difficult to interpret or apply, but the RTI model presents a means for doing so.

Box 9.1   Federal Regulations Governing Evaluation Procedures for All Disability Categories

(b) Special rule for eligibility determination. A child must not be determined to be a child with a disability under this part—

    (1) If the determinant factor for that determination is—

        (i) Lack of appropriate instruction in reading, including the essential components of reading instruction (as defined in section 1208(3) of the ESEA);

        (ii) Lack of appropriate instruction in math; or

        (iii) Limited English proficiency; and

    (2) If the child does not otherwise meet the eligibility criteria under §300.8(a).

Source: 20 U.S.C. 1414(b) *et seq.* §300.306 Determination of eligibility

---

Universal screening at Tier 1, where evidenced-based instruction is delivered to all students, can reveal whether students are progressing at an adequate rate. The addition of Tier 2 supplemental, targeted intervention for students who are at risk represents a further refinement of instruction. Students who fail to display an appropriate rate of growth and level of performance (i.e., those who are not responsive to either Tiers 1 or 2) are appropriate candidates for the Tier 3 case study, where the need for the specialized, intensive resources of special education can be demonstrated. More specifically, when the case study has confirmed the need for a high-intensity intervention, and the ineffectiveness of low- to moderate-intensity interventions has been established through progress monitoring, it may be concluded that appropriate instruction in reading and math was provided, thus ruling this factor out as an explanation for the child's problems (Vaughn & Fuchs,

2003). Of course, this assumes that the RTI process has been implemented with fidelity and that the "intervention" component of the process consisted of evidence-based practices implemented with integrity.

The diagnosis of some disabilities, such as sensory and orthopedic impairments, is linked closely and unambiguously to eligibility for special education and related services. Among the so-called "high-incidence" disabilities, however, definitive evidence of a disorder and its adverse effect on learning may not be so readily apparent. These categories of disability—SLD, (mild) mental retardation, and emotional disturbance—typically pose greater challenges to identification efforts, and they are particularly well suited to identification through the RTI process. For these disabilities in particular, the application of RTI and the case study process enables schools to "rule in" appropriate interventions in general education classrooms, build intervention plans around practices found to be effective, set goals based on research-based standards for performance, routinely and systematically monitor progress toward goals, and make decisions based on objective data that are directly descriptive of relevant academic and behavioral skills. These features of RTI underscore its relevance to the second principle framing this chapter, namely that the establishment of special education eligibility is secondary to the goal of developing an effective intervention.

RESPONSIVENESS VERSUS RESISTANCE

Christ, Burns, and Ysseldyke (2005) describe a "responsiveness" versus "resistance" focus in RTI models, wherein a child's resistance (i.e., failure to respond) to intervention is considered by some to be evidence for the existence of a within-child disability. Interventions are implemented in general education settings, and their ineffectiveness is documented through progress monitoring measures; evaluation is focused on conditions that do not work rather than conditions supporting effective intervention. The danger of this approach lies in its implicit endorsement of the notion that, for some children, the search for an effective intervention is doomed to failure. Consequently, special education "becomes" an intervention, and attempts to identify an appropriate intervention are pursued only half-heartedly or abandoned altogether. Ultimately, this approach differs little from traditional prereferral intervention practices and suffers from the same limitations described in Chapter 1 of this text.

In contrast, a "responsiveness" focus seeks first to identify conditions supporting effective learning and then determine how best those conditions can be created and maintained. Among the conditions supporting learning that might be identified in a case study are additional practice opportunities, modeling and prompting, and response contingencies—all of which may vary in frequency, intensity, and duration, as discussed in

Chapter 7. In some cases, the resources of general education are adequate (i.e., low- to moderate-intensity interventions); in others, special education and related services are needed (i.e., high-intensity interventions). The responsiveness model places instruction and intervention before diagnosis, and diagnosis follows a determination of the resources needed to implement an intervention whose effectiveness has been confirmed (Christ, Burns, & Ysseldyke, 2005). In this approach, which is employed in this text, a disability is suspected when the case study has revealed the need for a high-intensity intervention, and the eligibility evaluation includes a review of the circumstances and services necessary for its successful delivery.

As the reader no doubt is aware, changes in federal law and regulations have not necessarily eliminated problems with traditional eligibility determination methods; in fact, several new issues have arisen regarding the adequacy of the RTI model. Issues cited by critics include the limited range of academic skills and age groups for which an adequate research base has been established. Specifically, RTI research has concentrated on the academic (rather than behavioral) performance problems of students in the elementary grades (rather than middle school and secondary school), with emphasis on learning disabilities and the domain of reading (rather than math and other academic skill areas). It is encouraging to note that increased attention is being paid to these issues in the current RTI research.

USING CASE STUDY INFORMATION FOR SPECIAL EDUCATION ELIGIBILITY DETERMINATION

Figure 9.1 portrays Tier 3 as a two-phase process; the first phase, comprising the Tier 3a case study, is consistent with the requirement for comprehensive evaluation of all areas related to a suspected disability. Assessment seeks to pinpoint actual skill levels, determine the degree of discrepancy from expected performance, and measure the effects of brief experimental interventions for academic problems. Similarly, behavioral observation and interviews are used at Tier 3a to identify factors that may be contributing to behavior problems, and hypothesis testing lays the foundation for effective intervention. The RTI process delivers interventions of increasingly greater intensity until meaningful improvement is observed, providing a detailed framework for special education services as outlined in the IEP. This "increasing intensity" progression of intervention and assessment "defines and clarifies the least restrictive environment prior to the need for classification. Given adequate technical adequacy, increasing- and decreasing-intensity designs can be used as decision aids, to determine the least intrusive and most efficient and effective strategies" (Barnett, Daly, Jones, & Lentz, 2004, p. 76). The routine administration of

Figure 9.1   Special Education Eligibility Determination at Tier 3b

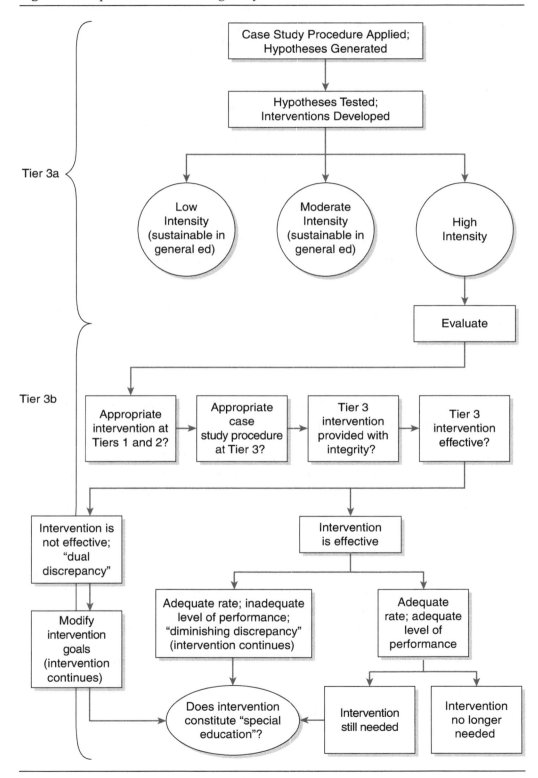

progress monitoring measures allows educators to assess children's progress over time (rather than during one testing event), increasing confidence in judgments about a student's progress and continued need for intervention, and reducing the bias that has characterized decision making in the past.

Assuming that the case study has determined that a high-intensity intervention is needed, the decision-making sequence moves to Tier 3b, where four questions are addressed: (1) Was appropriate instruction provided at Tiers 1 and 2? (2) Was the case study conducted with fidelity at Tier 3? (3) Were Tier 3 interventions provided with integrity? And (4) was the Tier 3 intervention effective? The first and third questions must be answered affirmatively in order to rule out the exclusionary criterion that applies to all disability categories; namely, that a lack of appropriate instruction is responsible for the child's continued poor performance. The second question, having to do with the adequacy and appropriateness of the case study, speaks to the need for a "comprehensive evaluation in all areas related to the suspected disability" as well as the validity of decisions about intervention outcomes. The fourth question, addressing the effectiveness of the high-intensity, Tier 3 intervention, has two possible answers, representing two general-intervention outcomes.

First, the intervention was not effective; that is, a "dual discrepancy" continues to exist, reflected in the intervention's failure to eliminate the discrepancy between actual and expected levels of performance as well as between actual and expected rates of growth. In this case, the finding of a dual discrepancy does not end the problem-solving process, although it would serve as the basis for suspecting a disability and initiating the legally mandated identification process, including required timelines for completing it. Indeed, the construct of *dual discrepancy*, which was discussed earlier in this text, has been found to reliably distinguish between low-achieving students (deemed "nonresponders"), and those whose deficits are more severe and wide ranging (Speece & Case, 2001). Assuming that other preconditions have been met—that appropriate instruction and intervention were provided at Tiers 1 and 2, that the Tier 3 case study was conducted properly, and that the resulting Tier 3 intervention was implemented with integrity—it is likely that the intervention did not enable the child to attain the prescribed goal because the goal itself was poorly matched to the child's capacity to perform, and the goal should therefore be modified. While "lowering goals" is not ordinarily an acceptable solution to the problem of inappropriate interventions, the circumstance under consideration is one in which even the most intensive level of appropriate intervention, tailored to the child's unique needs on the basis of tested hypotheses, has not yielded satisfactory results.

Inspection of the trend in progress-monitoring data would indicate that the current rate of progress cannot close the gap between the child's performance and expected levels of performance. Note that this recommendation to modify (i.e., reduce or change emphasis of) intervention goals differs from the basis on which a modification of goals has been recommended by others. Whereas some experts advise that intervention goals be reduced when problem identification/certification reveals a significant discrepancy between the student's current and expected performance before intervention (see Chapter 4), the procedure described herein recommends that goals be modified only when high-quality intervention has failed to yield satisfactory progress toward original goals. For example, Burns and Gibbons (2008) advise that, when testing reveals an instructional level that is two or more years below current grade placement, intervention goals should be set in materials one year above the instructional level, thereby modifying the level of performance expected as a result of intervention. In contrast, the case study model recommends that expected performance levels, or goals, be modified only when a high-quality, high-intensity intervention—implemented with integrity as the result of a valid case study—fails to yield performance consistent with initial expectations. Under these circumstances, the need to adjust goals (and use corresponding instructional and progress-monitoring materials that differ from those used with grade-level peers) might itself be considered evidence of the "specially designed instruction" that constitutes special education. Consistent with this perspective, the final hypothesis explaining academic problems that is considered in the formulation offered by Daly, Witt, Martens, and Dool (1997) (see Chapter 7) is that instructional demands are too difficult for the target student. The rationale for considering this hypothesis only after the other four hypotheses have been explored (*doesn't want to do it; hasn't had enough practice; hasn't had enough help;* and *hasn't had to do it this way before*) is that its acceptance implies that the only intervention likely to be effective is one in which goal modifications (i.e., lowering expectations) will be necessary.

The second possible outcome is that the intervention was effective; that is, the dual discrepancy was eliminated, and progress monitoring results reveal adequate levels of performance (i.e., a score consistent with expected levels of performance) and/or an adequate rate of growth (i.e., a rate of growth, or slope of trend line, consistent with expected growth rates). If the intervention resulted in an adequate level of performance, and there is no need for continued intervention, then special education is not appropriate. However, if continued intervention is deemed necessary to maintain the student's satisfactory performance, decision makers would analyze the needed intervention to determine whether it qualifies as "special education," and, if so, develop an IEP establishing the child's entitlement to the intervention using special education resources. If the intervention is found to be "promising"—that is, it resulted in a satisfactory rate of growth (but not an adequate level of performance, as yet)—the outcome, termed a *diminishing discrepancy,* would require decision makers to determine first whether the intervention qualifies as "special education," and then how, and under what conditions, the intervention should be maintained in order to preserve the rate of growth that will ultimately lead to a satisfactory level of performance. The team would determine either that the continuing intervention does not constitute "special education," or that it should be continued in the form of (anticipated) "short duration" special education, with entitlement certified in the form of an IEP.

RTI AND SPECIFIC LEARNING DISABILITIES

The RTI model is cited specifically in IDEA 2004 and federal regulations as an alternative method for determining special education eligibility for children with specific learning disabilities (see Box 9.2). Consistent with the first principle framing this chapter, IDEA's definition of a specific learning disability (see Box 9.3) should not be viewed as a state-of-the-art, evidence-based description summarizing what is known about the phenomenon of "learning disability." This point is pertinent to the question of what should be included in an evaluation for the purpose of SLD identification, and how such an evaluation should be conducted.

Experts disagree about whether there is a need to assess "basic psychological processes," since this phrase is included in the definition of specific learning disabilities. Some argue that tests of cognitive ability have evolved well beyond an assessment of g (general intelligence), and are useful in establishing the existence of a disability, reflected in differences in processing skill. Further, they express concern about the assumption that, when instructional explanations for children's problems have been eliminated (at Tiers 1 and 2), a disability is inferred, rather than affirmed, in the course of assessment (Kavale & Flanagan, 2007), and that RTI-based definitions of SLD (i.e., lack of responsiveness to intervention in general education) may compromise the integrity of the construct of SLD, threatening its standing as a funded disability category (Fuchs, Mock, Morgan, & Young, 2003). Others (Reschly, 2005a) argue that the IDEA definition of learning disabilities does not require the assessment of psychological processes and that, even if it did, such assessment would be invalid because research support for this approach to SLD identification and remediation is lacking.

Box 9.2   **Federal Regulations Governing Evaluation Procedures for Specific Learning Disabilities**

§ 300.307 Specific learning disabilities

(a) General. A State must adopt, consistent with § 300.309, criteria for determining whether a child has a specific learning disability as defined in § 30.308 (c) (10). In addition, the criteria adopted by the State—

(1) Must not require the use of a severe discrepancy between intellectual ability and achievement for determining whether a child has a specific learning disability, as defined in § 300.8 (c) (10);

(Continued)

(Continued)

    (2) Must permit the use of a process based on the child's response to scientific, research-based intervention; and

    (3) May permit the use of other alternative research-based procedures for determining whether a child has a specific learning disability, as defined in § 300.8 (c) (10).

Source: 20 U.S.C. 1221e-3; 1401(30); 1414(b)(6)

Since there is still no generally accepted, empirically derived definition of a learning disability, it would be premature to proclaim a "best-practice" standard for evaluation and diagnosis. Indeed, differences of opinion about the nature and evaluation of SLD are to be expected, and research to resolve these differences should be encouraged. For example, recent research suggests that *nonresponsiveness* is associated with neurophysiological processes implicated in reading; this offers a promising evidentiary link between psychological processing and the use of RTI procedures for SLD diagnosis (Simos, Fletcher, Sarkari, Billingsley, Denton, & Papanicolaou, 2007). In the meantime, practitioners are faced with the task of conducting evaluations and certifying special education eligibility using methods that are consistent with existing statutory (IDEA) and regulatory (Code of Federal Regulations) standards.

Box 9.3   Definition of Specific Learning Disability

The term "specific learning disability" means a disorder in one or more of the basic psychological processes involved in understanding or in using language, spoken or written, which disorder may manifest itself in the imperfect ability to listen, think, speak, read, write, spell, or do mathematical calculations.

    Such term includes such conditions as perceptual disabilities, brain injury, minimal brain dysfunction, dyslexia, and developmental aphasia.

    Such term does not include a learning problem that is primarily the result of visual, hearing, or motor disabilities, of mental retardation, of emotional disturbance, or of environmental, cultural, or economic disadvantage.

Source: 20 U.S.C. §1401 (30)

Table 9.1 presents language from federal regulations, and corresponding information obtained through the RTI process, that may be useful in documenting eligibility for special education services for a SLD.

Table 9.1   Regulations for SLD Identification and Relevant Elements of RTI and Case Study

Federal Regulation: Determining the Existence of a Specific Learning Disability (§ 300.309) 20 U.S.C. 1221e-3; 1401(30); 1414(b)(6)	*Relevant Elements of Response to Intervention and Case Study*

(1) The child does not achieve adequately for the child's age or to meet State-approved grade-level standards in one or more of the following areas, when provided with learning experiences and instruction appropriate for the child's age or State-approved grade-level standards:
 	
  (i) Oral expression
  (ii) Listening comprehension
  (iii) Written expression
  (iv) Basic reading skill
  (v) Reading fluency skills
  (vi) Reading comprehension
  (vii) Mathematics calculation
  (viii) Mathematics problem solving
	(1) Tier 1 universal screening results demonstrating satisfactory achievement (score level) and growth (slope of trend line connecting fall, winter, and spring data points) for peers. This demonstrates that appropriate learning experiences and instruction were provided.
	
	Tier 1 universal screening (and strategic monitoring) results demonstrating discrepancy between target student's performance and local and/or national norms and benchmarks.
	
	Sample Measures:
	
	  (iii) Written expression: CBM writing sample
	  (iv) Basic reading skill: DIBELS early literacy measures; CBM oral reading fluency
	  (v) Reading fluency skills: CBM oral reading fluency
	  (vi) Reading comprehension: DIBELS retell fluency; CBM Maze
	  (vii) Mathematics calculation: CBM math computation
	  (viii) Mathematics problem solving: CBM math concepts and applications; CBM tests of early numeracy

(2) (i) The child does not make sufficient progress to meet age or State-approved grade-level standards in one or more of the areas identified in paragraph	(i) Tier 1 strategic-monitoring results demonstrating student's inadequate rate of growth despite high quality, research-based instruction in general education;

(Continued)

Table 9.1 (Continued)

Federal Regulation: Determining the Existence of a Specific Learning Disability (§ 300.309) 20 U.S.C. 1221e-3; 1401(30); 1414(b)(6)	*Relevant Elements of Response to Intervention and Case Study*
(a) (1) of this section when using a process based on the child's response to scientific, research-based intervention	Tier 2 progress-monitoring results demonstrating student's inadequate score level and rate of growth despite research-based, supplemental, targeted intervention in general education. At Tier 3b, information about nature of intervention and progress-monitoring results demonstrating student's adequate score level and rate of growth, but only with specialized, high-intensity intervention planned and evaluated using case study procedures; or inadequate score level or inadequate rate of growth despite research-based, individualized intervention planned on the basis of case study findings.
(b) To ensure that underachievement of a child suspected of having a specific learning disability is not due to lack of appropriate instruction in reading or math, the group must consider, as part of the evaluation described in § 300.304 through 300.306: Data that demonstrate that prior to, or as a part of, the referral process, the child was provided appropriate instruction in regular education settings, delivered by qualified personnel; and Data-based documentation of repeated assessments of achievement at reasonable intervals, reflecting formal assessment of student progress during instruction, which was provided to the child's parents.	(b) (1) As above (universal screening results at Tier 1 and progress monitoring results of Tier 2 intervention in general education). (2) Records of universal screening (and strategic monitoring) conducted at Tier 1; graphs depicting progress monitoring conducted at Tiers 2 and 3.

DECISION MAKING IN ELIGIBILITY DETERMINATION

Because of the high-stakes nature of decisions about eligibility for special education, care must be taken to ensure the validity of decision-making practices and rules. Decisions resulting from RTI implementation have greater validity when the psychometric properties of the rules and criteria for decision making are reliable and valid (Fletcher, Lyon, Fuchs, & Barnes, 2007), and the problem-solving process is applied in a consistent manner. Macmann and colleagues (1996) defined reliable and valid decisions as those based on evidence of (1) a discrepancy between the critical behaviors of the target student and peers, (2) the functional, empirical relationship between the target behavior and intervention, (3) intervention integrity, and (4) specification of measurable outcomes. To this list, Barnett and colleagues (2007) added (5) use of technically adequate decision rules, and (6) application of intervention intensity criteria. Issues of technical adequacy for decision making can be distilled to three basic preconditions, depicted at the outset of Tier 3b (see Figure 9.1) for determining special education eligibility: (1) the requirement for appropriate, high-intensity intervention, (2) evidence of intervention integrity, and (3) evidence of case study fidelity.

Appropriate, high intensity intervention. Historically, prereferral intervention or problem-solving teams have been established to determine the best and most appropriate interventions for struggling students. As noted in Chapter 1, however, collaborative problem-solving efforts have not been without their challenges. An important concern relates to errors in identifying the cause of problems. Types of errors in identifying the cause of the problem include issues of (1) availability, (2) anchoring, and (3) insufficient adjustment (Barnett et al., 2007; Kahneman, 2003).

Availability errors occur when diagnoses and interventions are limited to an easy-to-find and implement list of options. Barnett and colleagues (2007) recommend that this type of error be minimized by choosing interventions that have a solid evidence base linking dependent (target behavior) and independent (intervention) variables.

Anchoring errors occur when a set of strategies becomes the sole source from which interventions are selected. This strategy of intervention selection is more closely associated with Tier 2 of the RTI process, in that methods are selected from a preestablished list of scientifically validated interventions to be implemented with groups of students who show similar deficiencies. However, interventions that have resulted in success for some children may or may not have relevance to the cause of the problem for the target student.

Errors of insufficient adjustment can be recast into the issue of biased decision making, which has already been discussed at length in previous chapters. Biased decision making is overcome through problem-solving procedures that are thorough and systematic and that employ decision rules for analyzing data. The Tier 3 case study, when conducted as recommended in this text, overcomes the problems of availability, anchoring, and insufficient adjustment. Case study fidelity, or adherence to procedures for conducting case studies, increases the likelihood of accuracy in identifying the cause of the problem and linking it to an effective intervention.

Special education services are provided to students who can be successful in academic settings only with the support of high-intensity interventions. Data from the Tier 3 case study are used to verify the need for high-intensity services, which are defined as those that are costly for the school district to provide due to their demands on time, effort, or resources. Group size and duration of intervention have been investigated as factors to consider for estimating cost effectiveness (Vaughn, Wanzek, Linan-Thompson, & Murray, 2007). A 1:1 ratio of change agents to students was found to result in stronger effects than ratios characteristic of small groups (two to eight students). However, duration of the intervention was not found to be an adequate predictor of interventions effects or cost. Although additional research is needed in this area, the variables that are currently regarded as a basis for estimating intervention costs include group size and time as well as resources needed for implementation.

A qualitative method has been configured from criteria proposed by Barnett and colleagues (2007) to determine whether intervention cost meets the "high-intensity" criterion for special education eligibility. Intervention teams determine the cost of the intervention by reviewing the time, effort, and resources needed for implementation. Table 9.2 offers a simple intervention intensity guide that could be used for this purpose.

Intervention integrity. Obviously, if high-intensity interventions are not delivered as designed, data resulting from their implementation will be invalid and cannot be used as evidence of the need for special education services. The logic underlying the importance of intervention integrity is exemplified in Table 9.3, where it is assumed that cases were conducted with a high level of case study fidelity, so there can be confidence that a credible reason for the problem has been identified along with a related set of empirically validated interventions. No conclusions can be drawn about the impact of the intervention on students 2 and 3 because the intervention was not delivered as intended. Although the high-intensity intervention for Student 3 was implemented with integrity, the possibility that the moderate-intensity intervention would have been adequate cannot be ruled out because that option was not offered as intended.

It is only in the cases of students 1 and 4 that there can be confidence that all interventions were implemented as planned. For student 1, positive results were obtained with a moderate level of intervention intensity, so the student would not require special education support. Results for student 4 indicate that a high-intensity intervention will be needed for successful performance; therefore, special education services are needed.

Table 9.2   Intervention Intensity Guide

Guiding Questions	Moderate Intensity	High Intensity
Can intervention implementation be embedded in the typical classroom routine?	Yes	No
Additional instructional or practice activities of less than one hour per week		
Provision of feedback/contingencies		
Can teacher planning and management be completed in less than one hour per week?	Yes	No
Modification of tasks or instructional formats		
Communication with stakeholders (e.g., parents)		
Progress-monitoring activities (e.g., assessment, graphing)		
Consultation and meetings between professionals		
Does the intervention require additional resources or costs?	No	Yes
Materials and tangible resources; modified curriculum		
Highly qualified providers (e.g., certified educators, paraprofessionals)		
Training for implementation		

Table 9.3   Decision Making Based on Integrity of Moderate- and High-Intensity Interventions

Student	Integrity of High-Intensity Intervention	Results of High-Intensity Intervention	Integrity of Moderate-Intensity Intervention	Results of Moderate-Intensity Intervention
1	100%	Positive	100%	Positive
2	50%	Positive	50%	Positive
3	100%	Positive	50%	Negative
4	100%	Positive	100%	Negative

Case study fidelity. To illustrate the importance of case study fidelity in special education decision making, consider the hypothetical fourth-grade students included in Table 9.4. Each has been the subject of a Tier 3a case study. Assume that interventions were implemented with 100% integrity for all students. Positive outcomes were obtained for students 1 and 3; however, only in the case of student 1 can there be reasonable confidence that the outcome was indeed a result of accurate identification of the cause of the problem. Poor case study fidelity leaves the impact question unanswered for student 3 because there is no way to know if results were due to the problem-solving effort or to some other unknown factor. Negative outcomes occurred for students 2 and 4. The case of student 4 requires more investigation and hypothesis testing so that confidence in the accuracy of decisions about the cause of problems can be increased.

Table 9.4   Case Study Fidelity and Judgments About Outcomes

Student	Case Study Fidelity	Intervention Results
1	100%	Positive Results
2	100%	Negative Results
3	50%	Positive Results
4	50%	Negative Results

TECHNICAL ADEQUACY OF DECISION-MAKING PRACTICES

Measurement issues. Decisions about special education eligibility in the context of the RTI model must be based on data and practices that are both reliable and valid (Barnett et al., 2007). Reliability is demonstrated through consistency of administration, scoring, and interpretation of appropriate instruments and procedures. Problems with procedural reliability result in lower effect sizes (Barnett et al., 2007; Cohen, 1988), and the ethical propriety of decision-making practices is questionable if decisions are made as if interventions were carried out as planned (Barnett et al., 2007; Gresham, 2004).

Several aspects of the case study approach increase confidence in the reliability and validity of decision-making practices. Generally, the greater the amount of evidence informing eligibility decisions, the greater the reliability and validity of the decisions (Fletcher, Lyon, Fuchs, & Barnes, 2007). The performance of students receiving interventions is monitored with brief assessments administered repeatedly over time, and reliability increases with the frequency of administration. If the case study is conducted with fidelity, the cause of the problem will have been appropriately investigated, and a functional (causal) link between independent and dependent variables will have been established. Verification of intervention integrity is a measure of reliability and validity; it ensures that the outcome of problem-solving effort is actually a result of the intervention and not another unidentified factor.

Validity research shows that RTI models lead to enhanced student outcomes and lower rates of referrals for special education (Fletcher, Lyon, Fuchs, & Barnes, 2007; McNamara & Hollinger, 2003). RTI validity is established in five areas: (1) construct, (2) internal, (3) social, (4) external, and (5) statistical conclusion validity (Barnett et al., 2007). *Construct validity* refers to the conceptual foundation for using data-based change-analysis techniques and decision rules targeting the most salient at-risk behaviors, proper selection of students, and identification and evaluation of the most effective and efficient interventions. *Construct validity* can be demonstrated through repeated successful application of the Tier 3 case study process along with evidence of validity in the other four areas.

Internal validity confirms the hypothesized cause of the problem when appropriately selected interventions have the desired effect on the targeted dependent variable. Tier 3 case studies ensure internal validity through a carefully designed process of data collection and hypothesis testing. Multiple measures of outcomes are used to verify the quality and magnitude of change in dependent variables, as expressed in the characteristics of variability, level, or trend.

Social validity is evidenced when the importance and acceptability of goals, procedures, and results is acknowledged by all stakeholders in the process, including the student, teacher, and family. The Tier 3 case study is a collaborative process that relies on input, planning, and agreement on evaluation strategies involving all relevant parties or stakeholders. In fact, the success of the RTI process in general is strongly dependent on the hallmark of collaborative participation.

External validity refers to generalization of the change in the target behavior to other settings and situations. External validity is also concerned with resources needed for the implementation of interventions. (In the RTI process, increased intervention intensity raises the cost of an intervention and is a criterion for special education eligibility.) The use of single-case designs in the case study is useful for ensuring that both generalization and intervention intensity requirements are met.

Statistical conclusion validity occurs when measures appropriately inform special education decisions. Recast as *decision validity*, it is characterized by the use of correct methods for making special education eligibility decisions as well as the accuracy of judgments based on those measures.

Growth models. Academic and behavioral goals for all students are based on normative expectations corresponding to age and grade levels. Instructional, and prevention and intervention strategies facilitate the attainment of these goals. Students who are at risk for school failure do not make progress toward goals at the same rate as their peers. Typically, they begin the academic year at a lower level of academic performance or demonstrate a higher rate of inappropriate behaviors, and it may be unrealistic to expect them to immediately "catch up" with their peers.

Growth models have been proposed to assist in goal setting and are described by Gresham (2007) in terms of their relevance to special education eligibility decisions. Two such models are especially relevant to special education eligibility determination: the *catch-up* and the *nonresponder models*. The catch-up model is based on the notion that the student should be able to catch up with same-age peers if provided with appropriate instruction and intervention. According to this model, the purpose of special education is to provide the extraordinary effort, time, or resources needed to sustain the successful intervention (Barnett et al., 2004; Hardman, McDonnell, & Welch, 1997). For example, the catch-up model is appropriate when interventions are used to compensate for missed instructional opportunities or to match instruction and intervention strategies to the unique needs of a student. In this scenario, high-intensity interventions that are equivalent to special education services are expected to be of limited duration, particularly if the student demonstrates a rapid rate of improvement. If the catch-up model is used to determine special education eligibility, weekly progress-monitoring data should predict that the student will catch up with peers over time (i.e., there will be a "diminishing discrepancy"). Special education services continue until the student functions at a level commensurate with peers, and the student is able to function at that level independently.

The nonresponder model predicts little to no growth toward the accomplishment of the goal when case study fidelity and intervention integrity are optimal and confidence in the problem-solving process is strong. In the nonresponder model, special education eligibility is established on the basis of low rates of growth in response to high-intensity interventions, where the logical conclusion is that student goals were inappropriate or too ambitious. This often occurs among students who have severe physiological, mental health, or other conditions that interfere with typical development. Without support over time, the student is expected to continue to fall further behind peers (i.e., displays a "dual discrepancy") and may begin to show other school-related problems. To prevent this downward spiral, goals need to be adjusted. When individual student goals are significantly different from goals for the class, special education services may be needed to provide intensive services over a longer period of time so students can attain these (modified) goals.

ELIGIBILITY DECISIONS

Table 9.5 uses the hypothetical data that were displayed in Table 8.2 (Chapter 8) to illustrate special education eligibility decisions for students who need high-intensity interventions.

Table 9.5   Special Education Eligibility Decisions

Student	Case Study Fidelity	Goal	Intervention Integrity	Magnitude of Change Using High-Intensity Intervention	GAS Score	Special Education Decision
		Stabilize Variable Data		ES_{var}		Small = .02 Moderate = .15 Large = .35
1	5/5 = 100%		95%	ES = 2.01	0	Eligible
2	3/5 = 60%		95%	ES = .01	0	Not eligible May be incorrect intervention target; check hypothesis
3	2/5 = 40%		40%	ES = 1.35	+2	Not eligible Change may be due to an external factor, not case study or intervention
4	5/5 = 100%		100%	ES = .17	+1	Eligible
5	4/5 = 80%		98%	ES = 3.29	+2	Eligible
		Change Level		ES (*d*-index) PND		ES (*d*-index) • Small = .2 • Moderate = .5 • Large = .8 PND • Ineffective = 49% • Questionably effective = 50%–69% • Moderately effective = 70%–89% • Highly effective = 90%
6	4/5 = 80%	Decrease	97%	ES = .2 PND = 54%	+2	Eligible

(Continued)

Table 9.5 (Continued)

Student	Case Study Fidelity	Goal	Intervention Integrity	Magnitude of Change Using High-Intensity Intervention	GAS Score	Special Education Decision
7	2/5 = 40%	Decrease	65%	ES = 3.1 PND = 70%	+1	Not eligible Change may be due to an external factor, not case study or intervention
8	5/5 = 100%	Increase	0	ES = .1, PND = 40%	−1	Not eligible Failure to implement intervention, target behavior deteriorated
9	5/5 = 100%	Decrease	89%	ES = 1.5 PND = 95%	+2	Eligible
10	2/5 = 40%	Increase	100%	ES = .4 PND = 61%	0	Not eligible Inappropriate target; check hypothesis
		Improve Trend		ES (g-index)		positive g-index = improvement negative g-index = deterioration
11	3/5 = 60%	Increase	91%	ES = .02	0	Not eligible Inappropriate target; check hypothesis
12	5/5 = 100%	Increase	50%	ES = −.58	−2	Not eligible Failure to implement intervention with integrity, target behavior deteriorated
13	4/5 = 80%	Decrease	90%	ES = +.35	+1	Eligible
14	5/5 = 100%	Increase	100%	ES = +.99	0	Eligible
15	5/5 = 100%	Increase	100%	ES = +1.77	+2	Eligible

Of the 15 students who were considered for special education services, 8 were found eligible. For each of these students, the team can be confident that a high-intensity intervention is needed. The remaining students did not qualify due to problems with case study fidelity or intervention integrity. Although not included in this chart, visual analysis of graphed data is important for predicting whether the student will need special education services for a limited period of time (diminishing discrepancy) or for a longer period of time (dual discrepancy). Data for the target student and normative data are compared to estimate whether it is possible for the student to catch up with peers or the goal for the target student should be changed.

In sum, special education eligibility determination using RTI for students for whom neither Tiers 1 nor 2 have been adequate occurs in the following order: (1) conduct a Tier 3 case study; (2) use data from the case study to establish that a high-intensity intervention is needed; (3) evaluate the intervention for appropriateness and integrity; (4) confirm the fidelity of the case study process; (5) establish special education eligibility with a high-intensity, effective intervention ("diminishing discrepancy") or with a high-intensity intervention that requires a modified goal because satisfactory results have not yet been attained ("dual discrepancy"); (6) continue progress monitoring; and (7) exit student from special education services if and when data indicate that the student is performing at a level commensurate with peers and that this level can be maintained without the support of a high-intensity intervention.

SUMMARY

Eligibility for special education and related services can be established in context of the RTI framework, as assessment results indicate the need for increasingly more intensive levels of intervention. When a student demonstrates the need for high-intensity intervention, the presence of a disability may be suspected. In this chapter, emphasis was placed on the importance of identifying an effective (or promising) intervention before considering special education eligibility. However, high-stakes decisions regarding special education eligibility require confidence in the technical adequacy of methods and standards used in the decision-making process.

Intervention integrity and the fidelity with which the case study process has been applied are of particular concern because special education eligibility is predicated on the assumption that students have received high-quality instruction and intervention and that the hypotheses and interventions resulting from the case study process accurately targeted factors that were functionally related to the student's performance problem. In the next and final chapter, Chapter 10, a rubric for evaluating the fidelity of the case study is presented, and its use is demonstrated with sample cases involving both academic and behavior problems.

10

Program Evaluation

S chool psychologists are expected to have a beneficial impact on the students they serve. Data-based outcomes from case studies, which are described in Chapter 8, attest to the value of their services. In addition, aggregated data from multiple case studies can be used by practitioners and school psychology service units for purposes of accountability and to improve professional practices. Case studies that generate a consistent pattern of strong positive results are eloquent testimonials to the effectiveness of school psychologists. Clearly, evaluation of case study implementation and outcomes is a critical responsibility of both school-based service delivery units and university-based school psychology programs.

There are two methods for unit or program evaluation. The first method uses the case study rubric to evaluate the skills of the case study facilitator. The rubric is then used to analyze a completed case study. The second method uses aggregated data to detect general patterns of effectiveness. Data analyzed through the second method include case study fidelity, treatment integrity, and case study outcomes. An example of aggregated data is included in this chapter to illustrate the manner in which such data can be used for evaluation and improvement of a school psychology graduate program.

This chapter is divided into four sections. The first section provides a case study rubric that can be used to determine the facilitator's (or case manager's) degree of proficiency and fidelity to the process. Two case study examples are offered in the second and third sections of the chapter. The first case study (Morgan) illustrates the process employed to address the problems of an elementary school student who struggles with academic performance. It is formatted to include the logic underlying the process, and it is annotated with a number corresponding to the stage of the case study rubric that is being addressed. Note that, for purposes of explication, this case study is quite lengthy in comparison to the type of report that would actually be used in the school setting. The second case study (Reggie) targets a behavior problem displayed by a high school student. It is written in a shorter, more practical format. This study offers two different evaluation scenarios for Reggie's case study. Scenario 1 demonstrates results that are successful and limited to Tier 3a, while evaluation Scenario 2 provides an example of a case in which special education services (Tier 3b) are considered.

In terms of implementation, both the Morgan and Reggie case studies would be rated as "Outstanding," so they can serve as a model for students and practitioners. In the fourth section of this chapter, the evaluation of school psychology services and programs using information generated by case studies is discussed.

CASE STUDY STRUCTURE

By regularly evaluating their skill in conducting case studies, school psychologists can improve student outcomes. One way of doing this is to use a case study rubric for evaluation and feedback about specific skills comprising the case study process. This type of evaluation is particularly important for graduate students who are learning how to conduct case studies and for the training programs responsible for facilitating their skill development. The case study rubric presented in this chapter also is a helpful method for school-based units to identify professional development needs.

The case study rubric is derived from a summary of best-practice literature and information and feedback obtained while the rubric was being developed. It can be used as a set of guidelines for conducting case studies as well as a measure of facilitator competency. It is also an invaluable tool that can be used by school psychology training program faculty to assess the progress of school psychologist candidates as they implement case studies. Furthermore, the rubric is designed to meet criteria for Standards Domains established by the National Association of School Psychologists for training and credentialing purposes.

The case study rubric is presented below, followed by two examples of case studies that would be rated as outstanding in their adherence to the rubric. Each of the sections of the rubric (e.g., Stage 2: Problem Identification) has been described in detail in previous chapters. The quality of case study components as implemented by the student or practitioner is rated as "Needs Development," "Competent," or "Outstanding." Although the criteria for each stage are specific and discrete, evaluation of case studies using this format should be approached holistically; failure to include or attain a satisfactory standard for all of the elements described in the rubric does not necessarily imply that the case study has been conducted poorly. If the case study follows the general guidelines and deviations from them have a sound rationale, the evaluation still may result in ratings indicating successful facilitation.

The rubric begins with an analysis of data from Tiers 1 and 2 of the RTI process, resulting in the decision to conduct a case study at Tier 3. It is possible to use the case study process without data from Tiers 1 and 2, but there would need to be documentation of the student's poor performance prior to and after implementation of less-intensive intervention strategies. In the absence of data from Tiers 1 and 2, the second stage of the case study (problem identification) would involve the collection of more extensive information about the student's background and school history, past interventions and their effects, and comparisons with the performance of typical peers, as well as direct behavioral observation and curriculum-based measurement of academic skills. This information would then be used to develop skill and performance hypotheses regarding the cause or causes of the problem.

Stage 3 of the rubric describes hypothesis testing in terms of brief implementation of empirically sound interventions and is highlighted as a major feature of the RTI framework. This stage provides the link between the referral problem and an appropriate intervention; for this reason, it requires careful consideration of data leading to empirically based hypotheses. Multiple hypotheses should be generated with the expectation that one or more of them will be rejected, and one or more will be accepted. Recall that the case study is conducted at Tier 3 because strategies at Tiers 1 and 2 were unsuccessful, making it necessary to identify the cause of the problem before an effective intervention can be developed. In most cases, both skills-based ("can't do") and performance-based ("won't do") hypotheses should be investigated.

Stage 4 of the case study rubric establishes procedures for implementing interventions and monitoring their delivery and effectiveness. The final stage of the process includes a report of intervention effectiveness using outcome data, a description of evaluation methods, and recommendations for follow-up. Multiple methods of outcome evaluation are used to describe the magnitude of the change, the quality of the outcome, and intervention integrity.

CASE STUDY RUBRIC

Note: Permission is hereby granted for use of the Case Study Rubric for purposes of training and evaluation of school psychology graduate students and professional service delivery units.

Stage 1.0   Local Norms: Local Norms and Outcome Goals Are Established for Class

	Outstanding	*Competent*	*Needs Development*
1.1	☐ Teacher consultation provided classwide behavioral and/or academic goals and a target date to accomplish the classwide goals.	☐ Teacher consultation provided classwide behavioral and/or academic goals.	☐ Teacher consultation did not occur.
1.2	☐ The class goal statement was written in observable, measurable terms, and it was based on all of the following: ☐ Review of curriculum for academic goals; ☐ Task analysis for academic and/or behavioral target goals; ☐ Description of classwide instructional methods to address the academic and/or behavioral target goals.	☐ The class goal statement was written in observable, measurable terms.	☐ The class goal statement was *not* written in observable, measurable terms.
1.3	☐ Local norms were established. (Classes that do not have established local norms will need to have at least three administrations of each measure conducted over several weeks to determine average rate of change per week, level, or variability/stability for class.)	☐ Local norms were available and used.	☐ Local norms were underdeveloped.
1.4	☐ Data from Tier 1 were used to identify Tier 2 students; *and* Tier 2 students received more intensive intervention prior to implementation of Tier 3.	☐ Data from Tier 1 were used to identify Tier 2 students.	☐ Data from Tier 1 were *not* used to identify Tier 2 students.

Rating for 1.0				
☐ Outstanding: All components in the *Outstanding* category are checked.	☐ Substantially Developed: Components in the *Competent* and *Outstanding* categories are checked.	☐ Competent: All components in the *Competent* category are checked.	☐ Threshold Development: Some components in the *Competent* category are checked.	☐ Needs Development: Multiple components in the *Needs Development* category are checked.

Stage 2.0   Problem Identification: The Student Who Is At Risk and Academic/Behavioral Concerns Are Investigated

	Outstanding	*Competent*	*Needs Development*
2.1	☐ The at-risk student's academic and/or behavioral concerns were identified *and* operationally defined using class goals *and* local norms.	☐ The at-risk student's academic and/or behavioral concerns were identified *and* operationally defined using class goals *or* local norms.	☐ The at-risk student's academic and/or behavioral concerns were identified but *not* operationally defined.
2.2	☐ A baseline for the at-risk student was established for the concerns and included seven or more data points.	☐ A baseline for the at-risk student was established for the concerns.	☐ A baseline for the at-risk student was *not* established or was inappropriate.
2.3	☐ Skill analysis was conducted and included ☐ Error analysis; ☐ Direct observation of skill; ☐ Criteria-based assessment, *or* curriculum-based assessment.	☐ Skill analysis was conducted and included one or two of the following: ☐ Error analysis; ☐ Direct observation of skill; ☐ Criteria-based assessment, *or* curriculum-based assessment.	☐ No skill analysis was conducted, or analysis was inappropriate for the identified concerns.

(Continued)

(Continued)

	Outstanding	*Competent*	*Needs Development*
2.4	☐ Performance analysis was conducted and included ☐ Record review for historical documentation of pertinent information; ☐ Student interview; ☐ Ecological or situational analysis of concern (e.g., routines, expectation-skill match, relationships, classroom environment, adult and/or teacher support, cultural issues); ☐ Direct observation (e.g., on-task); ☐ Parent interview.	☐ Performance analysis was conducted and included less than five of the following: ☐ Record review for historical documentation of pertinent information; ☐ Student interview; ☐ Ecological or situational analysis of concern (e.g., routines, expectation-skill match, relationships, classroom environment, adult and/or teacher support, cultural issues); ☐ Direct observation (e.g., on-task); ☐ Parent interview.	☐ No performance analysis was conducted, or analysis was inappropriate for the identified concerns.

Rating for 2.0				
☐ Outstanding: All components in the *Outstanding* category are checked.	☐ Substantially Developed: Components in the *Competent* and *Outstanding* categories are checked.	☐ Competent: All components in the *Competent* category are checked.	☐ Threshold Development: Some components in the *Competent* category are checked.	☐ Needs Development: Multiple components in the *Needs Development* category are checked.

Stage 3.0   Problem Analysis: Hypotheses Are Developed and Tested

	Outstanding	*Competent*	*Needs Development*
3.1	☐ Hypotheses were generated through team collaboration with teacher, parent, and other relevant parties.	☐ Hypotheses were generated through collaboration with teacher or parent.	☐ Hypotheses were *not* collaboratively generated.

	Outstanding	*Competent*	*Needs Development*
3.2	☐ Multiple hypotheses were developed to identify the cause or source of each problem.	☐ One hypothesis was developed to identify the cause or source of each problem.	☐ No hypotheses were developed.
3.3	☐ Each of the multiple hypotheses was tested, and data were used to confirm the cause or source of the problem using one or more of the following methods: ☐ Direct observation; ☐ Analogue assessment; ☐ Functional analysis; ☐ Self-monitoring assessment; ☐ Other.	☐ One hypothesis was tested to confirm the cause or source of the problem using one or more of the following methods: ☐ Direct observation; ☐ Analogue assessment; ☐ Functional analysis; ☐ Self-monitoring assessment; ☐ Other.	☐ Hypothesis testing did not occur.
3.4	☐ The hypotheses reflected awareness of individual differences (e.g., biological, social, linguistic, cultural), and the intervention for hypotheses was verified for acceptability.	☐ The hypotheses reflected awareness of individual differences (e.g., biological, social, linguistic, cultural).	☐ The hypotheses did *not* reflect awareness of individual differences (e.g., biological, social, linguistic, cultural).
3.5	☐ Evidence was provided to justify the use of the intervention as research-based practice that linked to the targeted problem.	☐ Hypothesis testing linked the academic and/or behavioral problems with the intervention.	☐ Hypothesis testing did *not* link the problems with the intervention.

Rating for 3.0				
☐ Outstanding: All components in the *Outstanding* category are checked.	☐ Substantially Developed: Components in the *Competent* and *Outstanding* categories are checked.	☐ Competent: All components in the *Competent* category are checked.	☐ Threshold Development: Some components in the *Competent* category are checked.	☐ Needs Development: Multiple components in the *Needs Development* category are checked.

Stage 4.0   Intervention: Intervention Is Implemented and Monitored

	Outstanding	*Competent*	*Needs Development*
4.1	☐ Goal-Attainment Scale was developed, prior to intervention implementation, using appropriate methods.	☐ Goal statement was written in observable, measurable terms.	☐ Goal statement was *not* written in observable, measurable terms.
4.2	☐ Intervention was developed collaboratively with teacher *and* parent.	☐ Intervention was developed collaboratively with teacher *or* parent.	☐ Intervention was *not* developed collaboratively.
4.3	☐ Intervention logically linked to all of the following: ☐ Referral question; ☐ Accepted hypothesis; ☐ Goal statement.	☐ Intervention logically linked to one or two of the following: ☐ Referral question; ☐ Accepted hypothesis; ☐ Goal statement.	☐ Intervention did *not* logically link to any of the following: ☐ Referral question; ☐ Accepted hypothesis; ☐ Goal statement.
4.4	☐ Treatment-integrity checklist was developed prior to intervention implementation, and logistics of setting, time, resources, and personnel required for intervention and data gathering were defined and implemented.	☐ Logistics of setting, time, resources, and personnel required for intervention and data gathering were defined and implemented.	☐ Intervention was *not* described in enough detail to ensure appropriate implementation.
4.5	☐ Intervention was implemented with integrity.	☐ Intervention was implemented.	☐ Intervention was limited to determination of eligibility for special education services or referral for services external to the school and/or the home.
4.6	☐ Acceptability of intervention by teacher, parent, and child was verified and reflected sensitivity to individual differences, resources, classroom practices, and other system issues.	☐ Intervention reflected sensitivity to individual differences, resources, classroom practices, and other system issues.	☐ Intervention did *not* reflect sensitivity to individual differences, resources, classroom practices, and other system issues.

	Outstanding	Competent	Needs Development
4.7	☐ Intervention was monitored and data were used to determine implementation integrity.	☐ Intervention implementation was monitored.	☐ Intervention implementation was *not* monitored.

Rating for 4.0				
☐ Outstanding: All components in the *Outstanding* category are checked.	☐ Substantially Developed: Components in the *Competent* and *Outstanding* categories are checked.	☐ Competent: All components in the *Competent* category are checked.	☐ Threshold Development: Some components in the *Competent* category are checked.	☐ Needs Development: Multiple components in the *Needs Development* category are checked.

Stage 5.0. Evaluation: Data Were Gathered, Documented, and Evaluated

	Outstanding	Competent	Needs Development
5.1	☐ Graphed data indicated measurable, positive impact toward stated goal.	☐ Progress-monitoring data were plotted on a graph or chart.	☐ Progress-monitoring data were *not* plotted on a graph or chart.
5.2	☐ Single-case design was specified (e.g., changing criterion, withdrawal, multiple baseline, multi-element) to prove effectiveness of intervention.	☐ Single-case design was implied by graphed data (e.g., changing criterion, withdrawal, multiple baseline, alternating treatments) to prove efficacy of intervention.	☐ Single-case design was *not* apparent.
5.3	☐ Data were evaluated through all appropriate methods and were presented in support of student's progress: ☐ Visual analysis; ☐ Magnitude of change statistics;	☐ Data were evaluated through one or more methods and were presented in support of student's progress: ☐ Visual analysis; ☐ Magnitude of change statistics;	☐ No evidence was provided in support of student's progress or methods were inappropriate.

(Continued)

(Continued)

	Outstanding	*Competent*	*Needs Development*
	☐ Goal-Attainment Scaling; ☐ Intervention integrity; ☐ Other.	☐ Goal-Attainment Scaling; ☐ Intervention integrity; ☐ Other.	
5.4	☐ Effectiveness of intervention, case study fidelity, and intervention integrity were examined collaboratively.	☐ Effectiveness of intervention was examined collaboratively.	☐ Effectiveness of intervention was *not* examined collaboratively.
5.5	☐ Strategies for changes in intervention and/or follow-up were implemented, and data were provided. Intervention limitations or side effects were described.	☐ Suggestions for changes in intervention and/or follow-up were provided.	☐ Suggestions for changes in intervention and/or follow-up were *not* provided.

Rating for 5.0				
☐ Outstanding: All components in the *Outstanding* category are checked.	☐ Substantially Developed: Components in the *Competent* and *Outstanding* categories are checked.	☐ Competent: All components in the *Competent* category are checked.	☐ Threshold Development: Some components in the *Competent* category are checked.	☐ Needs Development: Multiple components in the *Needs Development* category are checked.

Overall Rating for Case Study				
☐ Outstanding: Case study is rated *Outstanding* in all five sections.	☐ Substantially Developed: Case study is rated *Competent* or higher for all sections and *Substantially Developed* or higher in one or more sections.	☐ Competent: All five sections of the case study are rated *Competent*.	☐ Threshold Development: Some but not all sections are rated *Competent* or higher.	☐ Needs Development: Multiple sections are rated *Needs Development*.

CASE STUDY: MORGAN

The annotated case study of Morgan illustrates specific elements of the case study rubric as they are reflected in a successful problem-solving effort. Note that the case study follows the general sequence of the rubric, but it is flexible when it is appropriate to depart from standard criteria. For example, the first paragraph in Morgan's case study report makes reference to criteria presented later in the rubric, at 3.4, which attends to the issue of diversity. The report is quite lengthy and is not representative of one that would be written in actual practice, where a much shorter version would be both feasible and appropriate. However, extensive detail is included in this example because it is intended to summarize and examine the thinking of the case study facilitator as the process moves forward. References to corresponding sections of the case study rubric appear in parentheses throughout the report.

Morgan was selected for a Tier 3 case study due to insufficient progress with reading fluency, demonstrated in assessments of her performance at Tiers 1 and 2. Although she has a chronological age of 11, she is in the fourth grade rather than the fifth grade because she was retained in kindergarten due to failure to master the prereading skills required for first grade. Morgan's primary language is English and her social and cultural status is similar to that of her peers who are predominately Caucasian and of moderate socioeconomic means (3.4).

Consultation with the fourth-grade teacher at Harrison Elementary School revealed that Morgan's class is one of five 4th-grade classes in the school and is comprised of 26 students. It is a general education self-contained class with all major subjects taught by the same teacher except for music, art, and physical education, which students attend once a week outside their classroom (1.1).

According to the state Department of Education's curriculum standards, students should have developed the skills for independent reading by the time they are in the fourth grade. The teacher stated an academic goal priority for the class as follows: All students will be able to orally read fourth-grade level text at 118 or more correct words per minute (wcpm) by the end of the school year. This target is based on DIBELS oral reading fluency (ORF) national benchmark goals (1.2).

Fluent readers should be able to recognize and decode printed words by using the alphabetic principle (sound-symbol match) and demonstrate a growing stock of sight words and fluent oral reading. Fluent readers are able to read with speed, accuracy, and proper expression. To read with expression, readers must divide text into meaningful chunks and know when to change emphasis and tone. Word recognition in isolation is a necessary but not sufficient condition for fluent reading. Fluent reading sounds natural, as it would in a conversation (1.2).

The teacher uses a variety of instructional methods to help students grow as fluent readers, including independent reading, guided reading groups, literature circles, repeated reading, and oral reading. The teacher incorporates a variety of books in these formats, including informational books, fiction, nonfiction, fantasy, chapter books, historical fiction, biographies, and poetry. At the end of each day, the teacher spends 10 to 15 minutes reading aloud to the class. All students spend at least one and a half hours every day involved in reading and reading-related instruction, and students are encouraged to read at least 20 minutes a day at home (1.2).

A reading resource teacher spends an additional 30 minutes, three times a week, with students who are reading below grade level. The results of the last DIBELS classwide administration established a median ORF score of 126 wcpm, which is above the 50th percentile based on national norms. The 25th percentile for the class was 110.5 wcpm, with five students scoring below this level. These students are provided a supplemental Tier 2 intervention using the Read Now Power Up program published by Renaissance Learning (Educational Research Institute of America, 2003) for students in grades K–12. This program emphasizes the reading skills of phonological awareness, phonics, fluency, vocabulary, and comprehension (1.3, 1.4).

Morgan's median baseline DIBELS ORF score of 63 wcpm was the lowest in the class and well below the DIBELS national norms, even after Tier 2 interventions were provided. Students who read fewer than 96 wcpm are considered to be at risk and in need of intervention. To meet the teacher's goal of 118 wcpm by the end of a seven-week intervention period, Morgan would need to increase her reading fluency rate by 55 wcpm, a weekly gain rate of 7.8 wcpm. If the class median score did not change throughout the remaining year, and Morgan achieved the goal of 118 wcpm, her score would place her at the 33rd percentile ranking in comparison to her class. Though the classroom teacher and reading resource teacher questioned whether the ORF goal set for Morgan was realistic, they decided that it would be best to strive for the DIBELS end-of-year benchmark goal of 118 wcpm because the classroom teacher wants all of her students to read at this level by the end of the year (1.2, 1.3, 1.6, 2.1, 2.2).

Problem Identification

Morgan received both Tier 1 support and Tier 2 intervention services for reading fluency. Since her reading skills were not improving as anticipated, the case study process (Tier 3) was initiated to determine the cause of Morgan's academic problems. Her ORF skills were analyzed through an error analysis, criterion-based assessment, and direct observation of skills. Her general academic performance was analyzed through behavior observation, records review, and interviews (1.6).

An error analysis of Morgan's ORF was performed using the responses from the DIBELS ORF and through the administration of a program called Lexia (Lexia Learning Systems, 2001). Lexia is a computerized diagnostic reading assessment program that evaluates students' decoding skills, ability to use word-attack strategies, and ability to automatically recognize sight words. Test results indicated that Morgan struggled with simple short vowel (CVC) words (e.g., *lun, gat, het*), silent e-complex (CCVCe) words (e.g., *brile, flune,* and *trame*), silent e-simple words (e.g., *cale, jope, pite*), one-sound vowel combinations (e.g., *spoin, hoat, loy*), two-sound vowel combinations (i.e. *loum, fow, sout, drouk*), and multisyllable words (e.g., *meppe, rutton*) (2.3).

The Developmental Reading Assessment (DRA) was administered to examine the quality of Morgan's reading and determine her independent reading level. The DRA evaluates two major aspects of reading: (1) accuracy of oral reading and comprehension through reading, and (2) retelling of narrative stories. Morgan's rate of accuracy was 97%, and her speed was 74 wcpm. In terms of phrasing and intonation, Morgan read slowly in long phrases, but her reading was choppy at times, with frequent breaths taken between words. At times, she adjusted her intonation to convey meaning, and she attended to punctuation. When faced with difficult words, Morgan paused and made no effort to sound out the words. Morgan's comprehension was rated as "adequate" with a score of 17. Adequate comprehension means that Morgan told many events of the story in sequence, included many details, referred to the characters by name, provided adequate response to teacher questions, and responded with literal interpretation of the story's meaning. DRA results place Morgan at a level 30 for independent reading, which is an early third-grade reading level. Even when reading third-grade level text, Morgan's fluency rate of 74 wcpm is still low (2.3).

Morgan's behavior was observed, records reviewed, and interviews completed to determine if Morgan's academic problems represented a performance ("won't do") deficit. Morgan is new to the school and therefore has not had the same amount of time as her peers to establish relationships with her teacher and others, and she has not received the same instruction as her peers. She has attended eight different schools in the past five years, and she has lived at six different addresses. Attendance was most sporadic in third and fourth grade. Morgan missed 18 days of school in third grade, and she missed 14 days between September and December of the current school year (2.4).

Records from prior schools indicate that Morgan's grades began slipping in third grade, when she started earning Cs in reading, writing, and math. In the last school she attended prior to Harrison, she earned an F in math, a B in reading, a C in writing, and a C in science. Achievement test scores indicate that in first grade Morgan scored a 222 in reading and math on the Off-Grade Proficiency Test, which is above the proficiency standard of 217. The following year, she tested at a basic level of achievement with a score of 388 points in reading and math on the state achievement test (2.4).

Her teacher reports that Morgan sometimes appears lost during instruction, though she raises her hand at times to answer questions. Morgan requires individual assistance in reading and math. The teacher reports that Morgan's oral reading skills and vocabulary knowledge are significantly worse than those of her class peers. In reading comprehension, the teacher states that Morgan's relative strengths are in identifying the main ideas, identifying the plot, and identifying the main characters. Morgan's weaknesses lie in making predictions, recalling facts, synthesizing the story, and making inferences. In terms of behavior, Morgan stays on task, works quietly, and remains in her seat when required. She completes her homework on time, though not always accurately. During reading groups, Morgan sometimes volunteers answers, gives correct answers when called upon, and knows the appropriate place in the book to find an answer. Though quiet and reserved, she appears to get along well with her peers and seems to enjoy her day. Since starting school at Harrison, Morgan is gradually talking more to her teacher and peers (2.4).

Interviews with Morgan's aunt were completed via e-mail. Morgan lived with her mother until January of this year. She currently lives with her maternal uncle and his wife, their two children, and Morgan's two elder brothers, who are in their teens. The aunt believes that, with time, Morgan will catch up to her peers. The aunt reports that she had a similar experience with Morgan's brothers when they first came to live with the family. The aunt does not think that Morgan is accustomed to getting help with homework, and she would like to check Morgan's homework without being oppressive, believing that it must be difficult for Morgan to go from an unstructured environment to a structured one. Morgan reports to her aunt that she likes her class and the friends she has made. Morgan especially likes meeting with the reading resource teacher and enjoys the fact that her cousin, who is in the same grade, meets with the same reading resource teacher. Overall, the aunt expressed her appreciation for the school's concern with Morgan and desire to help her improve in reading (2.4).

I met with Morgan several times to establish rapport and help her feel comfortable. When I first met Morgan, she was very quiet and shared very little, but, over several meetings, she gradually talked more. Morgan told me that she sees her mother every weekend and misses living with her all the time. She reported that she likes it when her uncle takes her and her brothers to Indiana in the summer to visit her father and grandmother. When I told Morgan that I would be working with her on reading, she smiled in response and wanted to know if I would also work with her in fifth grade. When engaged in an exercise in repeated reading, Morgan appeared happy with her progress as we graphed each improvement in words read per minute. She asked about the computer program designed to improve phonic skills, and wanted to know when and how often she could work on it. She often asked when I would be returning to meet with her. Overall, she seemed to respond well to my attention and help with reading (2.4).

The Behavioral Observation of Students in Schools (BOSS) was used to record two direct observations of Morgan during a review of science facts and instruction on telling time. In addition, two informal observations were conducted and recorded in narrative form. Overall, the observations indicate that Morgan is passively engaged more frequently than she is actively engaged. Off-task behaviors are passive in nature, and occur about 10% of the time. When given the opportunity to participate in tasks requiring active engagement, Morgan will do so, depending upon her confidence level or ability to perform (2.4).

Observation during the science review of facts revealed that Morgan's active engagement (45.6%) was less than her peers (87.5%). Passive engagement (42.1%) was higher than her peers (12.5%). She displayed off-task passive behaviors 7.3% of the time. The teacher was directly instructing the class 58% of the time. The review of science facts consisted of the teacher asking questions and having students answer the questions independently by writing their answers on their white, erasable boards. Once the students knew the answer, they raised their hands. Morgan appeared as though she was thinking about the question, but she did not write the answer down as quickly, nor did she raise her hand as often as her peers. At times, she looked lost, glancing at her peers as though she was looking for an answer from them. This was a review session, not new information (2.4).

Observation during instruction on telling time revealed that Morgan's active engagement (38.4%) was less than her peers (57.89%). Passive engagement (43.5%) was higher than her peers (31.6%). She was off-task passively 16.67% of the time. Teacher-directed instruction occurred 57.89% of the time. The telling time instruction included the use of a hand-held paper clock that each student used to learn about time (2.4).

Observation of Morgan in music class was recorded in narrative form. Morgan appeared to enjoy the class by singing as prompted and smiling. When the music teacher asked volunteers to sing solo in the microphone, Morgan stepped forward as requested by the teacher to show that she wanted to be picked, but as each child was picked and the teacher got closer to picking Morgan, she stood back, indicating that she no longer wanted to be picked. During another singing exercise, the teacher asked volunteers to read different narratives while music played in the background. Morgan seemed fascinated by the music lesson, and after students had read five different narratives, she volunteered to read. However, the class ended before she had a chance to read. During another informal observation of Morgan interacting with peers in a small group project, she took direction from others on how to complete the project and did not offer her own ideas. She tends to stay back and watch others take action, looking as though she would like to do the same (2.4).

Problem Analysis

Hypotheses were generated in collaboration with the reading resource teacher and classroom teacher, and a plan for testing each hypothesis was developed. Three skills-based hypotheses and one performance-based hypothesis were generated from the accumulated data and information. Hypothesis testing occurred through brief applications of interventions that targeted the hypothesized cause of the problem (3.1, 3.2).

Hypothesis 1. Morgan reads only 63 wcpm of fourth-grade level material because she lacks some decoding skills and word-attack strategies for sounding out unknown words (including multisyllable words, silent e-complex words, and short vowel simple words), which consequently prevents her from reading in a more fluent manner.

This hypothesis is representative of the "not enough help" explanation proposed by Daly, Witt, Martens, and Dool (1997). It would be accepted if Morgan's ORF rate improved after she receives instructional feedback on how to decode words she mispronounced and apply word-attack strategies during an oral reading session. Conversely, the hypothesis would be rejected if Morgan's rate of fluency did not improve after receiving feedback on how to decode and use word-attack strategies for pronouncing unknown words.

Hypothesis testing was conducted with Morgan by giving her a fourth-grade level reading probe from DIBELS progress-monitoring passages. After she first read the passage, the examiner gave her explicit feedback on the words she mispronounced. A lesson was provided on how vowel sounds can be either short or long depending upon the silent e. In addition, Morgan was directed to break a multisyllable word into parts, and pronounce each syllable separately. Morgan practiced pronouncing the words correctly and reread the passage. Her fluency rate increased by eight wcpm. Therefore, this hypothesis was accepted (3.3).

The National Reading Panel (2000) concluded that the greatest improvements in reading resulted from systematic phonics instruction. Three methods for improving Morgan's phonics skills were integrated into her Tier 3 intervention plan to address this identified problem.

Parts of an intervention called 'Word Attack' Hierarchy (Haring & Eaton, 1978) were used, in which the instructor prompts the student to apply a hierarchy of word-attack skills when a word is misread. The instructor gives these cues in descending order. This part of the intervention was implemented when difficult words were being reviewed after Morgan completed a reading. Assistance was also provided on how to sound out words with the silent vowel sound, and words with the long vowel sound (3.5).

Parts of the Error Word Drill intervention were used to build Morgan's reading vocabulary of words that she can recognize automatically (Jenkins

& Larson, 1979). The instructor recorded the misread words from the repeated readings to review with Morgan after the reading. A log of difficult words was maintained for review throughout the intervention period. These words were rewritten on index cards and presented to Morgan for her to read. The goal was for Morgan to read these words automatically without having to sound them out (3.5).

Lexia Strategies for Older Students (Lexia Learning Systems, 2001) was also selected to provide computer-based Tier 3 support. It is designed to provide systematic opportunities for learning and applying phonic word-attack strategies to improve word-recognition skills. Studies that have investigated the use of computer-assisted instruction (CAI) in schools have found that CAI is particularly well suited for supplementary instruction in reading (Blok, Oostdam, Otter, & Overmaat, 2002; MacArthur, Ferretti, Okolo, & Cavalier, 2001). For example, an evaluation of the use of Lexia software in the Boston Public Schools (Faux, 2004; Macaruso, Hook, & McCabe, 2006) found that Lexia students statistically outperformed comparison students in third grade (3.5).

Hypothesis 2. Morgan reads only 63 wcpm of fourth-grade level material because she has not had enough help to read fluently with proper phrasing, prosody, and expression.

The hypothesis would be accepted if Morgan's ORF rate improved after she received explicit instruction and modeling on how to read more fluently with proper phrasing, prosody, and expression. Conversely, the hypothesis would not be accepted if Morgan's ORF rate did not improve after she received explicit instruction and modeling on how to read more fluently with proper phrasing, prosody, and expression.

Hypothesis testing was conducted with Morgan by giving her a fourth-grade level reading probe from DIBELS progress-monitoring passages. After she first read the passage, the examiner gave her explicit feedback on the words she mispronounced. Morgan reread the passage and her rate of fluency increased by 8 wcpm. Next, the examiner gave Morgan explicit feedback on how she could flow words together more smoothly, pause less often, and convey meaning with expression in her voice. The examiner also demonstrated fluent reading for her. Morgan read the passage again and her fluency not only sounded better but also her rate improved as well by another 5 wcpm. This hypothesis was accepted (3.3).

According to the National Reading Panel (2000), fluency is a separate component of reading that can be developed by providing students with instruction and practice in fluency as they read connected texts. Students learn about fluency by listening to good models of fluent reading. Students can focus on improving fluency when the text they are reading consists of words they already know or can decode easily. They learn how a reader's voice can help written text make sense (3.5).

Hypothesis 3. Morgan reads only 63 wcpm of fourth-grade level material because she has not had enough practice in oral reading to improve her fluency skills.

The hypothesis, corresponding with Daly and colleagues' (1997) explanation, "hasn't spent enough time doing it," would be accepted if Morgan's ORF rate improved after she practiced reading a passage aloud. Conversely, it would not be accepted if Morgan's ORF rate did not improve after she practiced reading a passage aloud.

Hypothesis testing was conducted with Morgan by giving her a fourth-grade level reading probe from DIBELS progress monitoring passages. Morgan took the passage home to practice reading it aloud to family members. Three days later, Morgan read the passage to the examiner, who timed her reading rate. Morgan reported that she had read the passage aloud twice, once to her aunt and another time to her grandma. Morgan's fluency rate increased to 95 wcpm, an increase of 18 wcpm. This hypothesis was accepted (3.3).

Research findings on fluency conclude, "Repeated and monitored oral reading improves reading fluency and overall reading achievement" (National Reading Panel, 2000). Reading practice is generally recognized as an important contributor to fluency. Based on a detailed analysis of the available research on repeated oral readings, the panel concluded that repeated oral reading procedures that include guidance from teachers, peers, or parents had a significant and positive impact on word recognition, fluency, and comprehension across grade levels (3.5).

Hypothesis 4. Morgan reads only 63 wcpm of fourth-grade level material because she is not interested in reading and therefore does not read enough to improve her fluency skills. Morgan's interest in reading will improve by tracking her own progress in reading and as a result of receiving consistent encouragement and praise from others.

This hypothesis exemplifies Daly and colleagues' citation of "does not want to do it" as an explanation for poor academic performance (1997). The hypothesis would be accepted if Morgan's interest in reading improves, with a consequent increase in fluency, by tracking her own progress in reading and receiving consistent praise and encouragement from others to read. Conversely, the hypothesis would be rejected if Morgan's interest in reading did not improve by tracking her own progress in reading and receiving consistent praise and encouragement from others to read.

This hypothesis was tested by graphing each improvement in ORF (words per minute) on a bar graph for Morgan to see after each repeated reading of a DIBELS oral reading fluency probe for fourth graders. She appeared happy to see her improvements on the graph. The examiner also tested the hypothesis by praising Morgan for her improved reading. Morgan smiled in response to the examiner's verbal praise, and she expressed interest in the time spent reading by inquiring about when she could read again with the examiner. Though Morgan's initial response to the self-monitoring method, encouragement, and praise was positive, indicating an improved interest in reading, it is difficult to conclude that this would translate into improved fluency over time. The hypothesis is only partially accepted since it cannot be fully tested (3.3).

As indicated by Sprick, Borgmeier, and Nolet (2002), praise can be a useful technique for increasing student motivation. To be effective, praise should be contingent, descriptive, and not embarrassing. Contingent praise follows an appropriate behavior that is new or difficult for the student or a behavior of which the student is proud. Descriptive praise focuses on what the student did, which over time will help students learn to evaluate and reinforce their own behavior. Research has also shown self-monitoring to be an effective method for improving academic skills (Shapiro, Durnan, Post, & Levinson, 2002) (3.5).

Intervention

The school psychologist, classroom teacher, and reading resource teacher discussed the intervention plan. The plan was described to Morgan and her guardian, who agreed with the proposed intervention. Morgan would participate in the intervention from March 6th to April 24th. Everyone agreed the long-term goal for Morgan would continue to be to "read fourth-grade level material at a rate of 118 wcpm by the end of the 7 weeks" (4.2, 4.6).

The benchmark technique was used to develop a Goal-Attainment Scale (GAS) for Morgan's reading fluency based on the end of year DIBELS norms. During baseline, the average weekly rate of ORF growth for Morgan was 2 wcpm. Without Tier 3 intervention, Morgan was expected to have an ORF score of 77 by the end of the seven-week intervention period. Her academic goal was to increase the ORF score from a baseline score of 63 wcpm to the DIBELS end-of-year benchmark goal of 118 wcpm. This goal would increase the rate of weekly gain from 2 wcpm to 7.85 wcpm (4.1). (See Figure 10.1.)

Figure 10.1   Goal-Attainment Scaling for Morgan's Oral Reading Fluency

−2	−1	0	+1	+2
<63	63 to 76	77	78 to 118	>118

Morgan continued in the Tier 2 instructional activities that included meeting with the reading resource teacher in a small group with other students two to three times a week. She also continued with Tier 1 activities such as reading from a third-grade level text every day for 30 minutes during independent reading, writing the main themes of each chapter on a sheet of paper, and reviewing a bookmark highlighting the necessary comprehension strategies to use that week. Morgan continued to discuss her independent reading book with her teacher and reading resource teacher once a week.

Based on the results of hypothesis testing, the Tier 3 intervention consisted of several components: (1) repeated readings with feedback related to decoding skills, word-attack strategies, and fluent reading (phrasing, flow, prosody); (2) error word drills to increase automatic word recognition vocabulary; (3) Lexia computer exercises targeted to improve decoding skills; (4) methods to self-monitor progress in reading fluency; and (5) verbal praise and encouragement for demonstrated progress and/or effort (4.3).

Time and availability of personnel to implement the repeated reading and Lexia interventions were limited. Interruption of instructional time or time spent with the reading resource teacher needed to be avoided. Therefore, with permission from the guardian and Morgan's agreement, the repeated reading intervention was provided by the instructional aid twice a week for 30 minutes per session, during the daily scheduled independent reading time. The classroom teacher planned to ensure that Morgan would work on the Lexia program twice a week for 20 minutes a session when free time would be available during the week, usually before class starts in the morning or at the end of the day before the students leave (4.4).

The intervention was monitored through a weekly assessment of ORF with DIBELS fourth-grade level progress monitoring probes. A new progress-monitoring probe was used to start each repeated reading session. The ORF rate was determined from the first minute of reading each new probe. The repeated readings continued with the same passage (4.4).

A treatment integrity checklist on repeated readings was followed during the intervention and is included, along with other recording forms, in this chapter. This checklist includes a space to record the type of praise or positive feedback that the instructional aid provided. Morgan tracked her reading activities and completion of Lexia exercises on a reading and computer log. Morgan tracked her progress in oral reading fluency by charting her rate of fluency on a bar graph after each repeated reading. A small binder for keeping these papers together was prepared for Morgan to use (4.4).

Repeated oral readings and word drills (4.4). Repeated oral readings occurred twice a week for 30 minutes and were intended to increase Morgan's rate of ORF, improve decoding skills, and increase automatic recognition of words. The reading passages were drawn from DIBELS fourth-grade progress-monitoring probes. Morgan was asked to read the entire text aloud. Errors were counted according to the DIBELS administration guidelines. A word log of mispronounced words was established and grew with each new reading passage. This list was reviewed at least every other week by having Morgan read each word from index cards. This type of error word drill was meant to strengthen Morgan's reading vocabulary of words that she could recognize automatically.

After the first reading was completed, feedback and/or instruction related to decoding skills and/or word-attack strategies was provided on how to pronounce the words that Morgan did not read correctly. After the second reading, feedback was provided on how Morgan could read the text more fluently in terms of phrasing, flow, and expression. Any mispronounced words were reviewed again. The instructor also demonstrated fluent reading by reading the text aloud to Morgan. After the third reading, feedback was provided according to Morgan's overall performance.

Toward the end of the repeated reading session, Morgan was instructed to take the passage home to practice reading it aloud at least twice to someone. She was also instructed to review the words from the passage that she had difficulty in pronouncing. These words were printed on index cards for her to take home. At the next meeting, Morgan read the practiced text aloud. Her rate was recorded and feedback was provided on her performance. This process continued with the same reading passage until Morgan had fluently read the passage aloud to the instructor at least four times.

Lexia computer instruction (4.4). Morgan spent 20 minutes twice a week involved in computer exercises targeted to improve her specific weaknesses in decoding skills and word-attack strategies. Morgan's classroom had several computers available for her to use. The reading resource teacher enrolled Morgan in the Lexia program, and it is available for Morgan to use at any time. The classroom teacher needed only to log into the program and pick the exercises that Morgan was supposed to work on that day.

Self-monitoring (4.4). At the beginning of each session after the first oral reading was completed, the instructor charted Morgan's rate of reading in wcpm on a bar graph. Rate of reading was determined by timing Morgan's reading for one minute with a stopwatch, and counting the number of wcpm. Morgan took this graph home to show her family members. In addition, Morgan recorded the times she read at home, reviewed her words, and worked on the Lexia program on a reading and computer log that she kept with her.

Praise and encouragement (4.4). The adults in Morgan's life, including her classroom teacher, reading resource teacher, school psychologist, and guardian, provided praise and encouragement to Morgan for demonstrated progress and effort in reading throughout the intervention period. Praise was specific and descriptive.

Summary and Recommendations (Morgan)

Because of proficiency testing and spring break, the intervention was implemented for five weeks instead of the proposed seven weeks. Given this shorter time frame, the team projected a reasonable end goal of 100 wcpm in ORF instead of the 118 wcpm goal expected after seven weeks of intervention. The intervention design implemented with Morgan was a single-case changing-criterion design. The revised plan slightly adjusted the expected weekly criterion for change from 7.85 to 7.4 wcpm. The GAS was altered accordingly (5.3). (See Figure 10.2.)

Figure 10.2   Revised Goal-Attainment Scaling for Morgan's Oral Reading Fluency

−2	−1	0	+1	+2
<63	63 to 72	73	74 to 100	>100

The treatment integrity checklist for the repeated readings intervention was completed on each day that the intervention was implemented. Overall treatment integrity for repeated readings was 97.65% during the intervention. A log was used to track the times and sessions that Morgan worked on the Lexia computer program to improve decoding skills. During the five-week intervention period, Morgan only worked on the computer two times for 20 minutes. Treatment integrity is only 20% for the Lexia computer program. The classroom teacher reported that there were technical problems with the computer, and she had difficulty in finding time for Morgan to work on the computer (5.3).

DIBELS fourth-grade progress-monitoring probes were used to assess Morgan's ORF on a weekly basis. A graph displaying Morgan's data is presented in Figure 10.3 (5.1, 5.2).

After five weeks of intervention, Morgan achieved an ORF score of 100 wcpm for a GAS rating of +2. The effect size of +.75 was calculated using the *g*-index and is considered to be a strong positive effect. In addition, Morgan's teacher reported that she volunteers to read aloud in class, which she rarely did before the intervention. From listening to her read aloud, the teacher noted that Morgan's fluency sounds significantly better (5.3).

Figure 10.3   Progress-Monitoring Results for Morgan's Oral Reading Fluency

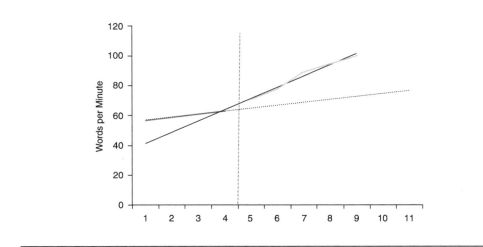

Morgan's vocabulary of recognizable words increased significantly. The words that Morgan had difficulty pronouncing were recorded on an error word log, which grew to 70 words during the intervention period. Morgan was able to pronounce 65 out of 70 words automatically without hesitation when presented with each word printed on an index card (5.3).

Morgan recorded the times she read aloud to someone at home on a weekly checklist. She also recorded the time that she spent reviewing difficult words. Morgan reported that she reads at home at least twice a week, sometimes every day. She appeared very happy when reporting on her progress in pronouncing difficult words. She reviewed the ORF graphs and commented when an improvement did not appear significant. She once asked, "How can I improve more?" after seeing that the last rate of reading was about the same as the prior rate of reading (5.3).

A limitation in using DIBELS ORF probes is the effect of certain types of text on oral reading fluency. Morgan's lowest fluency scores during baseline and the intervention were attained when she read science-related passages. Her highest fluency scores during baseline and the intervention were attained when she read stories about people and important events. Morgan is less familiar with words used in the science passages when compared to the words used in the stories. Morgan's background knowledge in science is more limited, and therefore she had more difficulty in reading about a subject that is unfamiliar to her. Consequently, it may be more helpful to track progress in fluency for science-related text separately from the progress made when reading stories about people (5.5).

Overall, Morgan appeared to be invested in her reading progress by completing the practice assignments at home, talking about new words she was learning, and reporting that she liked to read certain passages. She smiled when pronouncing a word that she once had difficulty in pronouncing. After the last reading about Wilma Rudolph, Morgan stated, "I really like reading about this person" (5.3).

All of the students, including Morgan, were given DIBELS end-of-year progress-monitoring probes. The class achieved a median score of 134 wcpm. Compared to 126 wcpm achieved 10 weeks before, the class showed an overall gain of 8 wcpm in ORF, again exceeding the DIBELS end-of-year benchmark. The 25th percentile increased from 110.5 wcpm to 115 wcpm and the 75th percentile increased from 140 wcpm to 149 wcpm. Though Morgan made the most significant progress in oral reading fluency when compared to every other student in the class, her fluency score still falls below the 25th percentile for the class (5.3).

The effectiveness of the intervention was discussed with the classroom teacher, guardian, student, school psychologist, and reading resource teacher. All members of the team were impressed with the progress Morgan made in oral reading fluency. However, all members of the team agreed that the intervention needed to continue in order to further decrease the gap between Morgan's ORF and the class norm (5.4).

The reading resource teacher expressed concern about Morgan's limited vocabulary and comprehension. To address the concern, the error word log would be expanded. In addition to recording difficult words on individual index cards, Morgan would be instructed to record on index cards words whose meaning she does not know. She would then be instructed to use a dictionary to find the meaning of these words and record their definitions on the back of each index card. When Morgan reviewed words to improve automatic word recognition, she would also review new definitions. The instructional aid would help Morgan feel more comfortable using a dictionary and ensure that Morgan is prepared to use the index cards as an aid in increasing word knowledge before the end of the school year (5.4, 5.5).

The team would like the intervention to continue throughout the summer. Repeated reading instructions along with eight different fourth-grade reading passages will be sent home with Morgan at the end of the school year. Her aunt agreed to assist Morgan with the repeated reading intervention during the summer. A simpler version of the repeated reading intervention is recommended for a parent volunteer to implement next year. The classroom teacher will ensure that information about Morgan's intervention, baseline data, and progress-monitoring data will be filed in Morgan's reading file, which will be given to her next teacher (5.4, 5.5). (Every student in the district has a reading file that follows them throughout their elementary school career.)

Recording Forms Used With Morgan's Intervention

REPEATED READINGS INTEGRITY CHECKLIST	
Title of Reading Passage:	
FIRST READING	Date:
1. Ask Morgan to read the passage.	
2. Follow DIBELS guidelines for scoring and counting errors.	
3. Time the first minute of reading. Record here.	
4. Record errors on DIBELS record form.	
5. Record rate of reading on DIBELS record form (words read correctly in one minute).	
This first recorded rate and retell score will serve as progress-monitoring scores.	
6. Chart the rate of reading on the bar graph.	
7. Give feedback/instruction on how to pronounce words that Morgan found difficult.	
8. Follow Word Attack Hierarchy to help Morgan decode words.	
8a. Try another way to say the word.	
8b. Finish sentence and guess the word.	
8c. Break word into parts and pronounce each one.	
8d. Cover parts of word so that only one part is visible to sound out.	
8e. What sound does _____ make?	
8f. Provide word and student repeats it.	
9. Instruct as needed on silent e complex words and short vowel simple words.	
10. Record the words that were difficult to pronounce on an error word log.	
SECOND READING	Date:
11. Morgan reads the same passage again from start to finish.	
12. Time the first minute of reading to determine the rate.	

(Continued)

(Continued)

13. After Morgan reads entire passage, review any missed words again.	
14. Provide specific feedback on how to improve phrasing, flow, and expression.	
15. Chart rate of reading on the bar graph.	
16. Read the passage aloud to demonstrate fluent reading.	
THIRD READING	Date:
17. Morgan reads the same passage again from start to finish.	
18. Time the first minute of reading to determine the rate.	
19. After Morgan reads the entire passage, provide feedback on her performance.	
20. Morgan charts her rate of reading on the bar graph.	
FOURTH READING	Date:
21. Morgan reads the same passage again from start to finish.	
22. Time the first minute of reading to determine the rate.	
23. After Morgan reads the entire passage, provide feedback on her performance.	
24. Morgan charts her rate of reading on the bar graph.	
WORD REVIEW	Date:
25. Transfer words from the error word log onto individual index cards.	
26. Morgan reads each word printed on the index cards.	
27. Record number of words read correctly out of the total words read.	
28. Record words that still present difficulty for Morgan to review again.	
PRACTICE AT HOME	Date:
29. When time has ended, give the reading passage to Morgan to read aloud to someone at home.	
30. Give Morgan index cards with difficult words from the passage to review at home.	
31. Check Morgan's record of time spent reading aloud and reviewing words at home.	

SUMMARY
Morgan reports reading her passage at home _____ times. (Orally or Silently)
Morgan reports reviewing her error word list _____ times.
_____ wpm was achieved on _____ after the _____ reading.
Positive feedback provided included:

MORGAN'S READING AND WORD REVIEW							
Date							
Day	Mon	Tues	Wed	Thurs	Fri	Sat	Sun
I met with Mrs. Wilson today.							
I read independently at home.							
I worked on Lexia computer today.							
I read with Miss Adams today.							
I read my passage at home aloud to:							
I read my passage at home silently.							
I reviewed my words with someone.							
I reviewed my words alone.							
People I read to were:							
Words I need help with are:							

RECORD TIME ON LEXIA PROGRAMS				
Level and Name of Exercise	Start Time	End Time	Unit #	Date
1: Consonant Blast				
2: E-maze				
2: Find and Combine				
2: Letter Switch				
3: Sea Hunt				
4: Syllable Puzzler				

CASE STUDY: REGGIE

Background and Problem Identification

Reggie, a 10th-grade student, was referred for a Tier 3a case study due to his frequent disciplinary referrals, absences and tardies, and poor grades. He participated in both Tiers 1 and 2 with little success. The problem solving team, which included two classroom teachers, Reggie's mother, the school counselor, and the school psychologist, gathered information relevant to the concerns. On average, Reggie was referred for discipline once a week, was absent or tardy 3.5 times a week (compared to the class average of less than 1 time a week), and his grade average was a D. In addition, he demonstrated lack of engagement in academic activities by sleeping in class and failing to complete assignments. Sleeping in class occurred approximately 20% of the time (compared to the class average of 2% of the time), and assignments were turned in 50% of the time (compared to a class average of 85% of the time).

A review of records showed that Reggie lived with his mother in subsidized housing. He had attended the same school district since second grade. His absences had gradually increased over the years with the greatest period of missed school occurring during a six-week period in October and November of last year, due to incarceration. Although Reggie had a greater than average number of disciplinary referrals, they were usually for being late to class. In elementary school, his grades typically averaged in the B range, and in junior high school, they had steadily dropped to a D average. Stanine scores on standardized tests consistently ranged from three to five, suggesting average to low-average performance.

The Central District High School has established "Respect, Responsibility, and Achievement" (RRA) as its three positive behavior support (PBS) goals. The ultimate schoolwide "respect" goal for each student is zero disciplinary referrals. The "responsibility" goal is 100% attendance, and the achievement goal is a GPA of C or above. At Tier 1, schoolwide and classwide strategies for encouraging students to accomplish goals include instruction, periodic review of the expectations, and various reinforcement methods. At Tier 2, small groups of students participate in an afterschool program called Twelve Together, an evidence-based peer-support intervention listed on the What Works Clearinghouse Web site (http://ies.ed.gov/ncee/wwc/reports/dropout/12_together/). The program goals are to encourage school completion and advancement.

Students are monitored in their progress toward the goal of respect through tabulation of discipline referrals. Attendance is monitored to determine levels of individual responsibility, and grades are reviewed as a measure of achievement. Responsibility and achievement were the areas of concern for Reggie. In his case, responsibility was expanded to include both attendance and engagement. Baselines for attendance and tardies (three times a week) and engagement (sleeping 20% of the time) were determined through record review and observations. Achievement baselines were indicated through GPA (D), and assignment completion rate (50%). The goals for Reggie were to increase attendance, engagement, GPA, and assignment completion.

Interviews with Reggie and his mother indicated that he had been experiencing difficulty engaging in school since the death of his friend last year. His friend was one of the group of Hispanic students with whom Reggie associated, and he was killed by a local man who was now in prison. This group of students was described by Reggie as "his family in the hostile environment" of his multicultural neighborhood. Reggie's incarceration was reported to have been the result of a car theft. His mother described Reggie as talented with his hands and very respectful to her. She worked two jobs to make ends meet and said that she wished that she had more time to spend with her son.

Interviews with several of his classroom teachers indicated that Reggie has had problems since he enrolled at Central District High School in ninth grade. However, they all agreed that Reggie could be charming, and he had well developed social skills. One teacher suggested that Reggie's reading skills were weak and thought that his academic progress might be impaired by this problem.

Problem Analysis

Four hypotheses were generated by the team (teachers, mother, school psychologist, and counselor). Failure to accomplish the PBS goals of responsibility and achievement represent a behavioral deficit (rather than "excess"), and, according to Witt, Daly, and Noell's (2000) general hypotheses for behavior problems, appear to be a matter not of an absence of skill, but a lack of motivation in the form of appealing and meaningful opportunities for engagement. More specifically, factors that may be implicated in Reggie's failure to perform satisfactorily include: (1) lack of academic motivation, (2) need for more time in an adult relationship, or (3) lack of sleep. A skill-based hypothesis in the area of reading was proposed as well.

Hypothesis 1. Lack of motivation. In a follow-up interview, Reggie indicated that school was boring, and he did not see the value of "sitting in class all day." He also reported that on a scale of 1 (not at all) to 10 (all the time) his level of depression was usually about 8. He recognized that he had been upset after the death of his friend last year, but stated that this was similar to other events in his life, such as the death of his brother from cancer seven years ago. When asked how he dealt with these losses, Reggie said that working on cars and electronic projects helped to clear his head. Additionally, he said that he was recognized by his peers as a "genius" in working on cars. His goal was to become an auto mechanic. Based on this interview, the "lack of motivation" hypothesis was accepted. The intervention should include vocational opportunities for Reggie in the area of auto mechanics to increase motivation.

Hypothesis 2. Need for a supportive adult relationship. Reggie reported that when he was feeling really down, he had a hard time getting out of bed. He also thought that talking about it with his mother was helpful, but she was not home much. This hypothesis was tested by pairing Reggie with the physical education teacher as a mentor for one week. Each morning, Reggie reported to the gym to talk and play basketball with the teacher. This hypothesis was accepted because his absenteeism and tardiness was reduced from a baseline of three to zero incidents per week during the intervention. An adult mentor was viewed as an important component of the intervention plan.

Hypothesis 3. Poor reading skills. This hypothesis was tested through the administration of Curriculum-Based Measures (CBM). Reggie's performance for ORF and reading comprehension was well within the level of expected performance, and similar to that of average students at his grade level. Written language and math were also examined through CBM and yielded similar results. Consequently, this hypothesis was rejected.

Hypothesis 4. Lack of sleep. Reggie's mother agreed to track his sleeping habits for one week to test the hypothesis that there was a relationship between his nightly bedtime and sleeping in class. Reggie went to bed every night between 11:00 p.m. and 1:00 a.m. There was no clear pattern that defined the relationship between bedtime and sleeping in class; however, his mother agreed that she would be more vigilant about encouraging him to go to bed by 11:00 p.m. This hypothesis could not be definitively rejected or accepted.

Hypothesis testing led to the conclusion that Reggie possessed the skills to succeed academically, but his performance was negatively affected by a lack of motivation and a need for adult support and supervision. The team agreed that he could benefit from an intervention that included (1) vocational opportunities in the area of auto mechanics and (2) an adult mentor. Research has demonstrated that both mentoring and vocational activities in areas of interest have been shown to improve student resilience and engagement.

Intervention

During the second grading period, Reggie was enrolled in the vocational school and linked with a mentor. He took courses in electronics and auto mechanics. His mentor was a local volunteer who owned an auto mechanic shop. Reggie began working in the shop after school every day. The intervention was monitored for time spent with the mentor and time spent working with automobiles (during school and with the mentor). Each day, Reggie and his mentor spent the last five minutes of the day completing the intervention checklist.

Following are two possible outcomes of the intervention plan that was developed for Reggie:

Reggie: Evaluation Scenario 1

The intervention was implemented with 95% integrity. His mentor missed work due to illness for a brief time, accounting for less than 100% integrity.

Progress-monitoring data showed marked improvement in Reggie's grades during the second term. At the end of the term, Reggie's grade average was a C, with a B in his auto mechanics course. Reggie's goal attainment reached the +1 level for assignment completion (see Figures 10.4 and 10.5). Assignment completion improved from an average of 50.4% during baseline to 91.3% during intervention, with 100% nonoverlapping data points and a large effect size (d-index = 1.78).

Sleeping in class was reduced, as indicated, by 100% nonoverlapping data points (NDP) and a large effect size (d-index = −2.01). Reggie's goal attainment reached the +2 level because during the intervention period, sleeping was reduced from 20% of the time to 1.7% of the time (see Figures 10.6 and 10.7).

Figure 10.4   Progress-Monitoring Results for Reggie's Assignment Completion (Scenario 1)

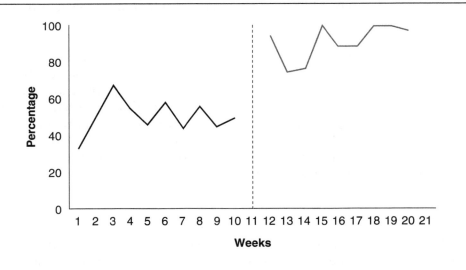

Figure 10.5   Result of Reggie's Goal-Attainment Scaling for Assignment Completion (Scenario 1)

−2	−1	0	+1	+2
0	>0 to <50%	50%	>50% to <100%	100%

Figure 10.6   Progress-Monitoring Results for Reggie's Sleeping in Class (Scenario 1)

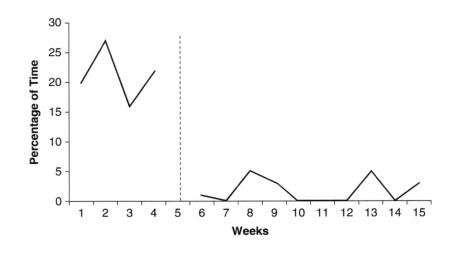

Figure 10.7   Result of Goal-Attainment Scaling for Reggie's Sleeping in Class (Scenario 1)

−2	−1	0	+1	+2
100%	<100% to > 20%	20%	>20% to >2%	<2% = Class average

Finally, as displayed in Figures 10.8 and 10.9, Reggie reached the +2 goal for decreasing the frequency of absences and tardies from an average of 3.5 per week during baseline to .5 per week during the intervention. The effect size (d-index = −1.74) and the PND (90%) indicated that the intervention had a large effect on attendance.

Figure 10.8   Progress-Monitoring Results for Reggie's Attendance (Scenario 1)

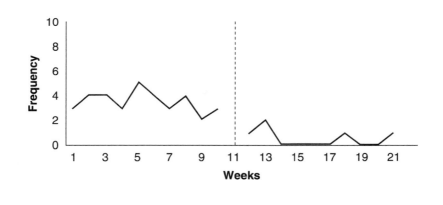

Figure 10.9   Result of Goal-Attainment Scaling for Reggie's Attendance (Scenario 1)

−2	−1	0	+1	+2
>3	>3	3	1 to 2	0

Summary and Recommendations (Reggie, Evaluation Scenario 1)

Evaluation data indicate that the Tier 3a intervention that incorporates opportunities for vocational course work in auto mechanics and electronics along with a mentorship was effective. It is recommended that Reggie continue to participate in this intervention.

Reggie: Evaluation Scenario 2

The primary intervention was implemented with 95% integrity. Reggie's mentor missed work due to illness for a brief time, accounting for less than 100% integrity. Progress-monitoring data did not show the desired level of improvement in grades during the second term. At the end of the term, Reggie's grade average was a D. However, his grade in his auto mechanics course was a C.

Reggie did not accomplish his goal of increasing his rate of assignment completion, as shown in Figures 10.10 and 10.11. The rate changed from an average of 50.4% during baseline to 51.4% during intervention, with 20% NDP in the desired direction and a small effect size (d-index = .05). The team noted that the data during the intervention period were more variable than during the baseline period. Further investigation revealed that

Figure 10.10   Progress-Monitoring Results for Reggie's Assignment Completion (Scenario 2)

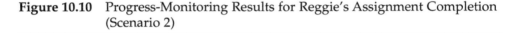

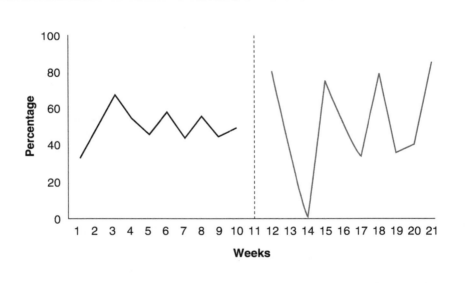

Figure 10.11   Result of Goal-Attainment Scaling for Reggie's Assignment Completion (Scenario 2)

−2	−1	0	+1	+2
0	>0 to <50%	50%	>50% to <100%	100%

higher rates of assignment completion occurred during the weeks after each of the four occasions that Reggie's mentor met with the team to review his progress in school. There were 100% NDP between the baseline and those 4 data points. In addition, the GAS for these 4 data points was a +1, and there was a large effect size (d-index = 1.84). Reggie stated that he felt compelled to do better during those periods so that he would not let his mentor down. The team concluded that the intervention was successful when the intensity of monitoring and mentoring exceeded what was typically possible in the regular education setting.

The goal of reduced sleeping in class followed a pattern similar to that of assignment completion. Reggie's sleeping changed from an average of 21.25% of the time during baseline to 19.2% during intervention (see Figures 10.12 and 10.13). There were 20% NDP in the desired direction and a small effect size (d-index = −.16), with a GAS of −1.

Figure 10.12 Progress-Monitoring Results for Reggie's Sleeping in Class (Scenario 2)

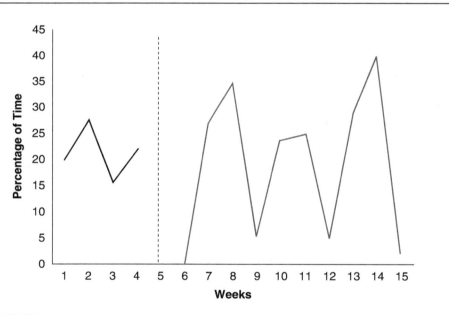

Figure 10.13 Result of Goal-Attainment Scaling for Reggie's Sleeping in Class (Scenario 2)

−2	−1	0	+1	+2
100%	<100% to >20%	20%	>20% to >2%	≤2% = Class Average

However, during the first, fourth, seventh, and tenth weeks (following team meetings), sleeping in class was reduced. There were 100% NDP between the baseline and the intervention phase data for those four weeks, with a change in mean scores from baseline to intervention from 21.25 to 3. The GAS for these four data points was a +1, and there was a large effect size (*d*-index = −1.77).

Classroom teachers indicated that during the four weeks after the meetings, they were more cognizant of the sleeping issue, and tended to wake Reggie up more frequently. The team concluded that the intervention was successful when they added the component of waking him up in class. However, the team agreed that this type of intervention is only a short-term improvement strategy, and a more intense intervention consisting of a high level of monitoring and mentoring was needed to increase Reggie's engagement and responsibility in school in the long run.

The GAS for frequency of absences and tardies was 0, suggesting little to no improvement (baseline average = 3.5 and intervention average = 3.1). The effect size (*d*-index = −.3) and the PND (15%) indicated that the intervention had a minimal effect on attendance in the desired direction (see Figures 10.14 and 10.15). Again, during the four weeks after the team meetings, attendance and tardies were significantly reduced in comparison to the nonmeeting weeks. The GAS for the four weeks was a +1. Both the effect size (*d*-index = −1.74) and the PND (86%) indicated that the intervention was effective during these periods. The team agreed that the reason for these successes during those weeks was that Reggie's mentor called him before school started each day to be sure that he was awake and got to school on time. Again, this was only a short-term solution.

Summary and Recommendations (Reggie, Evaluation Scenario 2)

The results of the interventions implemented during the second term of the school year revealed that there was a pattern of success based on a more intensive version of the established interventions. Importantly, during the second team meeting, the team recognized that the addition of more intense monitoring and feedback for assignment completion, sleeping, and attendance and tardies seemed to improve Reggie's school performance. Therefore, they tested this hypothesis by systematically implementing and withdrawing the more intense support during the fourth, seventh, and tenth weeks of the term. More intense support consisted of daily pep talks and morning phone calls by Reggie's mentor and consistent monitoring of sleeping in class by his teachers. The hypothesis was confirmed.

Although the hypothesis was confirmed, the team reported that they had difficulty with the extra expectations during the four testing weeks and would not be able to sustain this effort over a longer period of time. These difficulties were apparent in the lower rates of intervention integrity.

Figure 10.14   Progress-Monitoring Results for Reggie's Attendance (Scenario 2)

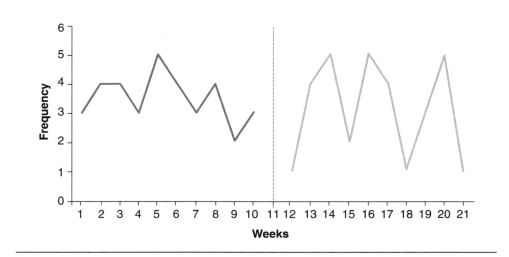

Figure 10.15   Result of Goal-Attainment Scaling for Reggie's Attendance
(Scenario 2)

−2	−1	0	+1	+2
>3	>3	3	1 to −2	0

(See the Intervention Checklist for the format for recording integrity.)
The mentor pep talk was completed with 85% integrity, the morning call was
completed with 75% integrity, and the teacher waking intervention
was completed with 90% integrity. The team recommends that Reggie be
considered for special education services because his needs extend beyond
the normal level of supports available in general education. Documentation will be submitted to the special education team to review his eligibility and will include a copy of the case study for confirmation of case
study fidelity, treatment integrity, and student-outcome data.

The team recommends that Reggie continue to participate in the vocational coursework and the mentor intervention. In addition, the case study
team concluded that more intense adult support and supervision were
needed. Therefore, Reggie should be considered for participation in the
special education intervention Check and Connect. The Check and Connect

program, presented as an evidence-based intervention on the What Works Clearinghouse Web site (http://ies.ed.gov/ncee/wwc/reports/dropout/check_conn/), is an intensive program that incorporates adult supervision and mentorship throughout the day, and it is offered within the special education program in Central District High School. This program has empirical validation for efficacy with students who need a high level of monitoring and supervision.

Recording Form Used With Reggie's Intervention

Time Spent in Class and with Mentor (completed sample)

Date	Activity	Time and Comments
	Electronics class	55 minutes out of 55 minutes = 100%
	Auto mechanics class	55 minutes out of 55 minutes = 100%
	Mentor	60 minutes out of 60 minutes = 100%
	Electronics class	45 minutes out of 55 minutes = 82% (late for class)
	Auto mechanics class	0 minutes out of 55 minutes = 0 (did not attend class)
	Mentor	120 minutes, 60 minutes greater than expected = 200%
	Mentor pep talk	Yes
	Mentor call in the morning	Yes
	Teacher waking in class	Yes

EVALUATION OF SCHOOL PSYCHOLOGY SERVICES AND PROGRAMS

Aggregated data can be used to monitor the skills of, and outcomes achieved by, one or more case study facilitators across multiple case studies. Patterns that emerge from the evaluation can reveal professional development needs and serve as accountability information in school settings. In colleges and universities, the data provide feedback and accountability information to school psychology candidates as well as their preparation programs. Figure 10.16 includes aggregated data for Stage 2 of the case study rubric, problem identification. A school psychology program uses these data to determine how well their program has trained the candidates to implement case studies. In this instance, they will attend to improving components 2.1 and 2.2, as 20% of the interns still need development in these areas.

Figure 10.16   Aggregated Data Describing Candidates' Competence in Various Components of the Case Study

Stage 2: Problem Identification			
	Number and % of Interns (N = 10)		
Case Study Component	Very Effective	Effective	Needs Development
2.1	5 (50%)	3 (30%)	2 (20%)
2.2	4 (40%)	4 (40%)	2 (20%)
2.3	7 (70%)	2 (20%)	1 (10%)
2.4	5 (50%)	5 (50%)	0
Overall rating for problem identification	4 (40%)	5 (50%)	1 (10%)

Evaluation of school psychology services and programs is optimal when it includes consideration of case study fidelity, treatment integrity, and data-based outcome information. Data-based outcome information is evaluated using the techniques listed in Chapter 8, in Tables 8.1 and 8.2. Specifically, aggregated outcomes can be represented by data describing the magnitude of change and by measures of goal attainment. Data patterns were analyzed in Chapter 8 in isolation through the use of hypothetical examples. However, as noted in Chapter 8, data from each measure should be considered contextually in relation to data from all other measures.

CASE STUDY FIDELITY

Patterns in case study fidelity indicate the degree to which the facilitators were able to integrate knowledge and apply skills to deliver services that resulted in measurable positive effects on the children they serve. The case study rubric can be used as a measure of case study fidelity. Lack of fidelity to the process is especially problematic when the outcome of the case study indicates that improvement has not occurred. In most cases, the likely cause of the lack of improvement is the failure to have identified the actual underlying cause of the problem and a corresponding appropriate intervention. When this type of problem is detected as a consistent pattern in school-based practice, professional development is needed to address specific areas of concern. University training programs that identify consistent patterns of poor case study fidelity across school psychology candidates may need to consider changes in the program curriculum or instructional practices.

Consider the patterns of case study fidelity that were presented in Table 8.2 in Chapter 8 of this text. Five of the fifteen cases had fidelity ratings of 3/5 or less. This means that one-third of the cases were conducted with poor fidelity. In three of those cases, improvement was not observed, and outcomes for the remaining two could not be linked to the case study process. If the majority of the cases with poor fidelity were facilitated by one person in a school setting, professional development would be recommended for that individual.

INTERVENTION INTEGRITY

Intervention integrity is an important component of the case study. Often, the intervention is implemented by someone other than the school psychologist, making this component difficult to assess. However, intervention integrity must be considered for program or unit evaluation. Poor intervention integrity can result in poor outcomes and may occur for any number of reasons. The most likely reasons include lack of intervention acceptability or contingencies for accurate implementation, failure to secure needed resources, or lack of skills required for implementation. Patterns of poor intervention integrity should be addressed by the case study facilitator through collaborative problem solving with the individual who is responsible for implementing the intervention.

Returning to Table 8.2, note that 4 out of the 15 case studies were implemented with less than 80% integrity. Two of those cases resulted in poor outcomes, and outcomes of the other two could not be attributed to the intervention. However, it can be concluded from these aggregated data that this service unit's collaboration with interventionists is adequate, as 73% of the interventions were implemented with 80% integrity or better. On the other hand, if all 4 of the cases with poor integrity were conducted by one case study facilitator or in one school, further investigation as to the cause of the problem would be needed.

MAGNITUDE OF CHANGE

Aggregated data revealing general patterns of the magnitude of change across case studies provide a powerful index of school psychologists' impact on the students that they serve. However, in order to avoid the "apples and oranges problem" of aggregating statistics that are not comparable, data should be organized according to the goal of the case study. Table 8.1 serves as a guide for choosing appropriate statistics, and Table 8.2 provides an organization strategy for data aggregation.

The "magnitude of change" data for cases in which the goal was to reduce the variability of targeted behaviors were calculated by ES_{var}, and presented in Table 8.2. The average effect size for these five cases is 1.37, indicating that, overall, these case studies were highly effective. All of the cases except one in this category yielded moderate to large effect sizes. Taken one step further, if these hypothetical data are related to mental health case study outcomes, then we could interpret them to mean that, in general, the mental health intervention strategies are effective.

In order to determine the magnitude of change in level for the five case studies in Table 8.2, the d-index and the PND were calculated. Aggregated d-index scores generated an average effect size of 1.06, indicating a strong overall effect. However, the range of scores was fairly wide, from .1 to 3.1. Two effect sizes were small, one was moderate, and two were large. Four of the cases resulted in questionable or ineffective outcomes, with PND scores of 70% or less. For purposes of illustration, imagine that further evaluation reveals that all of these cases addressed severe behavioral issues and were facilitated in one school by one school psychologist. Follow-up investigation would be recommended to determine whether the problem is a systematic school-based issue or is related to the skills of the practitioner.

When the goal of the case study is to increase or decrease the trend, the g-index is calculated as a measure of magnitude. In Table 8.2, four out of the five cases (80%) in this category revealed a positive measurable improvement. Trend data are not averaged and are limited to a summation of aggregated effectiveness because they are not generated from raw data. If this summary pertained to five case studies targeting academic improvement conducted in one school psychology training program, it could be concluded that the program generally prepares students to be effective facilitators.

GOAL-ATTAINMENT SCALING

Goal-Attainment Scaling (GAS) standardizes outcome data across cases, allowing for evaluation of aggregated data. Since this evaluation approach neutralizes the impact of the type of problem, the measures used to monitor performance, and the lack of symmetry across the ratings, behavioral, academic, and mental health problem-solving data can be combined in the aggregation. In Table 8.2, over 50% of the case studies had GAS ratings of +1 or +2. If the expectation of the service delivery unit was that half of the students receiving Tier 3 support would be successful, then these aggregated data would indicate that the unit met its goal. Examination of data associated with the case study rubric suggests that the rate of success for properly implemented case studies is higher than 50%. However, more extensive investigation is needed.

Since GAS also monitors the adequacy of predictions for goal attainment, aggregated data can reveal patterns of inadequate predictions across cases, such as under- or overestimation of expected levels of change. Consistent underestimation of predicted outcomes could result in high GAS scores (+2), but this would not reflect a strong impact of the intervention on the target behavior, as goals were set too low. Similarly, consistent overestimation of expected change in the target behavior would result in low GAS scores (−2), but that may be a reflection of inappropriate goals rather than actual failure to accomplish the goals. Case study facilitators who consistently over- or underestimate GAS outcomes may need to consider that their goals for the students are unrealistic or that the pattern reveals a need to improve their own skills in this area. One way to address problems with over- or underestimation patterns is to adopt specific methods for creating the GAS scale, such as those described in Chapter 8.

SUMMARY

Throughout this text, data collection and interpretation have been emphasized as keys to the successful implementation of case studies. Accurate and complete data regarding conditions surrounding academic and behavior problems are essential for meaningful hypothesis testing and intervention, while judgments about student outcomes require appropriate progress monitoring data and interpretation strategies that fit both the goals of intervention and the nature of the data.

In this chapter, a comprehensive plan was presented for use in evaluating the fidelity with which case study procedures were applied. The case study rubric can be used as a set of guidelines for implementation, an instrument to evaluate fidelity, or both. Finally, an examination not only of student outcomes but also of patterns of case study implementation yields information useful for demonstrating accountability of school psychological services and reveals areas in which additional training may be needed. For this reason, the case study evaluation procedures described in this text are of potential value to both school psychology service units (practitioners) and university-based school psychology graduate preparation programs.

References

Alberto, P. A., & Troutman, A. C. (2008). *Applied behavior analysis for teachers.* Columbus: Prentice Hall.

Allen, S., & Graden, J. (2002). Best practices in collaborative problem-solving for intervention design. In A. Thomas & J. Grimes (Eds.), *Best practices in school psychology IV* (pp. 565–582). Bethesda, MD: National Association of School Psychologists.

Anderson, A. R., Christenson, S. L., Sinclair, M. F., & Lehr, C. A. (2004). Check & connect: The importance of relationships for promoting engagement with school. *Journal of School Psychology, 42,* 95–113.

Arter, J. A., & Jenkins, J. R. (1979). Differential diagnosis—prescriptive teaching: A critical appraisal. *Review of Educational Research, 49,* 517–555.

Bahr, M. W., Fuchs, D., Stecker, P. M., & Fuchs, L. S. (1991). Are teachers' perceptions of difficult-to-teach students racially biased? *School Psychology Review, 20,* 599–608.

Barlow, D. H., & Hensen, M. (1984). *Single case experimental designs: Strategies for studying behavior change* (2nd ed.). New York: Pergamon Press.

Barnett, D. W., Daly, E. J., Jones, K. M., & Lentz, F. E. (2004). Response to intervention: Empirically based special service decisions from single case designs of increasing and decreasing intensity. *The Journal of Special Education, 38,* 66–79.

Barnett, D. W., Elliott, N., Wolsing, L., Bunger, C. E., Haski, H., McKissic, et al. (2006). Response to intervention for young children with extremely challenging behaviors: What it might look like. *School Psychology Review, 35* (4), 568–582.

Barnett, D. W., Hawkins, R., Prasse, D., Graden, J., Nantais, M., & Pan, W. (2007). Decision-making validity in response to intervention. In S. R. Jimerson, M. K. Burns, & A. M. VanDerHeyden (Eds.), *Handbook of response to intervention: The science and practice of assessment and intervention* (pp. 106–116). New York: Springer.

Batsche, G. M., Castillo, J. M., Dixon, D. N., & Forde, S. (2008). Best practices in linking assessment to intervention. In A. Thomas & J. Grimes (Eds.), *Best practices in school psychology V* (pp. 177–194). Bethesda, MD: National Association of School Psychologists.

Batsche, G. M., Curtis, M. J., Dorman, C., Castillo, J. M., & Porter, L. J. (2007). The Florida problem-solving/response to intervention model: Implementing a statewide initiative. In S. R. Jimerson, M. K. Burns, & A. M. VanDerHeyden (Eds.), *Handbook of response to intervention: The science and practice of assessment and intervention* (pp. 378–395). New York: Springer.

Bergan, J. R., & Kratochwill, T. R. (1990). *Behavioral consultation and therapy.* New York: Plenum.

Blok, H., Oostdam, R., Otter, M. E., & Overmaat, M. (2002). Computer-assisted instruction in support of beginning reading instruction: A review. *Review of Educational Research, 72,* 101–130.

Bloom, M., Fischer, J., & Orme, J. G. (2003). *Evaluating practice: Guidelines for accountable professionals* (4th ed.). Needham Heights, MA: Allyn & Bacon.

Bradley, R., Danielson, L., & Hallahan, D. P. (2002). *Identification of learning disabilities: Research to practice.* Mahwah, NJ: Erlbaum.

Browder, D. M. (1991). *Assessment of individuals with severe disabilities: An applied behavior approach to life skills assessment* (2nd ed.). Baltimore, MD: Paul H. Brookes.

Browder, D. M. (2001). *Curriculum and assessment for students with moderate and severe disabilities.* New York: Guilford.

Brown-Chidsey, R., & Steege, M. W. (2005). *Response to intervention: Principles and strategies for effective practice.* New York: Guilford.

Buck, G. H., Polloway, E. A., Smith-Thomas, A., & Wilcox Cook, K. (2003). Prereferral intervention processes: A survey of state practices. *Exceptional Children, 69,* 349–360.

Burns, M. K., Appleton, J. J., & Stehouwer, J. D. (2005). Meta-analysis of response-to-intervention research: Examining field-based and research-implemented models. *Journal of Psychoeducational Assessment, 23,* 381–394.

Burns, M. K., & Gibbons, K. A. (2008). *Implementing response-to-intervention in elementary and secondary schools: Procedures to assure scientific-based practices.* New York: Routledge.

Burns, M. K., Jacob, S., & Wagner, A. R. (2008). Ethical and legal issues associated with using response-to-intervention to assess learning disabilities. *Journal of School Psychology, 46,* 263–279.

Burns, M. K., & Symington, T. (2002). A meta-analysis of prereferral intervention teams: Student and systemic outcomes. *Journal of School Psychology, 40,* 437–447.

Burns, M. K., VanDerHeyden, A. M., & Jiban, C. (2006). Assessing the instructional level for mathematics: A comparison of methods. *School Psychology Review, 35,* 401–418.

Burns, M. K., Vanderwood, M., & Ruby, S. (2005). Evaluating the readiness of pre-referral intervention teams for use in a problem-solving model: Review of three levels of research. *School Psychology Quarterly, 20,* 89–105.

Calderhead, W., Filter, K., & Albin, R. (2006). An investigation of incremental effects of interspersing math items on task-related behavior. *Journal of Behavioral Education, 15,* 51–65.

Campbell, D. T., & Stanley, J. C. (1967). *Experimental and quasi-experimental designs for research.* Chicago: Rand McNally.

Carnine, D. (1976). Effects of two teacher presentation rates on off-task behavior, answering correctly, and participation. *Journal of Applied Behavior Analysis, 9,* 199–206.

Carter, M., & Kemp, R. (1996). Strategies for task analysis in special education. *Educational Psychology, 16,* 155–170.

Chandler, L. K., & Dahlquist, C. M. (2002). *Functional assessment strategies to prevent and remediate challenging behavior in school settings.* Upper Saddle River, NJ: Merrill Prentice Hall.

Christ, T. J., Burns, M. K., & Ysseldyke, J. E. (2005, November). Conceptual confusion within response-to-intervention vernacular: Clarifying meaningful differences. *Communique, 34*(3), 1–7. Bethesda, MD: National Association of School Psychologists.

Christ, T. J., & Hintze, J. M. (2007). Psychometric considerations when evaluating response to intervention. In S. Jimerson, M. Burns, & A. VanDerHeyden (Eds.), *Handbook of response to intervention: The science and practice of assessment and intervention* (pp. 93–105). New York: Springer.

Clarizio, H. E. (1992). Teachers as detectors of learning disability. *Psychology in the Schools, 29,* 28–35.

Cohen, D. A. (1988). *Statistical power analysis for the behavioral sciences* (2nd ed.). Hillsdale, NJ: Erlbaum.

Cohen, J. (1992). A power primer. *Psychological Bulletin, 112,* 155–159.

Cooper, J. O., Heron, T. E., & Heward, W. L. (1987). *Applied behavior analysis.* New York: Macmillan.

Curtis, M. J., Castillo, J. M., & Cohen, R. M. (2008). Best practices in system-level change. In A. Thomas & J. Grimes (Eds.), *Best practices in school psychology V* (pp. 887–901). Bethesda, MD: National Association of School Psychologists.

Daly, E. J., Martens, B. K., Hamler, K. R., Dool, E. J., & Eckert, T. L. (1999). A brief experimental analysis for identifying instructional components needed to improve oral reading fluency. *Journal of Applied Behavior Analysis, 32,* 83–94.

Daly, E. J., Persampieri, M., McCurdy, M., & Gortmaker, V. (2005). Generating reading interventions through experimental analysis of academic skills: Demonstration and empirical evaluation. *School Psychology Review, 34*(3), 395–414.

Daly, E. J., Witt, J. C., Martens, B. K., & Dool, E. J. (1997). A model for conducting a functional analysis of academic performance problems. *School Psychology Review, 26,* 554–574.

Deno, S. (2002). Problem solving as "best practice." In A. Thomas & J. Grimes (Eds.), *Best practices in school psychology IV* (pp. 37–55). Bethesda, MD: National Association of School Psychologists.

Deno, S., & Mirkin, P. (1977). *Data-based program modification: A manual.* Reston, VA: Council for Exceptional Children.

DiPerna, J. & Elliott, S. (2002). Promoting academic enablers to improve student achievement: An introduction to the mini-series. *School Psychology Review, 31,* 293–297.

DuPaul, G. J., & Eckert, T. L. (1994). The effects of social skills curricula: Now you see them, now you don't. *School Psychology Quarterly, 9,* 113–132.

Educational Research Institute of America. (2003). *A study of the instructional effectiveness of Power Up! Building Reading Strength* (Tech. Rep. No. 120). Austin, TX: Harcourt Achieve, Available from http://steckvaughn.harcourtachieve.com/HA/correlations/pdf/e/ERIApowerup.pdf

Ehrhardt, K., Barnett, D. W., Lentz, F. E., Stollar, S. A., & Reifin, L. H. (1996). Innovative methodology in ecological consultation: Use of scripts to promote treatment acceptability and integrity. *School Psychology Quarterly, 11,* 149–168.

Eidle, K., Truscott, S., Meyers, J., & Boyd, T. (1998). The role of the prereferral intervention teams in early intervention and prevention of mental health problems. *School Psychology Review, 27,* 204–216.

Engelmann, S., & Carnine, D. (1982). *Theory of instruction.* New York: Irvington.

Faux, R. (2004). *Evaluation of Lexia software in Boston public schools: Final report.* DavisSquare Research Associates. Retrieved May 18, 2009, from http://www.lexiauk.co.uk/docs/fauxt.pdf

Fletcher, J. M., Lyon, G. R., Fuchs, L. S., & Barnes, M. A. (2007). *Learning disabilities: From identification to intervention.* New York: Guilford.

Flugum, K., & Reschly, D. (1994). Prereferral interventions: Quality indices and outcomes. *Journal of School Psychology, 32,* 1–14.

Fuchs, L. S. (2002). Best practices in defining student goals and outcomes. In A. Thomas & J. Grimes (Eds.), *Best practices in school psychology IV* (pp. 553–564). Bethesda, MD: National Association of School Psychologists.

Fuchs, D., & Fuchs, L. (1986). Effects of systematic formative evaluation: A meta-analysis. *Exceptional Children, 53,* 199–208.

Fuchs, D., Fuchs, L. S., Bahr, M. W., Fernstrom, P., & Stecker, P. M. (1990). Prereferral intervention: A prescriptive approach. *Exceptional Children, 57,* 128–139.

Fuchs, D., Mock, D., Morgan, P., & Young, C. (2003). Responsiveness-to-intervention: Definitions, evidence, and implications for the learning disabilities construct. *Learning Disabilities: Research and Practice, 18,* 157–171.

Fullen, M. G. (1991). *The new meaning of educational change.* New York: Teachers College Press.

Gansle, K. A., & Noell, G. H. (2007). The fundamental role of intervention implementation in assessing response to intervention. In S. Jimerson, M. Burns, & A. VanDerHeyden (Eds.), *Handbook of response to intervention: The science and practice of assessment and intervention* (pp. 244–251). New York: Springer.

Gickling, E. E., & Havertape, S. (1981). *Curriculum-based assessment (CBA).* Minneapolis, MN: School Psychology Inservice Training Network.

Ginsburg-Block, M., Rohrbeck, C., Fantuzzo, J., & Lavigne, N. (2006). Peer-assisted learning strategies. In G. Bear & K. Minke (Eds.), *Children's needs III: Development, prevention, and intervention* (pp. 631–645). Bethesda, MD: National Association of School Psychologists.

Good, R. H., Gruba, J., & Kaminski, R. A. (2002). Best practices in using dynamic indicators of basic early literacy skills (DIBELS) in an outcomes-driven model. In A. Thomas & J. Grimes (Eds.), *Best practices in school psychology IV* (pp. 679–700). Bethesda, MD: National Association of School Psychologists.

Graden, J. L., Casey, A., & Bonstrom, O. (1985). Implementing a prereferral intervention system: Part II. The data. *Exceptional Children, 51,* 487–496.

Graden, J. L., Casey, A., & Christenson, S. L. (1985). Implementing a prereferral intervention system: Part I. The model. *Exceptional Children, 51,* 377–384.

Graden, J. L., Stollar, S. A., & Poth, R. L. (2007). The Ohio integrated systems model: Overview and lessons learned. In S. R. Jimerson, M. K. Burns, & A. M. VanDerHeyden (Eds.), *Handbook of response to intervention: The science and practice of assessment and intervention* (pp. 288–299). New York: Springer.

Gravois, T., & Gickling, E. (2002). Best practices in curriculum-based assessment. In A. Thomas & J. Grimes (Eds.), *Best practices in school psychology IV* (pp. 885–898). Bethesda, MD: National Association of School Psychologists.

Greenwood, C. R., Horton, B. T., & Utley, C. A. (2002). Academic engagement: Current perspectives in research and practice. *School Psychology Review, 31,* 328–350.

Gresham, F. M. (1989). Assessment of treatment integrity in school consultation and prereferral intervention. *School Psychology Review, 17,* 211–226.

Gresham, F. M. (2002). Responsiveness to intervention: An alternative approach to the identification of learning disabilities. In R. Bradley, L. Danielson, & D. Hallahan (Eds.), *Identification of learning disabilities: Research to practice* (pp. 467–519). Mahwah, NJ: Erlbaum.

Gresham, F. (2004). Current status and future directions of school-based behavioral interventions. *School Psychology Review, 33*, 326–343.

Gresham, F. M. (2007). Evolution of the response-to-intervention concept: Empirical foundations and recent developments. In S. R. Jimerson, M. K. Burns, & A. M. VanDerHeyden (Eds.), *Handbook of response to intervention: The science and practice of assessment and intervention* (pp. 10–24). New York: Springer.

Gresham, F. M., VanDerHeyden, A. M., & Witt, J. C. (2005). *IQ—Achievement discrepancy in the identification of reading disabilities: Conceptual, measurement, and policy issues.* Retrieved September 14, 2009 from http://www.joewitt.org/Downloads/RTI%20and%20LD%20Paper%20Gresham%20VanDerHeyden%20Witt.pdf

Hall, G. E., & Hord, S. M. (1987). *Change in schools: Facilitating the process.* Albany: State University of New York.

Hardman, M. L., McDonnell, J., & Welch, M. (1997). Perspectives on the future of IDEA. *Journal of the Association for Persons with Severe Handicaps, 22*, 61–77.

Haring, N. G., & Eaton, M. D. (1978). Systematic instructional technology: An instructional hierarchy. In N. Haring, T. Lovitt, M. Eaton, & C. Hansen (Eds.), *The fourth R: Research in the classroom* (pp. 23–40). Columbus, OH: Merrill.

Havelock, R. (2005). *The change agent's guide to innovation in education* (2nd ed.). Englewood Cliffs, NJ: Educational Technology.

Hosp, M. K., Hosp, J. L., & Howell, K. W. (2007). *The ABCs of CBM: A practical guide to curriculum-based measurement.* New York: Guilford.

Howe, K. B., & Shinn, M. M. (2002). *Standard reading assessment passages (RAPs) for use in general outcome measurement.* Eden Prairie, MN: Edformation.

Hunley, S. A. (2008). Best practices for preparing learning space to increase engagement. In A. Thomas & J. Grimes (Eds.), *Best practices in school psychology V* (pp. 813–826). Bethesda, MD: National Association of School Psychologists.

Hunley, S. A., & Schaller, M. (2006). Assessing learning spaces. In D. Oblinger (Ed.), *Learning spaces* (Ch. 13). Educause. Retrieved April 13, 2009, from http://www.educause.edu/learningspaces

Individuals with Disabilities Education Improvement Act (2004). Public Law 108-446 (20 U.S.C. 1400 *et seq.*)

Irvin, L. K., Horner, R. H., Ingram, K., Todd, A. W., Sugai, G., Sampson, N. K., et al. (2006). Using office discipline referral data for decision making about student behavior in elementary and middle schools: An empirical evaluation of validity. *Journal of Positive Behavior Interventions, 8*, 10–23.

Jenkins, J. R., & Larson, K. (1979). Evaluating error-correction procedures for oral reading. *Journal of Special Education, 13*, 145–156.

Jones, R. R., Vaught, R. S., & Weinrott, M. R. (1977). Time-series analysis in operant research. *Journal of Applied Behavior Analysis, 10*, 151–166.

Joseph, L. (2007). *Understanding, assessing, and intervening on reading problems.* Bethesda, MD: National Association of School Psychologists.

Kahneman, D. (2003). A perspective on judgment and choice. *American Psychologist, 58*, 697–720.

Kampwirth, T. J. (1987). Consultation: Strategy for dealing with children's behavior problems. *Techniques, 3,* 117–120.

Kaplan, J. S. (1995). *Beyond behavior modification: A cognitive-behavioral approach to behavior management in the school* (3rd ed.). Austin, TX: Pro-Ed.

Kavale, K. A., & Flanagan, D. P. (2007). Ability-achievement discrepancy, response to intervention, and assessment of cognitive abilities/processes in specific learning disability identification: Toward a contemporary operational definition. In S. R. Jimerson, M. K. Burns, & A. M. VanDerHeyden (Eds.), *Handbook of response to intervention: The science and practice of assessment and intervention* (pp. 130–147). New York: Springer.

Kavale, K. A., & Forness, S. R. (1999). Effectiveness of special education. In C. R. Reynolds & T. B. Gutkin (Eds.), *The handbook of school psychology* (3rd ed.) (pp. 984–1024). New York: Wiley.

Kennedy, C. H. (2005). *Single-case designs for educational research.* Boston: Allyn & Bacon.

Kiresuk, T. J., Smith, A., & Cardillo, J. E. (1994). *Goal attainment scaling: applications, theory, and measurement.* Hillsdale, NJ: Lawrence Erlbaum Associates.

Kirk, R. E. (1996). Practical significance: A concept whose time has come. *Educational and Psychological Measurement, 56,* 746–759.

Kline, R. B. (2004). *Beyond significance testing: Reforming data analysis methods in behavioral research.* Washington, DC: American Psychological Association.

Knoff, H. M. (2002). Best practices in personality assessment. In A. Thomas & J. Grimes (Eds.), *Best practices in school psychology IV* (pp. 1281–1301). Bethesda, MD: National Association of School Psychologists.

Knoster, T. P., & McCurdy, B. (2002). Best practices in functional behavioral assessment for designing individualized student programs. In A. Thomas & J. Grimes (Eds.), *Best practices in school psychology IV* (pp. 1007–1027). Bethesda, MD: National Association of School Psychologists.

Kovaleski, J. F. (2007). Potential pitfalls of response to intervention. In S. R. Jimerson, M. K. Burns, & A. M. VanDerHeyden (Eds.), *Handbook of response to intervention: The science and practice of assessment and intervention* (pp. 80–89). New York: Springer.

Kratochwill, T. R. (2007). Preparing psychologists for evidence-based school practice: Lessons learned and challenges ahead. *American Psychologist, 62,* 829–843.

Kratochwill, T. R., & Bergan, J. R. (1990). *Behavioral consultation: An individual guide.* New York: Plenum Press.

Kratochwill, T. R., Clements, M. A., & Kalymon, K. M. (2007). Response to intervention: Conceptual and methodological issues in implementation. In S. Jimerson, M. Burns, & A. VanDerHeyden (Eds.), *Handbook of response to intervention: The science and practice of assessment and intervention* (pp. 25–52). New York: Springer.

Kratochwill, T. R., Elliot, S., & Callan-Stoiber, K. (2002). Best practices in school-based problem-solving consultation. In A. Thomas & J. Grimes (Eds.), *Best practices in school psychology IV* (pp. 503–608). Bethesda, MD: National Association of School Psychologists.

Kromrey, J. D., & Foster-Johnson, L. (1996). Determining the efficacy of intervention: The use of effect sizes for data analysis in single-subject research. *The Journal of Experimental Education, 65,* 73–93.

Lee, S., & Jamison, T. (2003). Including the FBA process in student assistance teams: An exploratory study of team communications and intervention selection. *Journal of Educational and Psychological Consultation, 14,* 209–239.

Lehr, C. A., & Christenson, S. L. (2002). Best practices in promoting a positive school climate. In A. Thomas & J. Grimes (Eds.), *Best practices in school psychology IV* (pp. 929–947). Bethesda, MD: National Association of School Psychologists.

Lentz, F. E., Jr., Allen, S., & Ehrhardt, K. (1996). The conceptual elements of strong interventions in school settings. *School Psychology Quarterly, 11*, 118–136.

Lexia Learning Systems. (2001). *Strategies for older students.* Lincoln, MA: Author.

MacArthur, C. A., Ferretti, R. P., Okolo, C. M., & Cavalier, A. R. (2001). Technology applications for students with literacy problems: A critical review. *The Elementary School Journal, 101*(3), 273–301.

Macaruso, P., Hook, P. E., & McCabe, R. (2006). The efficacy of computer-based supplementary phonics programs for advancing reading skills in at-risk elementary students. *Journal of Research in Reading, 29*(2), 162–172.

MacLeod, I. R., Jones, K. M., Somers, C. L., & Havey, J. M. (2001). An evaluation of the effectiveness of school-based behavioral consultation. *Journal of Educational and Psychological Consultation, 12*, 203–216.

Macmann, G. M., Barnett, D. W., Allen, S. J., Bramlett, R. K., Hall, J. D., & Ehrhardt, K. E. (1996). Problem solving and intervention design: Guidelines for the evaluation of technical adequacy. *School Psychology Quarterly, 11*, 137–148.

Marolt, D., & Telzrow, C. F. (2007). Working smarter, not harder: Use of a standard treatment protocol approach to facilitate RTI implementation. *The Ohio School Psychologist, 52*(4), 4–10.

Marston, D., Lau, M., & Muyskens, P. (2007). Implementation of the problem-solving model in the Minneapolis public schools. In S. R. Jimerson, M. K. Burns, & A. M. VanDerHeyden (Eds.), *Handbook of response to intervention: The science and practice of assessment and intervention* (pp. 279–287). New York: Springer.

McCook, J. E. (2006). *The RTI guide: Developing and implementing a model in your schools.* Palm Beach Gardens, FL: LRP.

McDougal, J. L., Chafouleas, S. M., & Waterman, B. (2006). *Functional behavioral assessment and intervention in schools.* Champaign, IL: Research Press.

McKevitt, B. C., & Braaksma, A. D. (2008). Best practices in developing a positive behavior support system at the school level. In A. Thomas & J. Grimes (Eds.), *Best practices in school psychology V* (pp. 735–747). Bethesda, MD: National Association of School Psychologists.

McMaster, K. L., Fuchs, D., & Fuchs, L. S. (2006). Research on peer-assisted learning strategies: The promise and limitations of peer-mediated instruction. *Reading and Writing Quarterly: Overcoming Learning Difficulties, 22*, 5–25.

McNamara, K. (1998, April). Ohio's implementation of intervention-based assessment: Reactions of key stakeholders. In C. Telzrow (Chair), *Ohio's implementation of intervention-based assessment.* Symposium conducted at the meeting of the National Association of School Psychologists, Orlando, FL.

McNamara, K. (2000). Outcomes associated with service involvement among disengaged youth. *Journal of Drug Education, 30*, 229–245.

McNamara, K., DeLamatre, J., & Rasheed, H. (2002, February). *Problem-solving teams: What are they, what do they look like, and does it really matter?* Paper presented at the meeting of the National Association of School Psychologists, Chicago.

McNamara, K., & Hollinger, C. (2003). Intervention-based assessment: Evaluation rates and eligibility findings. *Exceptional Children, 69*, 181–193.

McNamara, K., Rasheed, H., & DeLamatre, J. (2008). A statewide study of school-based intervention teams: Characteristics, member perceptions, and outcomes. *Journal of Educational and Psychological Consultation, 18,* 5–30.

Mueller, M. M., Sterling-Turner, H. E., & Moore, J. W. (2005). Towards developing a classroom-based functional analysis condition to assess escape-to-attention as a variable maintaining problem behavior. *School Psychology Review, 34*(3), 425–431.

National Reading Panel (2000). *Report of the national reading panel: Teaching children to read: An evidence-based assessment of the scientific research literature on reading and its implications for reading instruction* (NIH Publication No. 00-4769). Washington, DC: U.S. Government Printing Office.

National Research Center on Learning Disabilities (2004). *Executive summary of the NRCLD symposium on responsiveness to intervention* [Brochure]. Lawrence, KS: Author.

National Research Center on Learning Disabilities. (2007, Winter). *Responsiveness to intervention in the SLD determination process.* Retrieved July 10, 2007, from http://www.nrcld.org

No Child Left Behind Act (2002). Public Law No. 107-110, 115 Stat. 1425, 2002 U.S.C.

Noell, G. H., Witt, J. C., LaFleur, L. H., Mortenson, B. P., Ranier, D. D., & LeVelle, J. (2000). A comparison of two follow-up strategies to increase teacher intervention implementation in general education following consultation. *Journal of Applied Behavior Analysis, 33,* 271–284.

Noell, G. H., Witt, J.C., Slider, N. J., Connell, J. E., Gatti, S. L., Williams, K. L., et al. (2005). Treatment implementation following behavioral consultation in schools: A comparison of three follow-up strategies. *School Psychology Review, 34,* 87–106.

O'Neill, R. E., Horner, R. H., Albin, R. W., Sprague, J. R., Storey, K., & Newton, J. S. (1997). *Functional assessment and program development for problem behavior: A practical handbook* (2nd ed.). Pacific Grove, CA: Brooks/Cole.

O'Shea, L. J., Sindelar, P. T., & O'Shea, D. J. (1985). The effects of repeated readings and attentional clues on reading fluency and comprehension. *Journal of Reading Behavior, 17,* 129–142.

Olson, S. C., Daly, E. J., Andersen, M., Turner, A., & LeClair, C. (2007). Assessing student response to intervention. In S. Jimerson, M. Burns, & A. VanDerHeyden (Eds.), *Handbook of response to intervention* (pp. 117–129). New York: Springer.

Park, H., Marascuilo, L., & Gaylord-Ross, R. (1990). Visual inspection and statistical analysis of single-case designs. *Journal of Experimental Education, 58,* 311–320.

Reese, H. W. (1997). Counterbalancing and other uses of repeated-measures Latin-square designs: Analyses and interpretations. *Journal of Experimental Child Psychology, 64,* 137–158.

Reschly, D. (2005). Learning disabilities identification: Primary intervention, secondary intervention, and then what? *Journal of Learning Disabilities, 38,* 510–515.

Reschly, D. J. (2008). School psychology paradigm shift and beyond. In A. Thomas & J. Grimes (Eds.), *Best practices in school psychology V* (pp. 3–15). Bethesda, MD: National Association of School Psychologists.

Reschly, D. J., & Ysseldyke, J. E. (2002). Paradigm shift: The past is not the future. In A. Thomas & J. Grimes (Eds.), *Best practices in school psychology IV* (pp. 3–20). Bethesda, MD: National Association of School Psychologists.

Rhode, G., Jenson, W. R., & Reavis, H. K. (1993). *The tough kid book: Practical classroom management strategies.* Longmont, CO: Sopris West.

Richards, S. B., Taylor, R. L., Ramasamy, R., & Richards, R. Y. (1999). *Single Subject Research*. San Diego, CA: Singular Publishing.

Roach, A. T., & Elliott, S. N. (2008). Best practices in facilitating and evaluating intervention integrity. In A. Thomas & J. Grimes (Eds.), *Best practices in school psychology V* (pp. 195–208). Bethesda, MD: National Association of School Psychologists.

Saudargas, R. A. (1992). *State-event classroom observation system (SECOS)*. Knoxville: University of Tennessee, Department of Psychology.

Schulte, A. C., & Osborne, S. S. (2003). When assumptive worlds collide: A review of definitions of collaboration in consultation. *Journal of Educational and Psychological Consultation, 14*, 209–239.

Scruggs, T. E., & Mastropieri, M. A. (1998). Summarizing single-subject research: Issues and applications. *Behavior Modification, 22*, 221–242.

Scruggs, T. E., Mastropieri, M. A., Cook, S. G., & Escobar, C. (1986). Early intervention for children with conduct disorders: A quantitative synthesis of single-subject research. *Behavioral Disorders, 11*, 260–271.

Shapiro, E. S. (1996). *Academic skills problems workbook*. New York: Guilford.

Shapiro, E. S. (2004). *Academic skills problems: Direct assessment and intervention*. New York: Guilford.

Shapiro, E. S., Durnan, S. L., Post, E. E., & Levinson, T. S. (2002). Self-monitoring procedures for children and adolescents. In A. Thomas & J. Grimes (Eds.), *Best practices in school psychology IV* (pp. 433–454). Bethesda, MD: National Association of School Psychologists.

Shinn, M.R. (1989). *Curriculum-based measurement: Assessing special children*. New York: Guilford.

Shinn, M. R., Shinn, M. M., Hamilton, C., & Clarke, B. (2002). Using curriculum-based measurement to promote achievement in general education classrooms. In M. R. Shinn, G. Stoner, & H. M. Walker (Eds.), *Interventions for academic and behavior problems: Preventive and remedial approaches* (pp. 113–142). Bethesda, MD: National Association of School Psychologists.

Simos, P., Fletcher, J., Sarkari, S., Billingsley, R., Denton, C., & Papanicolaou, A. (2007). Altering the brain circuits for reading through intervention: A magnetic source imaging study. *Neuropsychology, 21*, 485–496.

Slavin, R. E., Leavey, M. B., & Madden, N. A. (1984). Combining cooperative learning and individualized instruction: Effects on student mathematics achievement, attitudes, and behaviors. *The Elementary School Journal, 84*, 408–422.

Slonski-Fowler, K.E., & Truscott, S. D. (2004). General education teachers' perceptions of the prereferral intervention team process. *Journal of Educational and Psychological Consultation, 15*, 1–39.

Speece, D.L., & Case, L. (2001). Classification in context: An alternative to identifying early reading disability. *Journal of Educational Psychology, 93*, 735–749.

Sprick, R. S., Borgmeier, C., & Nolet, V. (2002). Prevention and management of behavior problems in secondary schools. In M. R. Shinn, H. M. Walker, & G. Stoner (Eds.), *Interventions for academic and behavior problems II: Preventive and remedial approaches* (pp. 373–401). Bethesda, MD: National Association of School Psychologists.

Stading, M., Williams, R. L., & McLaughlin, T. F. (1996). Effects of a copy, cover, and compare procedure on multiplication facts mastery with a third grade girl with learning disabilities in a home setting. *Education and Treatment of Children, 19*, 425–434.

Stanovich, K. E. (1986). Matthew effects in reading: Some consequences of differences in the acquisition of literacy. *Reading Research Quarterly, 21,* 360–407.

Sterling-Turner, H. E., Watson, T. S., & Moore, J. W. (2002). The effects of direct training and treatment integrity on treatment outcomes in school consultation. *School Psychology Quarterly, 17,* 47–77.

Swanson, H. L., Hoskyn, M., & Lee, C. (1999). *Interventions for children with learning disabilities: A meta-analysis of treatment outcomes.* New York: Guilford.

Taylor, J., & Miller, M. (1997). When timeout works some of the time: The importance of treatment integrity and functional assessment. *School Psychology Quarterly, 12,* 4–22.

Telzrow, C. F., & Beebe, J. J. (2002). Best practices in facilitating intervention adherence and integrity. In A. Thomas & J. Grimes (Eds.), *Best practices in school psychology IV* (pp. 503–516). Bethesda, MD: National Association of School Psychologists.

Telzrow, C. F., McNamara, K., & Hollinger, C. L. (2000). Fidelity of problem-solving implementation and relationship to student performance. *School Psychology Review, 29,* 443–461.

Topping, K., & Ehly, S. (1998). *Peer-assisted learning.* Mahwah, NJ: Erlbaum.

Truscott, S. D., Cohen, C. E., Sams, D. P., Sanborn, K. J., & Frank, A. J. (2005). The current state(s) of prereferral intervention teams. A report from two national surveys. *Remedial and Special Education, 26,* 130–140.

United States Department of Education (2003). *Identifying and implementing educational practices supported by rigorous evidence: A user-friendly guide.* Washington, DC: Author.

U.S. Department of Education. (2006). *National assessment of Title I interim report: Executive summary.* Washington, DC: Author.

Vaughn, S., & Fuchs, L. S. (2003). Redefining learning disabilities as inadequate response to instruction: The promise and potential problems. *Learning Disabilities Research and Practice, 18,* 137–146.

Vaughn, S., Wanzek, J., Linan-Thompson, S., & Murray, C. S. (2007). Monitoring response to supplemental services for students at risk for reading difficulties: High and low responders. In S. R. Jimerson, M. K. Burns, & A. M. VandDerHeyden (Eds.), *Handbook of response to intervention: The science and practice of assessment and intervention* (pp. 234–243). New York: Spring Science & Business Media.

Watson, T. S., & Steege, M. W. (2003). *Conducting school-based functional behavioral assessments: A practitioner's guide.* New York: Guilford.

Webb, K. M., Schaller, M. A., & Hunley, S. A. (2008). Measuring library space use and preferences: Charting a path toward increased engagement, *Portal, 8,* 407–422.

Witt, J. C., Daly, E. M., & Noell, G. (2000). *Functional assessments: A step-by-step guide to solving academic and behavior problems.* Longmont, CO: Sopris West.

Ysseldyke, J. E., & Algozzine, B. (1982). *Critical issues in special and remedial education.* Boston: Houghton Mifflin.

Ysseldyke, J. E., & Christenson, S. L. (2002). *Functional assessment of academic behavior: Creating successful learning environments.* Frederick, CO: Sopris West.

Zandvliet, D. G., & Fraser, B. J. (2005). Physical and psychosocial environments associated with networked classrooms. *Learning Environments Research, 8,* 1–17.

Index

CORWIN

A SAGE Company

The Corwin logo—a raven striding across an open book—represents the union of courage and learning. Corwin is committed to improving education for all learners by publishing books and other professional development resources for those serving the field of PreK–12 education. By providing practical, hands-on materials, Corwin continues to carry out the promise of its motto: **"Helping Educators Do Their Work Better."**

NATIONAL ASSOCIATION OF SCHOOL PSYCHOLOGISTS

The National Association of School Psychologists represents school psychology and supports school psychologists to enhance the learning and mental health of all children and youth.